# MICHEL de GHELDERODE

## THE SIEGE OF OSTEND

## THE ACTOR MAKES HIS EXIT

## TRANSFIGURATION IN THE CIRCUS

edited and translated
by
David Willinger

HOST PUBLICATIONS, INC.
AUSTIN, TEXAS

©Copyright 1990 by Host Publications, Inc.

First Edition 1990. All rights reserved.

No part of this book may be reproduced or transmitted in any form or by any means, electronic or mechanical, including photcopy, recording, or any information storage or retrieval system now known or to be invented without permission in writing from the publishers, except by a reviewer who wishes to quote brief passages in connection with a review written for inclusion in a magazine, newspaper or broadcast.

Research for this volume was made possible by the Fulbright Foundation, the National Endowment for the Humanities, a grant from PSC-CUNY and a grant from the Wheatland Translation Fund.

Publication of the volume was made possible in part due to support from Service des Lettres, Services Générale de la Culture, Ministère de la Communauté Française of Belgium, and particularly to M. Marc Quaghebeur.

Permission to translate *The Actor Makes His Exit* comes from Editions Gallimard. Permission to translate *The Siege of Ostend* and *Transfiguration in the Circus* comes from Mme. Josette Marchant-Gérard.


Joe Bratcher, Design and Layout
Eric Elshtain, Copy-editor
Romuald Szoka, Technical Assistance


Printed in Austin, Texas.

ISBN: 0-924047-03-8

# TABLE OF CONTENTS

## INTRODUCTION
1

## THE SIEGE OF OSTEND
42

## THE ACTOR MAKES HIS EXIT
172

## TRANSFIGURATION IN THE CIRCUS
254

## BIBILIOGRAPHY
285

This volume is dedicated to
my remarkable teachers:
Beth Althofer
Albert Bermel
Joseph Chaikin
Daniel Gerould
Robert Silber

# INTRODUCTION

## *THE SIEGE OF OSTEND*

The *Siege of Ostend* (1933) is truly unique in the Ghelderode canon. It shows our playwright at his most uninhibited, mirthful, and inventive.

### ANALYSIS OF THE PLAY

This "military epic for marionettes," as it is subtitled, is a loosely strung-together series of nineteen scenes which satirically go for the jugular of many of Ghelderode's favorite *bêtes noirs*: war, the Catholic Church, nationalism, the medical profession, prudery, and hypocrisy. In the process of pitching darts at his targets, Ghelderode has loads of fun, unleashing a veritable fiesta of sexual and scatological antics and, above all, a panoply of creative word-play, the spirit of which is hard to capture in translation.

The play departs from the historical incident of the siege of Ostend (1601-1604), during which the forces of Spain, then imperialistically occupying the Lowlands, attempted to remove the Dutch occupying force from the coastal city, Ostend, in order to gain unimpeded trade routes and political hegemony. By historifying his play in a remote, forgotten past, Ghelderode succeeds in disguising the contemporary nemeses he really wanted to attack, and his way is clear to make his satire all the more savage.

Ghelderode alternates scenes between those at court in Brussels, seat of Spanish repression and prudery, and on the Atlantic coast at Ostend, where the siege is idling along its languorous course. The latter is also home of Sir Jaime, leader of the Ostendish resistance, who anarchically embodies ultimate freedom of feeling and expression. Many of the prankish assaults the Spanish duchess, Isabella, has to fend off, designed to offend her "Catholic modesty," oblige her to find solutions to such problems as unceasing rain, showers of turds, rats, and farts from the Ostendish fishwives manning the battlements. The lot are products of Sir Jaime's profane, irrepressible imagination and a rich source of outlandish comedy.

In the first scene, Isabella, who along with her husband Albert were the archdukes sent by King Philip II of Spain to oversee his colony, states her intention to lay siege to Ostend until the Dutch have been set to flight. To put muscle behind her resolve she vows not to take off her "chemyse" and refrain from sex for the duration of the siege. In Scene Three, Albert countermands her orders, telling his generals not to take Ostend, thus having his peevish revenge on her for withholding her favors. This marital squabble, then, is seen to be the cause of the siege's endless duration. Following the scene of Albert's reversal of Isabella's order, the siege of Ostend goes slack so far as gain or loss of the conflagration is concerned, since any urgency to fulfill the vow to take the city has been neatly eliminated from the start. The incident of the "chemyse" consequently provides pretextual armature for a vast parade of tangential matters — the real stuff of the play — to unfold. We are provided with a series of glimpses into society's corrupt and hypocritical corners which are, at one and the same time, revealing and dramatically inessential.

Forms reign supreme in Brussels — forms of religion and forms of court (read bureaucratic) pomp. Control from this seat of power is deployed over Ostend, but the daunting realities of military combat turn all forms to ridicule, rendering them irrelevant and impotent. Isabella is as bankrupt of authority as her coffers are of gold. The Duchess, ostensibly the repository of ultimate power, is revealed to have none: she cannot win the siege through any exertion of authority, since her husband has undermined her ability to do so from the outset and since topographical and meteorological circumstances are adverse. She ultimately achieves her ends only by accident. Thus the patriotic mystification of military aggression is decisively debunked.

Further, the formal life at court, inextricably bound up in censorious religious piety, is revealed to be a veritable cesspool of hypocrisy and licentiousness. In one of the play's culminating scenes, Tableau XV, the entire court, including most of the military High Command, Isabella's spiritual confessors and advisors, and Archduke Albert himself, are discovered disporting themselves at the local brothel. Although the ladies of Brussels have all imitated Isabella in refusing to doff their "chemyses" under normal conjugal conditions, they merrily continue to do so in the murky light of the brothel, where they romp not only with random Spanish grandees, but indeed with their own husbands, all disguised in masks!

The Spanish reign means to quash all artistic, intellectual, sexual, and emotional freedom of expression, and it does so on paper; but the play reveals that even those on the side of repression find ways to live out their natural impulses. No one really wants to fight, and no one (except Isabella, who is portrayed as a rigid bigot) really wants to abstain from love-making.

Indeed, love-making and military combat are frequently juxtaposed and interpolated in *The Siege of Ostend*. Military glory is equated with super-human virility, and both are demystified in the process. This technique trivializes nationalistic fervor and stands the usual patriotic admiration society bestows on war heroes on its head. In Tableau VII, General Spinola, giving instructions to his corps of "Pickers," employs the word pick so that the distinction between the military weapon and the sexual object whose name is quite similar become hopelessly garbled. The withholding of sex by Isabella is, from the first, linked with success in war. Military achievement (of which there is none) is identical to success in amorous combat (which abounds). Witness Don Juan and Don Horace in Tableau XI, both of whose military prowess are rated according to the number of nuns they can deflower in a circumscribed amount of time. Hobbesian virtues of size and quantity are what count. One of the play's principle casualties is the "wee-wee" of Ambassador Miralobar, which gets blown off following the ceremony in honor of a tree being planted to commemorate the start of the siege. And the Spanish army is eventually undone through the efforts of the women of Ostend who "man" the battlements and continually distract the sexually deprived troops with sights of their favors, the ladies continually lifting their skirts to reveal "enormous, mossy thighs." Reports give out that, for want of heterosexual commerce, the Spanish soldiers are setting up quaint domestic arrangements with each other on the field of honor, further overturning the notion that military combat and virile manhood go hand in hand.

Insofar as it is an anti-war play, *The Siege of Ostend*'s premises are second cousin to those in Aristophanes' *Lysistrata*. In the ancient Greek comedy, the women, in order to thwart their husband's bellicose ventures, refuse to make love with them until the men relinquish their pursuit of war. In the modern Belgian play, the premise is inverted so that the source of war, Isabella herself, is the one keeps her clothes on and her husband out of conjugal contact with her. Isabella never expected the siege to last for four years, although it does so as an effect of her own manufacture. The "chemyse" she won't remove grows to be a symbol of the absurdity, not only of such vows, but of nationalistic zeal, and consequently of war itself. As the undergarment becomes more and more infested with "beasties," and comes to smell viler and viler, as it grows tougher in consistency so it ultimately has to be cracked open with a hammer and chisel, it comes to stand for the rigidity of Isabella's mind and the putrefaction of her ideas which crystallize until they nearly suffocate the warmaker in just retribution for waging war.

The coup de grace to the glorification of war comes when Ostend is finally surrendered. After four years of feckless scrambling to capture the city, which has involved much time, loss of life and scratching, the prize turns out to be a void. As one character says, the Spanish flag is now waving over "little scraps of what used to be one big scrap." In other words, the city is uninhabited and devoid of spoils of any sort, thus reducing the Spanish victory to an entirely Pyrrhic one.

To Isabella, who imagines she has power, but in reality has none, is juxtaposed Sir Jaime, who knows he is a king only in his imagination, but wields enormous power in that acknowledgedly fictional domain. He is the embodiment of the artist, and as such, there is no limit to the reprisals he can (in his imagination) heap on his enemies. Ghelderode gives the artist (personified by Sir Jaime, but surely including himself as well) endless power: over heaven, hell, and the weather. He presides over his court of entities of his own invention with a smoked herring in lieu of a scepter in hand. His courtiers are the fishwives of the neighborhood and the devils and demons he keeps locked up in his closet. Far more than Isabella's captains and priests, these demons and fishwives are effective combatants, wreaking havoc on the enemy. This play, then, is the ultimate artist's fantasy of omnipotence in which he takes vengeance on the mighty of the world for having overlooked or undervalued his existence, and provides a restoration of standards of fair play and good living to the remainder of mankind. As he knows very well, the artist for all his frankness and idealism, is an outcast from the central strongholds of societal power and bereft of any actual impact on affairs of state. The boundless imagination he wields, though, gives him true, however marginal, strength over his opponents — hypocrisy and societal mores in all their guises. Sir Jaime's final speech is a paean to this power and how he will choose to capriciously use it in time to come. He dreams a world in which all imposed standards and etiquettes are overturned. This fantasy, though only articulated at the end of *The Siege of Ostend*, informs the play in its entirety.

## JAMES ENSOR AND SIR JAIME

Ghelderode wrote *The Siege of Ostend* for the delectation of Belgian artist James Ensor (1860-1945). Ghelderode imbued the play with Ensor's spirit; Ensor in the guise of "Sir Jaime" is one of the central characters, Ghelderode hoping that Ensor would be the play's ideal audience. Ensor, one of the most prominent painters and draughtsmen of this century, had recently written an elegy to Ghelderode; it figured as part of the special 1932 issue of *La Nervie* devoted to Ghelderode. In the artist's page-long tribute to the playwright, he wrote:

> Fighting spirit, biting clawing writer, crackling moralist, trenchant scratching stylist, molesting, upsetting, rejoicing extremist, you tickle our unsated self-loves at every turn.
>
> To you the serene smile of Isabella, the White smirk of Godelieve! To you the incense of tears, the accent of flowers and colors! To you the sovereign history and mysteries of a Flanders haloed in gold, art, and sorrow!
>
> Following the laws of Flanders, Antwerp, and other Lowlands, we are all made to love fat, buttered, potted, larded, waffled, sugared painting, encrusted with mashed potatoes, and forced with farce...
>
> And bim-bam and bam-bim! Flower works and candy-coated bombs, fire crackers, black eyes, rockets and bam! Bam! Ratabam! To salute Michel de

Ghelderode the good Fleming, bold of accent and of color. Let's celebrate the fire of his machine-gunned roses, his concerns, his proses.

To you, to us, dear Michel De Ghelderode, to you the rose!

Ghelderode, who worshipped Ensor, and knew the siege of Ostend was one of his favorite episodes out of military history, had already written and was yet to write several plays using Ensor's canvasses as sources of inspiration (*A Night of Pity*, *Ostend Masks*, and *La Farce des Ténébreux*). Ghelderode wrote *The Siege* as an appendix to a prose tribute to Ensor (which he never completed) while basking in the afterglow of the tribute Ensor deigned to write for him. The play is littered with images, both verbal and visual, from Ensor's work and references, both obscure and generally known, to Ensor's life. And Sir Jaime's (very long, rambling) speeches intentionally ape Ensor's oratorical style of address, one for which he was famous and put him in great demand at official functions.

See, taste our Ostendish masks. Yes, they're evolving to the four winds of the spirit, clothed in tenderness, enriched in prettiness, purpled, azured, mother-of-pearled, clammed, oystered, mussel-bounded, ray-fished, turbotted, catfished, bacaloaded, smoked soled, mermaided, stuffed with fantasy, they fill our hearts with joy.

Ghelderode saw in Ensor (the ideal version of the painter he fleshes out, at any rate) as the quintessential artist, who assumed the most fascinating stance vis-a-vis society. Jacqueline Blancart-Cassou delineates a certain type of "mystic or historic" hero in Ghelderode's plays as one who fullfils three main functions, and Sir Jaime conforms to this prototype in every respect:

1) To be themselves [the historic figure] with the aura of their prior legend trailing in their wake.
2) To act as avatars of Ghelderode and
3) To offer the spectators a neo-Romantic vision of Man, "the fallen god who remembers the heavens."

In many ways, Ensor and Ghelderode had much in common, and Ensor (the older man), also a French-speaking Fleming, was the most apt stand-in for Ghelderode to hand. As Blancart-Cassou points out, Ensor in 1895, at his most creative and least appreciated phase, was thirty-five, the same age as Ghelderode when he wrote *The Siege* in 1933. In his youth, Ensor had opposed all the same things Ghelderode opposed.

Thirty eight years before Ghelderode wrote his *Siege*, Ensor was as Ghelderode saw himself: misunderstood by critics, unloved by the public, and alone. Ensor, throughout his early life, was on a campaign against official academic art. Having enjoyed mediocre success at the art academy in Brussels, he forever after harbored a well-publicized contempt for the pedestrian techniques promulgated there. This accounts for the devils' cries in *The Siege* of "Long live the red cabbages and fat asses of the Academy!" and "Down with Stevens," alluding to the brothers Alfred (1823-1906) and Joseph Stevens (1816-1892), the latter famous for his sentimental portraits of dogs and other animals. At first friends and fellow students of Ensor at the Academy, the brothers Stevens were later numbered among his artistic enemies due to jealousy and contempt, damned by his trenchant wit with the title "revomited musketeers." He went so far as to deliver an entire speech running them down for opportunism and lack of creativity. As Ensor himself put it, "All rules, all canons of art, vomit death — vain labels..."

Ensor was also dead-set against what Sir Jaime calls "ministerial mucous," the bureaucratic establishment, one of Ghelderode's own pet peeves. Also like Ghelderode, he was stigmatized during his early years (but lionized later), was full of histrionic and playful pranks (they both loved a good practical joke), and had penchants for puppetry, darts, the harmonium, and the recorder. In several instances Ensor painted himself as a Christ figure, an identification Ghelderode felt keenly and which is most evident in his early play *Blockheads*. Both Ghelderode and Ensor tended to laugh at and lash out at the agencies of society they deemed insufficiently appreciative of their accomplishments, feeling themselves to be persecuted victims, in fact, the locus of all society's unjust barbs.

But Ghelderode was cautious not to let his wild satire extend to Sir Jaime, his admiration for the celebrated painter leading him to do a dance of equivocation in depicting Ensor. Ghelderode fashions Sir Jaime as a robust rebel who could go to any length to offend and set himself apart from the common herd — an accurate representation of Ensor in his youth. But Ghelderode dispenses with truth whenever there is danger that Ensor will be shown in less than favorable light. For example, to render Ensor more sympathetic, he characterizes Sir Jaime as virtually penniless, when Ensor in fact came from a prosperous bourgeois family. The play would have Sir Jaime virtuously spurning titles and honors, when Archduke Albert (in Tableau IX) tries to buy his allegiance with the title of baron. In fact, not only did Ensor accept the title of baron when the real King Albert I of Belgium bestowed it in 1929, but Ensor, whose period of greatest fecundity and outspoken defiance was long since over, enjoyed a red-letter year for lionization by society in 1932, the year before *The Siege of Ostend* was written. He was paid homage by both Albert Einstein and Elizabeth, Queen of Belgium, and was awarded the Legion of Honor; in real life, as Franz Hellens has observed, he coveted awards and honors like a child with his toys.

Ghelderode himself took great pains throughout his life (in vain) to produce genealogical proofs that he descended from royalty and went to self-compromising lengths seeking out honors and awards, all the while pretending he was oblivious to them. His ideal artist (embodied by Sir Jaime) is indifferent to such vain trifles. In addition to the idealization of Ensor, Ghelderode backs off when dramatic truth brings his portrait to the verge of the truly scandalous. For example, in the brothel scene, Rosie the madam goes out of her way to point out that Sir Jaime enjoys coming to her establishment not to sleep with the prostitutes, but to touch up the masks. As for his relations with the prostitutes, they are limited to teaching court dances and good manners(!), the very etiquette Ensor flew in the face of. In this respect, the portrait has not the courage of its convictions, but founders in servile flattery.

The piquant irony is that, for his great efforts to cover all bases in pleasing Ensor, Ensor never made the slightest direct response upon reading *The Siege of Ostend*; only an oblique and ambiguous reference in a speech the existence of which Ghelderode was ignorant. But Ensor's silence (unbeknownst to Ghelderode he had stopped writing to any of his friends at that time), coupled with manifest dissapproval of the play from other of Ghelderode's friends, notably Jean van Caillie, left Ghelderode with a sufficiently bitter taste in his mouth that he began to doubt the play's value and put the play away in his bottom drawer for some time.

### ENSOR'S PAINTINGS WITHIN THE SIEGE

James Ensor's paintings and etchings pop up in the play in a plethora of ways. Ensor's most famous painting, *The Entry of Christ into Brussels*, is evoked at the climax of Tableau IX, in which Sir Jaime is denounced by Trullemans, as though mere mention of the blasphemous work were invested with sufficient dramatic power to bring down the curtain! Devils embodied by masks figure prominently as Sir Jaime's servants; and indeed, Ensor was more famous for his paintings of masks than any other subject. In one well-known painting, *Ensor Surrounded by Masks*, he depicts himself in a floppy artist's hat topped by a jaunty feather surrounded by masks. Further, his *Demons Taunting Me* of 1895 shows him in consternation as large-eyed skeletons and other satanic figures, one sprouting horns, beleaguer him. Ghelderode clearly used this series as an inspiration, although he decidedly realigns the masks and devils on Ensor's side, with Sir Jaime in full command over them, whereas Ensor portrays himself at their mercy.

In *The Haunted Furniture* (1888) Ensor depicts a stately floor-to-ceiling wardrobe closet, surrounded by ghoulish demons which peek out from behind and out from under it. In *My Portrait* (1886), the artist's own face is superimposed on the same closet, and in *The Bewitched Wardrobe* (1885), a young girl is sitting, peering out distractedly, her schoolbook open in front of her. Her mother sits impassively knitting beside her. She is placed directly in front of the same cabinet as in the other etchings, but this time, lurid masks peer down at her from the walls on all sides. The cabinet in the three works is based on an actual piece of furniture that was in the parlor of friends of the Ensor family. Ghelderode brings the cabinet to life in *The Siege of Ostend*, and the devils make merry with it, rocking it about and peeking out from all sides of it, as in the etchings.

Ensor loved making savage fun of authority figures. In his 1889 etching, *Doctrinaire Nourishment*, Ensor depicts five individuals in squatting position, facing away from the viewer. They appear to be a professor (identified by the signboard in his hand which reads "Instruction"), a cardinal, a politician wearing tails, and two versions of King Leopold II, one in the military garb he favored and one in his monarch's robes. The five are hovering over an assembled multitude and are excreting spirals, torrents, and dribbles of feces on the crowd's heads. This scatological work captures both the spirit and letter of *The Siege of Ostend* in its infantile but biting social statement. This etching is seconded by one no less startling, *The Bad Doctors*(1895). Four seemingly modern doctors are circling a patient, the latter a fat-paunched man, spread-eagled on his back. The doctors seem to have pinned him to the bed with a gigantic thermometer that protrudes from his belly. The doctors, meanwhile, are gallivanting around, brandishing a giant hypodermic needle, a chamber pot, and an umbrella respectively. This visual work seems to have provided direct inspiration for Tableau X, the scene in which three doctors do an autopsy on a living patient. Three doctors in that scene dub the fatal epidemic the "reassuring" title of *Spanish Flu*, an appellation applied in Ghelderode's own past to a virulent epidemic of typhus in 1914, to which he had succumbed and was a principle catalyst for his withdrawal from school that year.

Ghelderode also derived inspiration from Ensor's drawings: *The Battle of the Golden Spurs*(1895) and its fraternal twin, *The Baths of Ostend*(1899). The former work depicts the historical battle (1302) in which the Flemish forces defeated the French on the sands of the Belgian coast near Ostend, and the latter contains the present-day use of the beach as a site of modern-day recreational activities. Both the battle and the summer diversions are drawn in the same whimsical spirit and with the same spatial composition, in which an overcrowded grouping of cartoon-style figures are spread evenly throughout the drawing with no particular emphasis or focus. The battle takes on a Punch and Judy flavor similar to *The Siege*, while the image of the beach as the apogee of commercialism, with its bathing cabins and french fry stands, is exactly that envisaged and advocated by Father Trullemans in Tableau XIII.

In 1895 Ensor took a trip to Zeeland, Holland with his biographer and friend Eugène de Molder. There they saw peasants dancing and playing the flute. He translated this experience into a series of drawings and etchings depicting a miniaturized Zeeland landscape with windmills in the background, Eugène de Molder kicking up his heels peasant style, and a young James Ensor accompanying him on the flute. This series is called *Fridolin and Gragapanca from Yperdamme*, which explains the otherwise obscure references in *Siege of Ostend* to Gragapanca and Yperdamme (the latter being a neologism which combines the names of two Belgian towns). It also combines the image of Sir Jaime playing a recorder, as he does in *Siege of Ostend*, and perhaps the association of Ensor with Zeeland, Sir Jaime's ultimate destination in the play, where he has license to play his flute unimpeded. Sir Jaime sails for the free refuge of Zeeland (Netherlands) to escape the tyrannical Spanish rule, a flight which is symbolic of that taken by 150,000 Flemings in the sixteenth century. As a result of this mass exodus, Flanders lost the bulk of its artist and intellectual class for centuries to come, as they were far freer to pursue their creative endeavors under Calvinist Protestant rule in the north.

Ghelderode depicts Ensor/Sir Jaime in chummy relations with the fishwives of Ostend. And Ensor's plebeian neighbors were in fact the subject of an 1892 painting, *The Melancholy Fishwives*. An apocryphal story has it that the fishwives used to try to hit Ensor in the head with herrings when he went out for his daily stroll. The image of the herring is wrung to the utmost for every last drop of humor it might contain. Apart from the fact that herring must have been one of the dietary staples of both Spanish and Dutch forces during the actual military engagement, Ensor had a personal connection to the humble fish. "Hareng saur," (French for pickled or sour herring) is a homonym for "Art Ensor" when pronounced with a French accent. Ensor made much of the coincidence, and so became closely identified with the herring. Herring figures in his art work as well. For instance, in *Skeletons Disputing over a Pickled Herring*, (1891) two horrifying skulls are locked in conflict; like a bridge stuck between their oral cavities, painted the same mortuary color as they, is an ardent herring, which has the aspect of a phallic tongue and is producing a very palpable French kiss of death!

The pickled herring, in traditional Dutch and Flemish folklore, is associated with Lenten penitence and an array of other traits, such as capriciousness and mercuriality. The herring, along with bread, was the Netherlandish "food of liberty," which they traditionally ate every October third. The herring was considered a quintessentially patriotic fish, to which one sixteenth century poet even wrote an ode, "In Praise of Pickled Herring," for it was said to exemplify how "great things grew from humble beginnings," just like the lofty exodus with which *The Siege* culminates, which is certainly prepared for in startlingly unheroic ways.

No less than the herring, Ensor was identified with the frog — another key component in *The Siege of Ostend* iconography. On the occasion of communal elections in Ostend in 1903, Ensor wrote a series of virulent articles opposing "certain bellypotent government officials," to which he appended the ineffable warning that was to become his personal slogan, "The swashbuckling conceit will bring down the apocalyptic frog-smashing," the indecipherable phrase Ghelderode expanded into a limerick in Tableau II of *Siege of Ostend*. Frog imagery pops up repeatedly throughout the action as a symbol alternately for the Flemish and Spanish forces, which would ultimately be smashed like the croaking frog when stepped on.

It is uncertain how well James Ensor knew his Dutch history, but Simon Schama, in his exhaustive *The Embarrassment of Riches* tells us that the frog had special connotations in Netherlandish iconography as:

the stock type of... caricature: ugly, slippery, guttural in utterance and with comical pretensions to higher status in the heraldic bestiary. "Frogs in great number/Their land doth cumber/And such like Croaking People" ran the broadside.

The endless rain, together with the muddy, sodden terrain that was continuously having to be reclaimed and filled in by Flemish and Dutch, was the proper playground for the damp-loving frog. The lowlanders were endlessly associated with muck, mire, and dung, so it is exploited by the image of the scatological, but freedom loving frog, which aspires to gain dominion over its own muckheap.

Ensor's unique manner of verbal invention, turning nouns into verbs and adjectives into nouns, spewing forth endless streams of modifiers, is reproduced in Sir Jaime's speeches. Quirks from Ensor's own writing are lovingly exploited in *Siege* . Ensor wrote the scenario for a "ballet-pantomime," entitled *The Gamut of Love*, which was performed in 1920. His characters' names include such far-fetched creations as Fifrelin, Murmuramis, Frigouzir, Craco-Cigaret, and Popofigue. Then a shock of recognition arises on looking at the devils' names in the cast-list of Ghelderode's *Siege*: Fifrelin, Clistheret, Vociferan, Colodion, and Crepitus. In general, each time a strange locution or incongruously inserted word pops up in the *Siege*, one has but to consult Ensor's collected writings to discover its source.

*The Siege*, patchwork of references that it is, draws its sources from a myriad of unlikely places. For example, when Spinola warns, "Toreador, beware," he is actually citing from *Carmen* . Both Spinola saluting, but refusing to remove his hat, in Tableau I, and Don Juan, who exclaims, "I'm gonna pull down my fly, but my sombrero stays on my head," in Tableau VI are interpolations of a phrase from *Hernani* by Victor Hugo. Another line from Offenbach's *La*

*Périchole* is used and re-used, when Ghelderode's characters repeatedly exclaim "It will grow for it is Spanish," referring to trees and phalluses alike.

## ALFRED JARRY AND *UBU*

But apart from these brief allusions to the great epoch of Romantic drama, whose heightened diction Ghelderode emulates while mocking it all the while, and the important inspirations of Ensor, Aristophanes, and Rabelais, the principle source for *The Siege of Ostend* was *Ubu Roi* by Alfred Jarry, and more than any of that turn-of-the-century visionary's specific works, Jarry's iconoclastic spirit. The first scene, with its exaggerated marital discord, with a bullying Isabella and a brutish but acquiescent Albert, is very reminiscent of the first scene from *Ubu*. In its blend of classical references (in Jarry's case to Shakespeare, in Ghelderode's both to the latter and to Victor Hugo) with the most contemporary slang and original verbal inventions, particularly scatological ones like "offishitios," Ubu is Isabella's immediate antecedent. Like Ubu, Isabella unleashes an obscene and far-reaching military disaster; like him, she succeeds despite an alarming ineptitude. Jarry, together with the Comte de Lautréamont, were the literary heroes of an entire generation for whom they represented a liberating defiance against conventional morality, a sneering at society's institutions, and an anarchic overturning of artistic convention. Ghelderode partook of this adulation:

> Jarry reminded me that there exists a laugh, a loud uncharitable laugh... but I haven't had occasion to hear it burst out in this century any too frequently, and yet it encumbers the monumental carcass of Pa Ubu. I have obtained and retained the recipe for this laugh and have often exploited it, I've catapulted it across the theater. It is this laugh and this laugh alone for which

they will never pardon me! [...] You will find it for example in *La Farce des Ténébreux*. This modulation of the mug, this satirical and panicked shout, which issues from Rabelais, and further back from Aristophanes, transmitted to Petronius and Juvenal, then through the Middle Ages of barking preachers to come down to us with Erasmus, Swift, Sterne, and yet others who, like Goya, if they do not write, hold an etcher's needle in their hand.

In fact, if Ensor were not such an immediate and avowed source of inspiration for *The Siege*, one might just as readily think of Goya's *Capriccios* as a stylistic and tonal forebear.

It is not accidental that *Ubu* was first performed as a puppet play and that Ghelderode, at least in his play's sub-title, suggested that marionettes were best equipped to perform it. Along with the Brabant tradition of marionette theater (upheld by generations of Toone marionettists, several of whom Ghelderode was on very friendly terms throughout his life and who continue to perform his plays today), it was Jarry who gave Ghelderode the cue that puppets were a liberating force for the stage; with them, as with the later art of screen animation, virtually anything became possible.

Also, with puppets, as Blancart-Cassou has noted, Jarry taught Ghelderode that the cruelty of peremptory slaughters and dropping of characters into the trap or sending them flying through the air, indeed, any elimination of humans in cursory fashion, is vastly mitigated when performed by puppets; the cruelty is cut with fun.

Whereas Jarry used extant dramatic texts (*Macbeth*, *Hamlet*, etc.) as springboards for *Ubu*, Ghelderode had recourse to an obscure chapter in Belgian history. The real siege of Ostend had absurd and grotesque facets all its own which drew Ghelderode's attention. But it is interesting to study in detail what he took from the historical incident and what he left out or distorted. It should not be imagined that, where Ghelderode did make alterations, that it was due to ignorance. He was an avid history buff; consequently any change he made was in the interest of dramatic expedience.

## THE HISTORICAL SIEGE OF OSTEND

Several months before his death in 1598, King Philip II of Spain bestowed his colony in the Lowlands on his daughter Isabella (1566-1633). Before setting out on her voyage to Flanders, Isabella faithfully attended on her dying father who, suffering from cancer, stank, so legend has it, "worse than Job on his dungheap." Undaunted, Isabella staunchly dressed his wounds and changed his bedclothes until he passed away.

She subsequently married her cousin, Archduke Albert, (1559-1622) who was already governor of the colonized territories. Under the reign of Isabella's grandfather, Emperor Charles V (fondly known as Keizer Karel), the Lowlands consisted of what is today known as the Benelux countries. When the archdukes assumed power in 1598, however, "Beligica," as it was then called, was in the process of coming apart at the seams. Under Philip's rule (and above all, that of his deputy, the ferocious Duke of Alba), the territory was rent by religious dissensions between Protestants and Catholics, culminating in Alba's notorious execution of the Counts Egmont and Hoorne.

During Alba's reign, the "Gueux," or Beggars, an insurgent group presumably consisting of commoners, rose up against Spanish domination, undermining it through both active and passive clandestine resistance. The legendary Thyl Uilenspiegel was the fictional incarnation of the mischievous Gueux spirit, who was immortalized in a nineteenth century novel by Charles de Coster. It is this self-same spirit of the Gueux, although wildly anachronistic, that Ghelderode has embodied in Sir Jaime, whose anti-tyrannical stance is meant to apply to all nations in all epochs.

In principle Spain continued to rule the entire territory. However, "The United Provinces" to the north (most of what is today known as the Netherlands), a largely Protestant agglomerate, declared its independence on economic, social, and religious grounds. This left the "Catholic Lowlands," (largely what is now Belgium) to the Archdukes who were trying to demonstrate that their territory could stand separate from Spain. Under the rule of the Archdukes, native Belgians retained a certain amount of civic authority on the provincial and communal levels. Ostensibly the Archdukes had the Spanish crown's approval to rule autonomously; nevertheless, they were continually stymied, having to demonstrate that Catholic interests could prevail within such a structure. This required the manifest approval of their leadership from the populace. They wanted to demonstrate that foreign rule need not be enforced with terror and in a fashion belligerent to the subjugated people. The Archdukes ultimately lost the battle for independent status at the time of Albert's death, when the southern Lowlands reverted to the Spanish crown.

According to the contemporary accounts, the arrival of the Archdukes to Brussels in 1600 was greeted with great approbation from the masses who expected prosperity and a measure of respite from the harsh side of Spanish rule. Albert and Isabella established themselves in a lavish palace (ultimately destroyed by fire in 1731) that was constructed for them in the center of Brussels. Their reign was noted for elaborate displays of conspicuous consumption on the one hand and adherence to rigid etiquette on the other.

Albert, in addition to his temporal title, held those of cardinal and archbishop of Toledo; both he and Isabella who did indeed wear a nun's habit on many occasions for expiatory purposes, were sincerely and fervently committed to the Catholic faith. They lived surrounded by chaplains, Castillian evangelists and militant Jesuits, who promoted the religious processions and protected artists and, to an even greater degree, the monks. The life of the court went forward in the combined atmosphere of ceremony and austerity. Ghelderode is not fictionalizing, only hyperbolizing, when he depicts the Archduke's court overrun and controlled by members of religious orders. Isabella's propensity for building churches is no less a fiction, for she sponsored a great many.

Isabella and Albert were under pressure to prove they could hold the Lowlands together. When diplomacy failed, Albert resolved to expel the Dutch occupying force, led by Maurice of Nassau, from the mouth of the Escaut River in Ostend, a coastal city where the Protestants were blocking all marine trade. Thus began the four-year long siege of Ostend.

In the beginning of the siege, contrary to Ghelderode's version in which Isabella keeps a safe distance from hostilities in Brussels, she actually joined her husband in his military camp on the coast and attended to his needs, even to nursing him when he sustained a wound. She was, in fact, known as "the Soul of the siege," ever exhorting the soldiers on to victory from close quarters. On the other hand, Ghelderode adheres to historical fact in that Isabella did swear not to remove her chemise until the siege was successfully concluded. As a result of her ordeal, Belgians even today refer to the "colors of Isabella" as anything dingy, grayish brown, and faded.

In Ghelderode's version, the siege goes on four years because Albert perversely but deliberately orders his army not to take Ostend. In reality, he set out to win the siege, but was a poor military strategist whose every scheme brought disaster on his troops. As the official history has it, the archdukes were "Unhappy in war and unhappy in negotiations." Albert was indeed handicapped by an army consisting of a mish-mash of poorly paid mercenaries of diverse nationalities: Italians (who mutinied at one point when their pay was not forthcoming), French, English, Scotch, Frisians, Goths,

Swiss, Flemish and Germans, the latter of whom comprised the main force that ultimately succeeded in taking Ostend, in addition to regular Spanish troops.

On land, Albert's forces were tormented by projectiles and continually foiled in a number of engagements. For example, Albert tried to take the stronghold by ruse, sending his troops creeping into the deep moat in order to gain entry to Ostend through a hole in the wall. Meanwhile, the Dutch opened the sluicegates, thus flooding the moat. Two thousand men were drowned in the rushing gulf. Further, Nassau's fleet offered continual provocation to Spain's naval forces led by Ferdinand Spinola (Ambrose's brother), the latter who was laid low by a cannonball in October, 1602. So disastrous were Albert's military efforts that, to his disgrace, Philip III (Isabella's brother, and successor to her father) sent Ambrose Spinola (1569-1630), a Genoan, to the Lowlands in late 1602 to replace Albert on the field of battle, contrary to Ghelderode's account, in which he takes part from the outset and in which he follows orders from the Archduke. In fact Spinola put Albert in the shadow not only militarily, but in statesmanship as well. Albert, embarrassingly, was gradually relegated to a purely ceremonial function while Spinola, with strong direct attachments to the Spanish crown, was the real power.

One of the principle reasons Albert did not forcefully protest when Spinola was retained to lead the siege was that the latter promised to pay the army out of his own pocket. The Archduke was forever in debt, a fact which Ghelderode exploits to comic advantage, and had trouble sustaining the siege financially as well as militarily. Albert's cause was greatly aggravated by the natural setting which was booby-trapped and militated against an easy victory. The terrain was sandy and marshy by turns, which actually obliged the Spaniards to use stilts which enabled them to negotiate the difficult terrain, but also made them very visible targets, as cannonballs dropped about them on all sides, an interesting anecdote Ghelderode chose not to include.

Another spectacular incident on which he drew but altered to form the basis of Tableau V, the scene with Klabotsky, the Polish engineer, occurred when Spinola did heed the advice of a certain Italian engineer who erected a gigantic contraption known as "the Big Cat." This apparatus consisted of two gigantic flat surfaces mounted on wheels and pulled by horses. One surface started in the vertical position, which shielded the Spanish assailants from shooting emanating from the fortress. As the Spanish approached, the vertical surface cranked down to a diagonal position and leaned against the fortress walls, and the Spanish forces could then storm the battlements. One day, however, after a torrid sunny spell, the wood of the Big Cat dried out, and a flaming projectile hurled from within the fortress turned the mechanical ruse into a blazing inferno. Another Italian engineer, a certain Targone, also designed a system of moving towers, mounted with cannon and sails, propelled by wind and long staffs, that apparently worked to better effect than the Big Cat. Thanks to such devices Ostend did indeed come to be known as "The New Troy."

It should not be assumed, however, as Ghelderode would have it, that the Ostendish (actually led by the Dutch) forces were spared from harsh conditions. They lined the battlements with old sacks which were forever catching fire. And they were assailed by bouts of both plague and dysentery which, together with military casualties, brought them losses in equal number to the Spanish. The natural forces which plagued the Spanish were no more gentle with the Dutch. One particular five-day storm from the sea swept the watchtower away, ripped off the fortress' enforcements, and drew artillery over the side. It cost the Dutch more lives than all of Albert's sallies put together.

Either the rain poured down or the sun beat down, as Ghelderode gleefully records, and Ostend was surrounded by deep moats which fended off attack by land, but allowed provisions, armaments, and reenforcements to be delivered to the Dutch forces by sea. Thus despite the many Dutch casualties, they were continually supplied with fresh recruits brought in from the oceanic entry. Still, by the end of the siege, the Dutch had gone through seven commanders! After four years of Spanish attempts to take the stronghold, 60,000 lives had been lost on either side. Ghelderode only exaggerates slightly in his depiction of an abandoned, vacant Ostend, for four thousand people did remain once the siege was ended; still the fort lay in ruins. On September 24, 1604, when Albert and Isabella (for Isabella was present for the occasion) made their triumphal entry into the fallen city, they were faced with a horrible blast of fetid stench from the quantity of corpses adorning the ground of Ostend.

Ghelderode's source for the scene with three doctors, in addition to Ensor's drawing, may have been an anecdote about a certain Dr. Courtemans. Although details of his treatment are not known, whomever did not die of it, immediately became immune to illness. The number of dead was extraordinary. There were daily excursions outside the citadel walls to dump that day's quota of corpses. In one such case, a military procession deposited a casket outside the wall which turned out not to contain a body, but gunpowder, that, when it exploded, finished off a goodly number of Spanish troops. The casualties on both sides were so great, often exceeding three hundred a day, that chroniclers speak of a gruesome condition in which the troops were constrained to battle upon seething mountains of corpses.

The accumulating corpses, which gradually were employed as land-fill for the region, are instances of great indignation for anyone opposed to war. And while *The Siege of Ostend* is unquestionably an anti-war play, Ghelderode, who is elsewhere an expert at evoking sinister atmospheres, in dramatizing these incidents spares the audience the most ghastly of the siege's consequences. When faced with a choice of horrifying or amusing the audience, Ghelderode skirts the horrors and goes for that which will elicit a childish snicker of half repulsion, half delight, after the Aristophanic model.

Ghelderode's vision of free and warm fraternizing between the Spaniards and the Flemish and Walloon populations seems an accurate representation of historic fact. The various groups not only socialized, but intermarried. The latter instance is given a satiric slant in Tableau XII when the illustrious Spinola discovers he is father to a Brussels dancer. Indeed the number of Spanish names, Spanish words in the Brussels patois (such as the name of the old prison, "The Amigo" and the famous "Faro" beer), not to mention Mediterranean facial features in many present-day Belgians bear lasting witness to the extent of the intermingling which went on through the epoch.

The same holds true for Ghelderode's depiction of the moral climate in Brussels. As early as the fifteenth century, Brussels had gained a reputation as a place where sensual pleasures were to be had in abundance. Saunas, centers of sociability and amusement, were legion, and by 1441 contemporary accounts denounce Brussels as a center of general "corruption and moral decay." Despite puritanical rules forbidding women from so much as entering establishments where alcohol was served under pain of having their clothing confiscated, prostitution had reached such vast proportions that a special district in the neighborhood of Fossée aux Loups was set aside for the exercise of that profession.

The savage rape of nuns and pillage of convents was common practice by Spanish soldiers, and occurred, for example, at Malines in 1572. Ghelderode's depiction of the Beguines of St. Schlongus as bitches in heat seems, from an enlightened viewpoint, a very reprehensible portrait of women subjugated by marauding invaders. Nevertheless Flemish history offers a model for this depiction. It appears that a certain group of "White Sisters" at the Convent of Jericho did bear resemblance to those in *The Siege* in their way of hosting passing squadrons. Duchess Isabella ultimately banished them as they "possessed few virtues apart from that of hospitality, which they dispensed with great prodigality." But the depiction of the women of Ostend lifting their skirts on the battlements and sending off volleys of farts against the Spaniards is pure Ghelderodian invention. In fact, all the women and children of Ostend were spirited off to Zeeland at the outbreak of hostilities. Still, the imaginative Ghelderode may have been inspired by entirely different incidents in which, as Simon Schama relates:

> ...the women of 's Hertogenbosch, led by 'Trijn van Leemput' (Catharijna Bergen), the wife of one of the city's magistrates, who mobilized another women's legion against [the Duke of] Alva in 1576, and those at Dordrecht in the fifteenth century who fired cannon from the city's walls.

Several other characters Ghelderode includes are hijacked from other periods in European history and implanted in the Ostend epic. The character Don Juan is not Don Juan Tenorio (although he seems to be endowed with the allure of the famous lover as well as his "love 'em and leave 'em" strategy in Ghelderode's presentation), but Don Juan of Austria. The latter was a bastard son of Charles V, who at 24 years of age, was governor of the Lowlands for two years, which, from 1576 to 1578, antedates the circumstances in *The Siege of Ostend* by twenty two years. Lamoral is based on Lamoral of Egmont, a victor over the French in a battle at Saint Quentin in 1557 (thus pre-dating *The Siege*) and subsequently governor of Flanders and Artois.

Admiral De Ruyter is yet another example of

forced anachronism. Michiel de Ruyter (1607-1676) started as a crewman on a whaling vessel and ultimately become a legendary admiral who sailed in opposition to the Spanish, but at a much later time than the siege. Although born three years after the siege had ended, Ghelderode uses him to embody Dutch attributes of hardiness, freedom, and hospitality.

Ghelderode's anachronisms are not limited to people. The epithet "architect" appears three times in *The Siege* as the height of an insult. This reference is incomprehensible unless one is aware that, in order to make room for the main law court in Brussels, *le Palais de Justice*, huge quantities of houses in the poor quarters of Brussels had to be razed. This injustice, effected at the instigation of the colorful King Leopold II in the 1880's (not the 1660's), led to a general distaste among the populace for builders and architects who bore the brunt of their disdain. "Lousy architect" is to this day a popular Brussels insult. Ghelderode's frequent references to Belgium are entirely out of joint with chronology, as Belgium was not so-called until 1830; before that it was the Lowlands, the southern Lowlands, Belgica, or an agglomerate of Flanders, Brabant, Hainaut, and Liege. His deliberate misnomer points up how thinly veiled his historification technique is. It is used to remind the audience that he is mocking present-day institutions and individuals more than long bygone ones.

References to people very much alive and recent historical events reveal Ghelderode's real targets. For example, when Isabella warns that "the Ostenders will pay," she is in fact quoting Poincaré who said "Germany will pay" during World War I. In Tableau XVII the soldiers are ordered to use up all their cannonballs to justify over-ordering so the High Command can get their kickbaks. Here Ghelderode includes what was revealed to be common practice in World War I. Don Horace, in the same scene, tellingly slips in, "They say this siege is nothing but a pretext for stirring up patriotic and fiscal enthusiasm," an able summation of the genuine motives behind many wars — to save the economy, justify over-taxation, and distract the populace from domestic ills. Many of the other nightmares of wars — disease, mass slaughter, flourishing of the military industrialization — all clearly refer to the horrible "war to end all wars" whose reverberations were still being felt throughout Europe in 1933 when Ghelderode wrote his "military" epic.

## THE PRIVATE HUMOR AND LANGUAGE OF *THE SIEGE*

To the extent that *The Siege of Ostend* is Ensorian (especially in the scenes where Sir Jaime figures prominently), it is also one elaborate in-joke. But there are several thinly veiled references to Ghelderode's own life and circle that are impenetrable without knowing their references. There is for example "The Mystery of Lost Innocence," a puppet play, performed in the brothel by one Jef Casteleynos, a pseudonym for Ghelderode's friend, Jef Contryn, a puppeteer who mounted many of the author's smaller works. Another puppet play, about the siege of Ostend, is also being performed at the brothel, one said to be written by a certain Don Miguel of the Blessèd Tree, a pseudonym for Ghelderode himself who was born at Rue de l'Arbre Bénit (Blessed tree) in Ixelles, Brussels. The name of the brothel, "The Farting Jackass," was also taken from the actual bar Ghelderode installed in his home the year after he wrote *The Siege*. Sir Jaime makes passing reference to "The Loves of Pope Joan," a swipe at Ghelderode's wife, Jeanne. A slew of other such private references were included in earlier versions of the play but eliminated by the final draft.

The language, which has been the subject of several detailed studies, is predominantly French, but liberally laced with Flemish turns of phrase and expletives, which are then, with the addition of an "io" or "os" suffix, endowed with a mock Spanish flavor. In any given sentence, these ethnic antics may be interspersed with both mock-heroic diction and the most plebeian of low-minded slang. Other terms, like "Sperloot," come directly from Ensor, and have no conventionalized meaning, except, in the personal iconography of the *Siege*, referring to those opposed to the Spanish frog.

The humor combines these elaborate hermetic references with pre-adolescent wallowing in humanity's baser sides: images of excretion ("What is the protocol for an archduke who has to shit?") and sexual organs ("Nothing, Milord, surpasses the spectacle of a good shot well-fired"). Jokes about the church charging parishioners to have bells rung and candles burnt in commemoration of war-like ventures abound, as well as those about myriad forms of torture (priests getting dunked in boiling wax for example), heroism ("valiant" pickers whose flies are down and whose noses are running), the Belgian rain, and drinking.

The rain ("It is seven in the morning, and it is not raining.") renders this giant mosaic more topical and local than universal. It is always "schpritzing" down, as even the casual visitor to Belgian will corroborate. A tremendous number of scenes end with the characters going off to the tavern for a drink of one beverage or another. All conflicts are resolved through communal swilling, and all personal sorrows are drowned in a flood of alcohol. All kinds of Belgian beer are invoked, including Kriek Lambick and Gueuze (named after the anti-Spanish rebels). And much is made of Schiedam, a kind of Dutch gin popular among the rebels. Thus the damp air and land are fitfully matched by the human landscapes inside the bodies of besotted Spaniards and Flemings.

## THE *SIEGE*'S UNFORTUNATE HISTORY

It is the "epic's" audacious nature that caused it never to be published or performed during Ghelderode's lifetime. Indeed it was first published eighteen years after his death, and only his widow's demise made that possible. It was to wait yet another eight years for its world premiere! A myth consequently arose around *The Siege* that its author had forbidden its dissemination. Nothing could be further from the truth; Ghelderode went to extraordinary lengths to entice directors and publishers to undertake it. The play's daring, often verging on defiant obscenity, together with its intermittent overflows of verbiage, tended to discourage directors. And the initially chilling response he received from his circle of friends, amongst whom he distributed copies, dampened his enthusiasm for writing in a similar mode, but did not eradicate his fondness for the play.

The few directors who came close to undertaking *The Siege* during Ghelderode's lifetime were prepared to do so with the stipulation that the author first cut it to a stageable length. This Ghelderode proved ultimately incapable of doing, and no production ever came to fruition. Mme. Ghelderode, who survived her husband by eighteen years and who apparently was one of the play's detractors, finding it too scabrous, forbade its publication; and it was only after her death that Mme. Josette Marchant-Gerard, Ghelderode's niece, permitted the play to see light of day. Ghelderode was ultimately vindicated when *The Siege of Ostend* was published by Louis Musin in 1980 and directed by Albert-André Lheureux at the Theatre de l'Esprit Frappeur in Brussels in 1988.

## TRANSLATORS' NOTE

A French man or woman attending a performance of *The Siege of Ostend* in the original French would probably be stupefied by one fifth of the verbal humor. That much of the play consists of Flemish, Brussels dialect, or in-jokes. In order to decode this bizarre linguistic stew we have had recourse to dictionaries of Brussels dialect, principally that by Louis Quievreux, and to the massive study of archaisms, regionalisms and neologisms to be found in the play written by Christine Miclotte. Even after consulting these official sources, a huge number of references remained incomprehensible and were only elucidated on generously offered consultation with Régine Van Belle, Prof. Roland Beyen, Jean Decock and Alain Piette.

We wished the play's humor to be somewhat more accessible to the average reader or audience member in English than it would be in French; leaving the references in their original impenetrable state (by literally transferring the Flemish and Bruxellois as we found it) was not a choice which we entertained for very long. Rather, once we had deciphered the literal meaning of each phrase for ourselves, we tried to find a comparable form of word-play in English. What follows then is an inexcusable combination of infantile nonsense words, New Yorkese, and pure invention. A certain percentage of word-play had to be sacrificed. And sometimes we had to move the playful part of a sentence to a different place, because it "felt" better there in English.

We hope we have captured the wildness of the original — its antic mixing of high and low forms, its weird flights of fancy, and its true originality.

## THE ACTOR MAKES HIS EXIT

The Actor Makes His Exit (Sortie de l'Acteur, 1935) is, in its own way, unlike any other play Ghelderode wrote. It resembles *Three Actors and Their Drama* (1926), in its Pirandellian presentation of actors on stage. But, whereas the latter is a schematic distillation of the theatricalist approach (with characters deliberately made anonymous with names like "The Actor," "The Ingenue," "The Young Male Lead," and "The Prompter"), *The Actor Makes His Exit* presents rounded multi-faceted characters in situations which elicit great passion from them. It is more an intensely personal cry from the heart than a fashionable intellectual exercise. This play, more than any other in the Ghelderode canon, places modern life in the foreground of the drama. His only other major play to do so, *Pantagleize*, is couched in the form of a modern fairy tale and parable, so that it retains a decided distance from contemporary life. Most of Ghelderode's other major plays from *Chronicles of Hell* to *Miss Jairus* to *The Grand Macabre's Stroll* (*La Ballade du Grand Macabre*) only reflect on the twentieth century by inference and allusion. Their theatrical force and originality are achieved to some degree from the pseudo-medieval ambience in which they are drenched.

Ghelderode makes only a small attempt to disguise the autobiographical nature of *Actor Makes His Exit*. Ghelderode himself called it his "theatrical last will and testament" and said it should rightfully be titled *The Author Makes His Exit*. In fact, the events it records did not occur exactly in life as they did in art. Still, the employment of the character of an author clearly intended to represent himself, grounds this play in the present in a way none of his other works do. Further, the important role of the actor Renatus is a transparent embodiment of the real-life actor Renaat Verheyen who played several principal roles in

Ghelderode's plays before he died an untimely death at age twenty-six.

Despite the play's modern settings (the stage of a theater in Act I, a squalid apartment in Act II, and the fringes of a cemetery in Act III), Ghelderode remains Ghelderode, uneasy with the century he was born in; consequently, he turns the play back into the past at every opportunity. The past coexists with the present and bleeds into it. The play-within-a-play the actors are rehearsing on the empty theatricalist stage of Act I is a medieval period piece, a pastiche of various other Ghelderode plays. Then Fago, the versatile prompter/mime/waiter/sacristan, appears in the Commedia mask of Pierrot strumming a haunting ukulele. Commedia crops up once more in Act II when Renatus in his delirium harnesses the looming shadows about him into a "doctor out of Molière," the ephemeral human form with which he communes during his last minutes of life.

One of the play's most intriguing facets is, in fact, the way in which light and dark are made in the first two acts to intimate the presence of the world beyond, a world which in Act III, set in the cemetery, erupts and takes center-stage. When Ghelderode leaves off the depiction of a "tasteless parlor" or bedroom, working in that most materialistic of genres, naturalism, and takes the leap into the spirit world of angels and ghosts, during which a Jacob's ladder to heaven materializes for Renatus to climb, one feels he is back home stylistically. Renatus's passage from corporeal existence in an infirm body to a divorce of his spirit self, which then rises above and away from the temporal world, follows the same trajectory as the play's structure — the movement from base realism (though injected with intimations of the beyond) to capricious fantasy.

The story behind the play is intimately based on Ghelderode's association with the Flemish Peoples' Theatre (De Vlaamse Volkstoneel). As a Fleming who had been brought up to write and speak French (his parents hoped this linguistic advantage would assist his rise through status-conscious Belgian society), Ghelderode first tried to gain a hearing in the French-speaking theater, but with very dim results. Only a few of his early small plays were performed, whereas his next few major experiments, *The Death of Doctor Faustus* and *Don Juan*, went unstaged. This impasse seemed to be overcome when the Flemish Peoples' Theatre, an itinerant group with both strong Socialist and Catholic leanings (and especially Flemish Nationalist tendencies) agreed to undertake this work. While they ultimately turned down many of the pieces he offered them, three major works were mounted with great success: *Images from the Life of Saint Francis of Assissi*, *Barrabbas*, and *Pantagleize*. So Ghelderode's first extensive experience with the practical stage saw his own plays being produced not in their original French but in Dutch translation, a language he spoke only in dialect and almost never wrote in. Still, at the time, he evinced a great sympathy for the Flemish Movement and wrote fervent articles on the subject for various newspapers; moreover, his fascination with Expressionism corresponded with the Flemish Peoples' Theater's enthusiastic forays into Expressionism, Constructivism, and other movements gleaned second-hand from Meyerhold, Tairov, and the German theater. Surviving photographs of their productions reveal actors tormenting their bodies at weird angles before geometricized, mechanized settings.

The actor Renaat Verheyen joined the Peoples' Theatre at age twenty in 1924 and played several important roles: Trufaldino in Goldoni's *Servant of Two Masters*, Mephistofeles and the Clown in Marlowe's *Doctor Faustus*, Rebolledo in Calderon's *The Mayor of Zalamea*, and the title role in Sophocles' *Oedipus Rex*. Ghelderode evokes each of these triumphs in one of Renatus's speeches in *Actor Makes His Exit*. As for Ghelderode's own plays, Verheyen created the title roles in *Pantagleize* (which he also directed) and

*Images from the Life of Saint Francis of Assissi*, as well as Judas in *Barabbas*, gaining the sobriquet "the Flemish Chaplin" for his diminutive stature and impish persona. Although he and Ghelderode were never intimate friends, the author did see him as the interpreter most capable of fulfilling his vision on stage and deeply regretted the split which divided the Peoples' Theatre in April, 1930. Occurring as a result of political differences, many members of the troupe also had labor grievances regarding the demanding rehearsal and performance schedules. Verheyen went with the more militant wing of the group, while Ghelderode, in great perplexity, maintained loyalty with Jan Boon and the original camp. In letters dated May 4 and June 15, 1930, Verheyen, on behalf of the splinter group, begged Ghelderode to give his faction a new play to perform. Ghelderode, in what was tantamount to a response, never followed through on certain projects he had half-promised to write for the secessionists, and on October 24th of the same year Verheyen passed away. Ghelderode was seized by feelings of guilt and sorrow. The eloquent obituary he wrote for the Flemish papers was not adequate to purge himself of both the loss of his best interpreter and remorse over the rift which had separated him from Verheyen at the time of the latter's death.

One full season went by with no Ghelderode play on the Peoples' Theater's roster. By 1932, when the group disbanded for good, they had rejected or dropped from season schedules several major works by Ghelderode and had produced a mere two minor works, *The Star Thief* and *Ocean Voyage*. Still the fact of the group's existence held out the promise that the playwright might be performed, a glimmer then decisively extinguished. His prime performance venue gone, Ghelderode next settled on writing what he considered closet dramas which, all hopes to the contrary, stood little chance of being produced. It was during this wave of turning inward and renouncing the practical theater that Ghelderode started writing *The Actor Makes His Exit* in 1933.

If there are echoes of Pirandello, Strindberg, and Wedekind in the writing, it is less a case of influence than testamentary permission these predecessors' plays furnish to delve into certain areas and introduce subject matter which reflected Ghelderode's own obsessions. Throughout his life he feared that, were he to write according to his own lights and give vent to his own voice, that he would be forever spurned by the boulevard theater and go unloved by his most beloved idols — actors and directors. Dramatizing this rejection as well as the writer's forswearing of his craft, Jean-Jacques flings his unperformed works into the fire, an act symbolic of Ghelderode's impulses, but one he didn't actually commit. Rather, he held onto his plays, reworking them continuously, until he was discovered by the Paris theater milieu after World War II.

The formula of actors playing actors, a conceit pervasive in the twenties and thirties, popular with playwrights as disparate as Pirandello and Thornton Wilder, permits the artist's rejection by peers and the artist's self-rejection to be played out onstage. Within the emotional logic of the play, what prevents the curtain from going up on Jean-Jacques's troublesome play? It is the lead player's, Renatus', death. And why does he die? Well, according to the accusation the actor hurls at the author, it is because by acting the role of a doomed man in the playwright's work, he has become infected by the playwright's fascination for death — he virtually dies of artistic morbidity. Thus it is Jean-Jacques's own gloom which undermines his chance at success and recognition. In fact, this drama is virtually internal, made external with Renatus as the projected agent of the writer's own would-be omnipotent mind. Through Renatus's fertile creativity he stood a chance of communicating his vision. But, accepting the accusation that it is he who is guilty of his tribune's demise, the author punishes himself accordingly: no more creation.

Alongside the troublesome wrestling match with death in which death triumphs, there is another one between man and woman. For unelucidated reasons, Jean-Jacques and the female lead Amanda are at each others' throats, in lieu of flinging their arms about each others' throats in an effusion of erotic passion. Despite a manifest attraction between them, they are only capable of exchanging barbed criticism and insults. These give way over the death-bed of their colleague Renatus, when the arms of caustic badinage are laid down in favor of passionate embraces which, in the tenebrous lighting, they yet resemble "two wrestlers locked in combat." Renatus's clattering death, along with Fago's entrance and discovery that the couple had relaxed their vigilance in favor of making-out, elicits a guilt so great in Jean-Jacques and Amanda that any positive feeling is smothered beneath resignation before death's ascendance. Thus a Strindbergian dance of love turns to a stand-off of death... and an end to writing. In a one-two assault, death divests Jean-Jacques both of capacity for fulfilled love and creativity, thus hollowing him out.

Without pressing the autobiographical parallel too far, this seems to have happened to Ghelderode in his own life. Not that there is any evidence for his having been unfaithful to his wife, but an incipient hypochondria, terror of death and loss of self-confidence set in and knocked the creative juices out of him during the last twenty years of his life. When he was belatedly discovered by the French theater world, which staged many Ghelderode plays in succession in the post-war period, he had no more plays in him to write. He spent virtually the remainder of his days re-writing old projects, fostering the world's image of him as a spooky hermit, and conceiving new projects which were never to see the light of day. The eminent Ghelderode scholar Roland Beyen regards the depredations of World War II together with an intensifying of his chronic asthma, as the causes for

Ghelderode's loss of creative energy. It may only be coincidental that both of his parents died around the same time (his father in 1943 and his mother in 1944), but full explanation for this lamentable occurrence is yet to be identified.

Within the play, the direness of this vision is mitigated by Renatus's return as a ghost in Act III. He is dressed in the Chaplinesque costume of Pantagleize, the famous Ghelderode role Verheyen originated. And he is desperately trying to hang onto life, despite being pursued by a squadron of angels who are determined to waft him off to heaven. Ghosts and apparitions are more common to the classical than the modern drama, but Wedekind provided a precedent in the final scene of *Spring's Awakening*, where the specter of Moritz appears to his guilt-consumed friend, Melchior, also in a graveyard. Both specters served the same dramatic function of absolving the protagonist of his nagging guilt for the other's death. Both Wedekind and Ghelderode balk at the prevailing positivist axioms which would preclude such an emanation from beyond, since for the positivists and naturalists there is no beyond, only material reality. One could plausibly argue in a Freudian spirit that the specter is nothing but an inner projection and that it has no actual existence; but Ghelderode's dramatizing is quite persuasive. One is inclined to accept the fantasy for reality. Here psychology, mysticism, and child-like fantasy weave together into a tangle of theatrical truth which defies reduction or logical explanation.

## *TRANSFIGURATION IN THE CIRCUS*

Ghelderode's politics fluctuated radically throughout his life and often seem to have been conditioned by which faction appreciated or might have potentially appreciated his work at any given moment. As a young man he wrote pro-anarchist articles under the pseudonym "Babylas." Interest in his plays by the Flemish People's Theatre greatly solidified his support of the Flemish Movement. Once the People's Theater's interest in his plays waned, his support of Flemish Nationalism faltered. With Nazis menacing an occupation of Belgium, Ghelderode privately exulted in the hope that the Germans would find value in and stage his plays. With the Occupation in full swing, its deprivations sapping Ghelderode's health, and none of his plays being produced, he came to despise Nazism.

Ghelderode's various contingent, pragmatic allegiances notwithstanding, he was temperamentally apolitical and had no lasting affiliation with any cause. His was a nature more suited to commentary from a far remove than one of engagement within the dynamic and perilous sweep of a political movement. *Transfiguration in the Circus*, like its more famous and elaborated cousin *Pantagleize*, presents just such a critical and distanced vision of a world in revolution. Written in 1927, immediately before the Russian Revolution had resolved itself into totalitarianism, it prefigures the multitude of juntas, overthrows, and coups d'états which have peppered this century and satirically reflects the genesis and consequences of an archetypal revolutionary process.

Ghelderode, who loved puppets, Commedia characters, and marionettes, had recourse to yet another popular entertainment, which took root in the Middle Ages (but only bloomed in the nineteenth century) — the circus. *Transfiguration in the Circus*, as its title suggests, is situated squarely in the tradition of the circus and knockabout physical farce, a genre which obviates the necessity for long *tirades* and trims the action down to essentials. And though its form is used to satirically mask his commentary on revolution, yet the Belgian playwright is quite faithful to the rules and regulations endemic to the traditional circus.

The various names Ghelderode assigns his clowns are classical clown titles, Mister Clown and August especially so. Gustave was the name of the first Fratellini brother, although Mister Clown in his position as dictator is reminiscent once again of Pa Ubu, or Chaplin in *The Great Dictator* . The jobs Mister Clown hands out to his cohorts correspond to categories of clown-types of the Garevich Circus System, which include the musical clown and the carpet clown. Cuckoldry was a typical circus episode, as was the idea of saturnalia in which the servants become masters. Revolution had been already been exploited as a circus act by Lucien Godard, a famed circus entrepreneur, whose staging of a clown revolution was prominent in his repertory.

*Transfiguration in the Circus* is a compendium of classic circus *lazzi* which are equated with the customary stages of revolution as Ghelderode sees them. For instance, the play repeats over and over again the prototypical comic situation of the hero who lays a trap in which he is the first to be caught. Both the Ringmaster and Mister Clown get shot by the trick gun with which each thought to kill the other. Luna is the focus of the plot that all the clowns hatch to outwit the others. Each in turn is caught in the trap of disillusionment she sets, even August, who appears to be the cleverest of the lot. And the final action of the play is constructed on this rhythm as well. Mister Clown intends to regain dominion over the situation by bringing about the end of the world with a bomb explosion. His trick holds within it, however, his own downfall, for who should pop out of the bomb to conduct their own massacre (including that of Mister Clown), but his adversaries, the Ringmaster and Luna.

The circus is a distancing metaphor for Ghelderode's preferred theatrical world, one which is in the process of dissolution and estrangement, one in which logical progression is obliterated and which ends in Armageddon. The arbitrary large and small peaks of action Ghelderode typically imposes are conveniently realized by classical clown tomfoolery, as described by Henri Bergson:

... the clowns came and went, collided, fell and jumped up again in a uniformly accelerated rhythm, visibly intent upon effecting a *crescendo*. And it was more and more to the jumping up again, the *rebound*, that the attention of the public was attracted.

Typical of the circus is the kind of routine in which a clown is injured or killed only to totally recover in the next moment, in total defiance of nature's laws. The clowns in *Transfiguration* die frequently and resurrect just as often. The first death is that of Mister Clown, who after announcing, "I am dead," raises his frame and requests a more upbeat funeral march from the bandleader. The next is the Ringmaster's death, which is followed by his surreptitious resurrection and escape. Mister Clown fails to observe the latter incident, which results, much later, in his own downfall. After a particularly frightful melee, the clowns skid to the ground in succession and dissolve in a flood of tears. August shouts, "Silence! You're all knocked out!" The clowns cooperate and go stiff, followed by an instantaneous revival upon August's exit. They attempt, and succeed in a mass suicide by tickling each others' feet, but immediately wake up when a real danger, Mister Clown's bomb, makes an appearance. The action of the dead coming back to life coincides exactly with Ghelderode's macabre taste for reviving corpses notable in larger plays such as *Miss Jairus*, *Chronicles of Hell*, *Magpie on the Gibbet*, and, as we have seen, in *The Actor Makes His Exit*

Other lapses of logic and sequentiality include the routine, "Mister Clown Doesn't Want to Work," a general strike in which clown logic entails a very literal interpretation of doing nothing, akin to Buddhist meditation: an eternal, static present. August demands that they "take a break" from the oppressive inactivity. They resolve to read the manifesto *after* the revolution is over, which both violates its inherent necessity, and points up its superfluity. The clowns characteristically wail about the shock that has struck them in the heart when they have actually been kicked in the derriere. The paradoxical clown logic is very much like that which dictators use. Mister Clown exults, "Long live liberty and liberated clowns," while shaking his billy club at his subjects, both belying their free choice and assuring instant assent.

Bergson speaks of other comic rhythms, such as "a great cause resulting in a small effect" and the literal interpretation of a figurative intent, both used in this play. The first cranking of Mister Clown's big bomb, constructed to blow them all to kingdom come, produces but a slight "pop". Starting from the premise that "revolutionary manifestoes are declarations of love," the clowns conclude that Luna, object of their love, is revolution. They equate a kick in the behind with the shock of love. "I'm sick at heart," moans Casimir, cradling his posterior. Since revolutions are well-known to set the world on its head, the clowns resolve to stand on theirs. All these conventions are generously interlarded with a plethora of sudden falls, blows, kicks, and somersaults, one series of which express Mister Clown's jubilation at his success as a revolutionary.

The sometimes pathetic figure of the clown, embodying both the idealist and the fool, is a perfect disguise for Ghelderode's hapless hero. Pathos is not absent from the circus world, and no one rejoices at an endearing clown's death. Mister Clown's epitaph: "Absurd clowns, painted clowns..." is poignant indeed, as is the beautiful final image of the clowns floating up by the flies in a bluish light. Once freed from their terrestrial constraints and the follies and pressures of revolutionizing, when they are ultimately seen circulating about in the heavenly sphere, the self-defeating, frivolous clowns acquire a touching nobility they never had in the circus rink of life.

David Willinger<br>New York, 1990

*The Siege of Ostend*
Théâtre Royale du Parc, Brussels 1987
photograph by Nicole Hellyn

# *THE SIEGE OF OSTEND*

translated by
**David Willinger and Gilbert Darbouze**

Characters of the Epic:

The Archduke Albert
The Infanta Isabella
General Marquis Ambrose de Spinola, Commander of the Spanish Armies
Sir Jaime, Baron of Sidney, Marquis of the Land-Fill, Artist, and Leader of the Resistance
Don Juan de Bel-Hombre y Mecton, Captain
Don Horace d'Antwerpia, Captain
Br'er Kletsaf, Capuchin friar, confessor to Isabella
Father Trullemans, religious advisor to Isabella
Don Lamoral, military advisor
Marquis of Miralobar, Ambassador from the Archduke
Don Mendoza, superior officer
Don Realgar, superior officer
Don Pachacrouto, colonel
Don Rambollo Bombardos, colonel
Admiral de Ruyter, Dutch Admiral
Santa Cruz
Captain Don Pacheco
Klabotsky, Polish engineer
Conchita, Baroness of Pierman
Don Pommados, Spanish doctor
Don Pillulos, Spanish doctor
Don Clysteros, Spanish dactor
Don Benèvolo, Major Army astronomer
Cleo, Spanish dancer
Aunt Rosie, dueña
Dom Faggot, documentary monk
Romero, Spanish soldier
Casanova, Spanish tenor
The Unknown Spanish Soldier
The Toreador

The Elder of the Nobles
Verdugo, Executioner
Mother Scopelor, Abbess of Saint Schlongus
The Six Beguines of the Abbey of Saint Schlongus
Paquita }
Conchita } señoritas at Aunt Rosie's
Marquita }
Carmencita}
The Tubercular Monkey
Bifrons, devil
Dom Cancrulor, bishop
Crapitus, devil
Israfel, devil
Fifrelin, devil
Zozo, devil
Rothomago, devil
Clistheret, devil
Vociferan, devil
Colodion, devil
Pruritan, devil
Peril, devil
Mirabel, devil
Assorted devils
Innkeeper of the Grand Mirror
The Hooded Brethren
Herring Mongers, Masks, Monks, Male Chorus, The Populace, Señors, Señorkas, Men and Women of Ostend, Flemish rebels, Men and Women of Flessingen. Tritons. Sirens. Nobles. Yeomen.

## Tableau I

*The Palace of Brusselos on the Montus Frigidus in the Hall of the Nobles. The great Spanish coat of arms is painted on the walls, the shields, and the servants' behinds. It is seven in the morning, and it is not raining. Albert and Isabella are in conversation:*

ALBERT: What offense have these Ostenders done you anyway? I foresee that your rage shall bring yet another great upheaval down on their heads, My Dryness.

ISABELLA: God so wishes, my Archduke. The citizens of the Lowlands have their nerve, as you very well know, and now these people of Ostend thumbing their noses at our royal person! I shall butt the Ostenders right into the sea and their city along with them. God wishes it, sir, since I so wish.

ALBERT: Pot-damitto, Milady Infanta, I smell a monk here somewhere. God's only wish is that the little folk of Belgium be happy. All they want is to play darts, shoot at birds with cross-bows, eat, drink, sleep, sing little ditties, and prance about, for which they're dead right, and make fun of our royal repute, in which they're consummately wrong. Also, bear in mind that the peseta is mighty weak, with no recovery in sight. .

ISABELLA: The people of Belgium are going to pay for this for I shall lay economic siege. They won't know what hit 'em. I'll have the Ostenders chucked into the drink before you can say one Our Father and one Hail Mary, you old archducal softy, you. Amen.

ALBERT: No amen say I to that! Who's boss around here in the palace of Brusselos anyway?

ISABELLA: You are, when, with pen of Toledo in hand, you sign decrees I tell you to that say: "We so wish" or "We so command." Thus, go to and straightway sign this foolscap with fine ink, and so forge the bull.

ALBERT: Are you calling this decree a bull?

ISABELLA: Bull I call it and bull it is!

ALBERT: She's saying her own idiotic decree's a crock. What foibles, Milady! Why, you're drunk on self-importance, you're potted, for Heaven's sake! Just let me know if you need to upchuck and I'll go look for the big bull bowl. [*He bestirs himself.*] She's had too much wine to drink at mass!

ISABELLA: May foul Beelzebub fix your wagon. I'll betake me to sound the alarum for the Capuchin monks. They'll come skin your buttocks and the Dominican fathers too. They'll stick the funnel inside you, the stocks, the ass-beveller, the water needles, and all other Christian devices. Hasten to my aid, my darling monks!

ALBERT: Have mercy, Milady, we shall sign and slice up the Ostenders and chop off both their thumbs and their noses. Then they'll think twice about thumbing their noses, my Infantility.

ISABELLA: Have at it, ballbuster, but that's not all. You must also sign this masterful act by which I mandate the construction of twelve new churches, for we're way short of churches, one dedicated to Our Lady of the Snows, one to Our Lady in Red, one to Our Lady of Good Odor...

ALBERT: I shall sign, my Catholic lovely, and the monks will be quite pleased. In exchange you shall demand of the blessèd chapters that they advance us blessèd pesetas so we can lay blessèd siege on Ostend, seeing as I have yet again scraped the bottom of the sacred coffers. My belovèd Treasurer just told me "Sire, take this nail, this blessèd nail, for that's all we've got left to scrape your sacred behind with..." Goddammit!

ISABELLA: We shall authorize the populace to fill the blessèd coffers and I shall call on the Grand Physcal to have a Te Deum sung over it, holding his great magnet in one hand and his great collection basket in the other, while all the gargoyles of all the cathedrals regargoylate holy water and all the tenor and baritone monks shall sing: "Cough up alms, make a down payment on Paradise." Amen!

ALBERT: Amen. What shall we nibble on this noonday, milady? Raw Ostender or else monk in caper sauce? Camphorated broth for my honeybunch, but the monks shall get nought but bones with marrow.

ISABELLA: They'll nibble their amens and misereres with holy sauce, and for you, guinea hen in white wine with balls of meat.

ALBERT: May I also have some of those snails the commoners call Chinese testicles in memory of the missionaries the Chinese people nibbled up?

ISABELLA: Be still my archduke, curl back your upper lip and smile according to protocol, for here come the military marquis and the others, all very noble.

*Here enters the retinue of Spinola, Br'er Kletsaf, monks and divers nobles. All salute, the monks belch.*

SPINOLA: My Highnynesses, I salute you without removing my hat, for I am a grandee of Spain. Why have you brought me to Brusselos?

ISABELLA: Saluto and down the hatch, Marquis van de Spinola. Have a seat for it is of laying sieges that we must. . .

SPINOLA: On what can your Highnyness instruct me besides how to lay my Spanish grandee behind into the seat and not in to the side?

ALBERT: The General got up on the wrong side of the bed. Amigo, I say to you . . [*He reads.*] We Albert, by the grace of God. . .

ISABELLA: Do order our valiant and sublime generals to assault Ostend forthwith by foot and by horse with the aid of the All-Mighty and ransack it in dos shakes of a lamb's tail as an example to those of our States who dare rise up against us and make a laughing stock of our sovereign royalty. Thus do we summon the famous Spinola and all the other rag-tags and tag-alongs of the militia and all other mercenaries and mess-tin-io voluntarios and all other offishitios and ambushadoros to cover themselves in great heroism as is customary for the greater glory of Spain and ours and the fair renown of our armies.

ALBERT: Assi nos ayde Dios.

MONKS: Y todos sus santos!

SPINOLA: Viva Hispania! I don't give a doodio, I'm Italian. Lord and Lady, it shall be done and undone according to military art. But I trust you realize that these Ostenders have nought in their heads save respect for you.

BR'ER KLETSAF: It makes no difference, milord, we shall pray for their quick and joyful pulverization. Give no quarter, kill, slice, carve, stab, phshew, phshew, phshew.

SPINOLA: Pray rather that it doesn't rain on our exploits. It hasn't let up yet.

ISABELLA: Spinola, what are you waiting for, to lay siege to Ostend?

SPINOLA: May Your Infanticide Highnyness deign to muster up her full powers and promulgate a decree enjoining all peasants to pull up all their carrots and send them without any carroting around to the Court of Brusselos where the said carrots shall be reduced to circular slices which will perforce have the value of the peseta and that the said spheres will cover the expenses of the siege of Ostend as we've done for previous sieges. Most Serene Highnynesses, I beg your leave to withdraw, since I must wax my boots, polish up my spiked bludgeon, and gather up my captains don Juan de Bel-Hombre and don Horace de Antwerpia who right this very minute are drinking Faro beer at the Caballo Blanco Tavern outside the Porte Namurcencis.

*He salutes and exits.*

ALBERT: Madama, do you think he might bring us back some shrimp? He's dead right to propose that we start minting carrots: there's need enough.

ISABELLA: Absolutely no talk of pesetas. The Ostenders will pay. Meanwhile let them raise an additional thirty-sixth penny on every glass of Lambick beer and let all backsliders be strung up. My little monk, very reverend Kletsaf, you have of late nibbled much pork in aspic, spam of Tartary, and ham-o of Congolo. Has your digestive track received no visitation from the Holy Ghost in consequence?

*Br'er Kletsaf goes into ecstasy.*

BR' ER KLETSAF: By Saint James of Campostella, [*He belches.*] I had a peppery vision in [*He belches.*] which I saw the Most Catholic Infanta [*He belches.*] who I heard in dialogue with Jesus-Mary-and-Joseph [*He belches.*] who said: Isabella, bella, bella, just build a church with all the trimmings [*He belches.*] and the Siege on Ostend'll be in the bag. [*He belches.*] Yes, answered the oh so venerable Infanta, but one's not enough... [*He belches.*] I shall build one before, one during, and one after in homage to the Holy Trinity.

[*He belches.*] It shall be as you wish and we accept gladly, continued Jesus-Mary-and-Joseph. [*He belches.*] However, don't expect it to go on greased wheels, since in Ostend, where they know how to fix your wagon for you, [*He belches.*] there is a great bearded devil surnamed the Fighting Sperloot [*He belches.*] who knows countless more tricks than you can shake a stick at. In the name of the Father [*He belches.*] of the Son [*He belches.*] and the Holy Ghost. [*He farts.*]

ISABELLA: I'll throw in one more church to confound the great bearded devil. And one more for the slaughter of all the nasty Knaves!

BR' ER KLETSAF: Deo Gratis, that makes five. I'm going off to make it known and have a Te Deum sung for the Spanish victory to come.

ALBERT: When is victory to be ours?

BR' ER KLETSAF: Jesus-Mary-and-Joseph did not deem it meet to inform me at this time.

ISABELLA: Holynamededios! We're giving away five churches and they can't even give us a deadline for the victory? Trumpet it forth throughout the land that the Infanta solemnly swears not to change her chemyse in major penitence until such time as the Ostenders are reduced to French fritos. Heaven marks me, monk, let the entire Catholic world know of my promise.

ALBERT: My Infantastic wife, what shall become of our conjugal duty with you in that chemyse?

ISABELLA: In this chemyse I stay. And let them shoot on it.

*The bombardment is heard.*

And let the churchbells be rung, the big ones especially, at the expense of the parishioners.

*The churchbells are heard.*

BR' ER KLETSAF: The big bells are bonging, ding, dong, ding. [*He laughs.*]

ISABELLA: Imbecile! And you Albert, don't pull such a face, if you please. Act archducal, if you please, and go eat the left-over meat from the royal broth, if you please.

ALBERT: My Dryness, I have no appetite for that slop. If you will allow, I'll go have a look at the bombardment bombarding. They're making some good hits.

BR' ER KLETSAF: Nothing, Milord, surpasses the spectacle of a good shot well-fired.

*Exeunt.*

## Tableau II

*Ostend. In the display room of the white-bearded Sir Jaime. Paintings, masks, skeletons, fairy slippers, artificial flowers, cushions, a huge Renaissance style wardrobe cupboard. Organs. Sir Jaime strides up and down, holding a ray-fish by the tail. Crystalline lighting.*

SIR JAIME: Oh ray, moon-bellied ray-fish, with a human grin, hanging limp. Before smearing you with black butter and eating you, I shall first lovingly paint your portrait. You are wingèd, floured, opalescent, masked, and in the great underwater fish carnival, you are the clown. Perfume my painting studio which overlooks the foamy pink wave, my salty lover, apple of my harpoon's eye. Praise unto you, O North Sea, you with your unabashed singing mermaids, and your tritons, cod-liver oil guzzlers, each and every one, and your aphrodisiacal shrimp, and your mussels, and your limp kippers. O sea, sidewalk rolling to infinity, I'll scoot away on you without a second thought if the herring eaters of Ostend keep ridiculing me for not doing the safe painting they want me to. How long must I keep flailing away at public opinion with my umbrella? Oh, how squalid it all is! But if that's how it's gonna be, I'll go off and join the last of the Aztecs. I'll emblazon them with esoteric tattoos, and I'll play the fife atop their fine pyramids to charm and tame the most amusing Rhesus Monkeys whose pinky posteriors are coated with absolutely indescribable hues. [*He tosses the ray-fish up to the ceiling where it remains suspended.*] Let's have us some fun, English style. [*He picks up a silver-colored glass ball and spins it.*] Spin luminous little world, spin like a sheep pissing. [*He puts the ball back down and picks up masks.*] My old friends, my masks, you're made of cardboard, Mr., Mrs., Miss, knight, my reverend. They're all aristocratically long-nosed, riddled with maggots and political axioms. Listen up, you villains. Jehova walked through the Garden of Eden and in the midst of all the nanny-goat turds, He found one male mask and one female mask. He filled them with earth and breathed His madness into them. You smell like the smashed frog, sui generis, and you still have the same monkey hair and ear wax as you did at the Creation. As for me, I was born of the conjunction between a jar of relish and the Ark of the Covenant on a British isle where acute Angles dwell. King Arthur plucked them and turned them into English. God save Arthur! [*He hurls down the masks.*] You look like you're crying, but you're laughing. And you, you look like you're laughing, but you're crying. You're silly and yet you seem bright. You, you're dead. Poof! Ratatatat! Tears, clown-white, doody, spit, I'll mix you all up with my colors, I'll paint you, heads sliced like cold cuts, with bay leaves, parsley, haloes, monacles, and horns of Cornwall. Heavens! The churchbells on Army Plaza keep tolling on and on, which means the hour has come for eating soggy bacalao and reheated crab. But I am poor, so I'll make a meal of ruddy pigment and the protruding schnozolas of my masks. And this frog, steeped in poetry, will be my appetizer:

*He salutes and recites:*

A Belgian frog saw a Spanish swashbuckler
Against the Moors swashbuckling conceitedly
Slaughtering in a fashion most terrible
Only in frescoes would you see such a slaughterer.

Then the frog
Its Belgian soul incensing
Told him in Belgian quite froggishly
You'd never see me brag so hoggishly
Atop a mast or on a blue flag.
"Death to the wag!" the Moor-killer cried.
And the frog was taken by so sudden a fright
That it smashed with a croak,
Its guts set to flight,
And the Belgians gave it a fine burial.

THE DEVILS: Yay for the poet! Aaaaooo! Down with the clown-white! House painter! You lousy Architek, you! You'll never get the Prix de Rome! Aaaaooo! Boo-boo-boo! Long live the Stevens Brothers, sell-out painters both of 'em! Long live the red cabbages and the fat asses of the Academy! Hairy rats! Scribbling, scrawling, and doodling! Aaaaooo! Aaaaooo!

SIR JAIME: [*Banging on the wardrobe*] Lice, roaches, fleas, and crabs, vroom, vroom, revroom, supervroom, or should I say shit-ah, shit-oo, shit-ay, whichever you prefer. I'm the only real artist alive in all the Netherlands and beyond. [*He returns.*] The devils I keep shut up in the haunted wardrobe are getting edgy. And they're beginning to sound like the French-speaking traitors of Flanders, making fun of my futurist poetry. Milord devils, "The *swashbuckling conceit*" — you know the rest. It's my baronly motto. C'mon, I'm waiting for you, I who challenge the lice-ridden beggars from Ypredamme with my faithful Gargapança. [*He picks up his shield and umbrella.*] Here I stand fully equipped and armed with my weapons bearing the image of the Sperloot quivering in battle on a crimson field of middle-class indignation. Come out indignant, scandalized, dejected, excited, shameless, riff-raffed masks. [*The Masks emerge from every nook and cranny and make cat-calls.*] We'll grab hold of those devils and seal them up alive in the portal of the cathedral to scare people away and make the clergy shit in their pants. Excelsior, my masks, you shall have Belgian chitlin's and stew. Excelsior, on greased wheels and with a swift wind from behind. Go on and make loop-dee-loops, tickle, taunt, take potshots, ah-jah, ah-jah, zim boom, forward march!

> *He looks absolutely magnificent, brandishing an umbrella. The masks take command of the haunted wardrobe which pitches from side to side. At that moment, a big commotion in Flanders Street. A dried flounder flies through the window and lands at Sir Jaime's feet. A rolled parchment is attached to its tail. Sir Jaime picks up the fish and takes a bite out of it.*

What is this gallant message, and since when are flounders used for homing-pigeons? It comes from the big-thighed, big-bottomed, big-bosomed, ladies of the noble Sorority of Fish-Mongers who come around to play practical jokes on me. [*The Masks go over to the window and lean out.*] Dear masks, spit torrents on the heads of my enemies, the Herring Maidens, those thick cod-fish, those sticky whitings. Spit green, purple, carmine, lilac, celadon, animal black, vomit and thumb your nose in proper classical, stylized fashion.

HERRING MAIDENS: Long live Sir Jaime!

SIR JAIME: They wish me well, do they? Let's read

their message. [*He reads.*] "We swear our fervent love and zeal for the famous artist, the eminent citizen, and matinee idol and let the very noble Sir Jaime, Lord of Sidney, Marquis of Multi-Color, and Prince of Engravomania, great virtuoso of both the stiff brush and the soft: Be advised that our city of Ostend and all our fine territory with its seven marvels which are the sea, dunes, light-houses, natural pools, light, oysters, and Sir Jaime, all dating from the time of Margaret of Constantinople, are in peril this Fifth of July, year of our Lord 1601, for the Spanish enemy mean to make compost of us through and through for our having been and remaining loyal to the United Dutch Provinces and to the brave rebellious Knaves. These same Spaniards mean to shear the hair on our asses as close as nuns' and reduce us to chopped meat according to their Catholic recipes. We patriotic Herring Maids beg the dashing Sir Jaime to head up the resistance, since he is a very learnèd engineer and the inventor of Tomfoolery Powder which in no wise harms his excellent relations with all the devils of hell. In witness of which, the suppliants declare themselves the very fecal and ornamental servants to Your Picturality." [*He sighs.*] Well I'll be a monkey's uncle, it's Greek to me, now that these Spaniards come along, trying to mess with me! They're cruel and fanatical busy-bodies, brimming over with Spanish conceit. They're known for skinning decent people alive and laying sculpted lands low. They're popish clergy adrip with popery. Excelsior, my devils, out of your box! [*He opens the haunted wardrobe.*]

*Twenty-seven devils come out of the wardrobe.*

Don your visored helmets, sallets, coats of mail, cuirass, leather corsets, iron masks, go get your catapults, seringes, bellows, Chinese head-splitters, spikes, lances, cutting shears, bayonets, and don't forget the military music with kettle drums and snare drums, flutes, bombardment machines, harmonicas and rattles. Festoon yourselves in feathers and hasten to the four ports and ramparts, for they're on their way with their stumps, crucifixes, gallows and scalpels... who? Why, the Spinach with their inquisitors and hangmen. Long live the devils and freedom of criticism. And you, sea-dwelling devils, out with you. And you sorcerers and witches of West Flanders, charge once more willy nilly on flying broomsticks armed with all your benevolent evil spells. I am the great devil in chief and master of Ostendish sorceries.

*The devils dance.*

THE HERRING MAIDENS: Long live the Scamp of all Scamps! Long live the devils and the sorcerers! Down with the clergy! Long live the war-like masks! Let's have a speech in Ostendish!

*Sir Jaime sets the wizard's hat of Saitafermes on his head and drapes himself in a cape covered with astrological signs. He holds a smoked herring as his sceptre, and goes to the window.*

SIR JAIME: Excelsior, my sisters, you're right up there with dames of olden times. You're in heat as usual my virgins. So, lacerate, vociferate, and eviscerate, toss forth stinking bubbles, seagull turds, mussel scales, fish intestines. Don your golden spurs and your giant diamond combs. Here you are — the women of Ostend, rising up from the ashes after centuries spent in gossip. Brandish your shields which bear crimson ovaries alternating with shark's teeth on a field of slandering brine. We must join in struggle against the enemy. Oo-oo-ah-ooo! Do like Joan of Arc, Joan of the Hatchet, she of the lovely thighs. Oh yeah! The Spinach are scared stiff of women. You are witches one and all, a vocation passed down from mother to daughter, and as a matter of course, whores. May glory rain down on you! Assemble the combatants and civil patrol together and all other shirk-fuzz and good-for-nothings, and pull them by the pudenda right into combat. The moralizing Spinach are coming to destroy my lovely lighting and shimmering expanses, to efface the soft profile of my beloved dunes, trouble the calm of my graceful pools, pettily oppose my loves, my delights, and my organ pipes. They mean to stifle my high fantasy and fine irony, smear my wondrous paintings with glue and blue. Their King Phillip, number three of three, is nothing but the leavings from filleted herrings. Long live the long-bearded, hairy, thick-lipped, big-bellied Knaves, long live the thick-skinned, forked-tongued Knavettes. To the ramparts my darlings, and as soon as you see the whites of the Spinach eyes, roll up your skirts and let 'em see your statuesque pilons and bear in mind that their swashbuckling conceit...

THE HERRING MAIDENS:   [*in unison*] *will bring down the apocalyptic frog-smashing!*

> *Sir Jaime salutes, puts the smoked herring between his teeth and goes to sit down at the organ. He majestically plays the solemn March of the Fighting Sperloot. All the masks, all the devils, and all the herring maidens shout and unfurl comic banners. The churchbells and the alarum sound.*

## Tableau III

*The tent of the Marquis de Spinola, before Ostend.*

SPINOLA: Would your Catholic and gracious majesty deign to wipe his Catholic and gracious feet on our unworthy doormat and make himself at home?

ARCHDUKE ALBERT: Holy damn and doodio, are the gunners shooting for real or is that pretend? [*Cannons are heard.*] Or else did you command this crackle in order to impress me? Well I'm impressed, down to my very guts General. But don't go to all this trouble on my account! If we fire on the Ostenders, then the Knaves'll shoot back and may inadvertently hit my gracious, Catholic and majestic person!

SPINOLA: Suffer me to say one thing Sire. In proper warfare, the belligerent parties do not shoot at their respective leaders. No cannon balls may strike Your Majesty any more than our artillery will bombard the castle of Sir Jaime, soul of the resistance. We have better manners than that.

ALBERT: They say this Sir Jaime is shrewd as a hundred monkeys, English to boot, noble even though not Spanish, and what's more, a breeder of demons. Yes, I'm well-informed. He reeks of heresy, he's a magician, a sorcerer, a cabalist, and an artist to boot.

SPINOLA: And a practical joker in the English manner. He is every inch a loafer just as I am grandee of Spain!

ALBERT: Well, since he's managed to get demons on his side, you'll have to lay siege without me. I'm high-tailing it back to Brusselos. [*cannon fire*] Heaven help me! Aahoo, aahoo! Do you by any chance have my chamber pot, the royal chamber pot with my coat of arms? No? Then, I shall hold back my load, thus setting an example of heroism before the enemy. General, what does protocol dictate that I do in these circumstances?

SPINOLA: You must go through the lines under fire and congratulate the soldiers.

ALBERT: General, what news of the siege of Ostend?

SPINOLA: Sire, the region is to my liking, the air is salubrious, the countryside fair. Ostend has not been taken despite a preliminary charge which was merely an exercise. But I can take it anytime it please Your Majesty.

ALBERT: No hurry! In these matters, the best strategy is to wait it out. And after both sides wait endlessly for the other to make a move, either the Ostenders will clear out, or else you'll clear out. He who remains will be the victor.

SPINOLA: Indeed My Lord... But I assure you that great courage will be required of us Spaniards not to be the first to flee. We'd be better off not to drag it out unnecessarily and simply to claim victory. Do you have any idea how these besieged Ostenders comport themselves? They've surrounded themselves with cauldrons filled with unbelievable quantities of salted herrings which they fling tirelessly on our troops and battlefield. Our hooded spies inform us that they have enough projectiles to herringfy us night and day for fifty years. And what effect does that have on us? Our charging soldiers slip on the herrings and fall, and on account of their Spanish pride, refuse to go one step further, a Spaniard preferring death and dishonor to flopping ludicrously in the stinking fish-slime. And that's not all. Our valiant Spaniards are right chaste by nature, and the fighting women of Ostend who adorn the ramparts lift their skirts and exhibit enormous downy buttocks, and, what's worse, loose horrid farts which resound ten leagues away and stink up the plain. Listen Sire, . . . we've never seen, never heard, and never smelled the like of these valiant fartomaniacs. Therefore the troop's morale is not at all up to snuff. They say it's not a fair match, that they're more than willing to die gloriously but not to be ignobly asphyxiated or engulfed in rotten fish.

*Albert bursts out laughing.*

ALBERT: That's news to me! I'm going over to have a look at these warriors in combat position and order our artiflows not to harm such magnificent human cannons. [*He rubs his hands together.* ] Now, my old Spinolo, mark well your Prince. He will reveal three things to you, all joking aside. . .

SPINOLA: The first?

ALBERT: It was my infanta who wished the siege of Ostend. And now she's got it. I wish to punish her. She has sworn not to take her chemyse off until such time as Ostend is taken. So be it! But she'll have to stay in the chemyse longer than she thinks. That'll teach her to rashly proffer foolish vows and endlessly erect churches. Spinola, I order you not to take Ostend. The siege will go on for one, two, three years, or however long we wish!

SPINOLA: Pobre Dryness!

ALBERT: Pity her not! Thus I take my revenge for all those times when I was in love with her. She's left me stuck in the bull-ring of conjugal love with hard-onero once too often, when by temperament I'd have been an ardent prickador.

SPINOLA: Shall we move on? The second point Sire?

ALBERT: The second: however agreeable Ostend may be, I know certain sectors in Brusselos no less marvelous, where I shall be able to observe the enemy at closer quarters, lay siege to it, and bring it under my control. You're familiar with those mighty strongholds and have oft battled there yourself. You shall publish dispatches announcing that the archduke will inspect this, do that, and then you shall rescind those dispatches and announce yet others, tra-la-la. And, meanwhile, I will take off for Brusselos incognito and you will lend me captains Don Juan de Bel-Hombre and Don Horace d'Antwerpia, proud conquistadores who hold the secret key to their strongholds, know the enemy's true value, and how to subdue them without great cost to us. [*He disappears behind the screen and returns, dressed in a dark cape and a large sombrero.*] The third thing... Caramba! How can I put it?

SPINOLA: Might your Majesty be in need of a few pesetas?

ALBERT: Who told you? Yes amigo, a mere trifle... five hundred.

SPINOLA: [*handing over his purse*] Here they are. But allow me to remind your Majesty that this makes it forty-five thousand.

ALBERT: I shall dub thee grandee of Spain, my palo!

SPINOLA: I already am, seventeen times over.

ALBERT: You will be for the eighteenth time, and this time I'll make it official. Adios! [*He shakes don Spinola's hand and exits.*]

SPINOLA: May your Majesty carry off multiple victories and return not too much worse for the wear. [*alone*] He's not as stupid as they say! While waiting for night to fall, let's have a look at the ramparts cast in Phoebus' last golden rays. [*He looks outside using a telescope.*] Mamma mía! How could a person ever choose between the blonde artillery or the brunettes? It must be quite a job to load cannonballs through their mouths. [*He throws down his telescope.*] This spyglass won't do at all. I shall order one which enlarges three hundred times the size!

## Tableau IV

*The Palace of Brusselos in the chamber of the Infanta.*

ISABELLA: The siege isn't breaking through! Sacramentos! And here I am, doing penitence every day, eating holy bread and enjoining Br'er Kletsaf to flog my backside! Lamoral, you were down there just now. I demand to know why the forts of Ostend are still standing. And in the meantime I'll write an isabellian ordinance enjoining the Belgian people to fast for the success of the siege.

LAMORAL: Highnyness, the Belgian people haven't stopped fasting since they've been under Spanish rule, and that's been a good century now. You're going to kill them.

ISABELLA: Let them die then if that's what it takes for the siege to break through! You'd better have a good explanation Lamoral, or I shall have you interrogated by the inquisitors.

LAMORAL: Highnyness, if the siege is stuck in the mud, it is not for want of reasons. Firstly, that the Ostenders are arrant rebels who show no righteous fear of Spaniards and make no secret of it, enshitting and enpissing them without respite. Our brave soldiers' honor is so offended that they refuse to do battle against such ignominious enemies. Secondly, that the Ostenders possess in their urban escutcheon three keys to an exit door which opens on to the North Sea through which are delivered simply exquisite, strong beverages from England and Holland, veritable potions known as Scotch and Schiedam of which they drink prodigiously, and which vouchsafe them courage, enthusiasm, and shield them from epidemics. The Spanish army, on the other hand, drinks nought but salted, contaminated water, and that renders them melancholic not to say sick to croaking. Thirdly, that the Ostenders are aided by Hell, no less, and all its devils. Their walls are guarded by horrible, impudent, rabid masks. All the devils and masks are commanded by a notorious rebel, one Sir Jaime, an amazing sorcerer, as eloquent as he is evil. He depicts Spain in her greatness as an infamous frog, great with foul wind, that's about to explode. Fourthly, in addition to the Ostendish rebels, devils, and masks, there are the women of Ostend, and whatever I might say of them Your Highnyness' chaste ears must not hear. Fifthly that the High Command is in need of pesetas.

ISABELLA: Don't speak to me of finance Lamoral. All these reasons are lame. What is my divine Master doing?

LAMORAL: The archduke? Ahem. . . he is doing inspection. . . ahem. . . He's trying to raise morale. . . ahem. . .

ISABELLA: No, I mean my Divine Master, the Lord God. Is He standing behind our armies?

LAMORAL: Oh, Him. He's gone AWOL, Highnyness. On the other hand, we see a lot of lazy, knavish monks running around that we could easily do without. Whenever the Ostenders lay their hands on one of them, they skin them like rabbits and boil them live in crab vat.

ISABELLA: Pobre martyrs! I will build a church in their honor. So command!

LAMORAL: [*calling out the door*] One more church.[*He comes back.*]

VOICE OF BR'ER KLETSAF: Boom! So be it!

ISABELLA: And my general Ambrose de Spinola, how the hell is he employing all his military genius?

LAMORAL: He is considering, Your Dryness. He has a plan.

ISABELLA: Is he going to be considering long? I shall straightway dispatch him a dozen of my Dominicans.

LAMORAL: He has plenty of them on his high command already.

ISABELLA: That way I shall exorcise the army, outwit the devils, and have the Ostenders excommunicated along with their leader who flaunts his flute right in the face of our royal honor. Lamoral, I have had more than enough! I've had it up to here with this chemyse! I am sick and tired of wearing a chemyse that isn't immaculate as an altar cloth. We won't talk about the color, but there reign in these Belgiums and foremost in Brusselos incredibly tiny critters, which I will not deign to name, that dare to gnaw on my royal flesh. Father Trullemans has composed prayers designed to get rid of them. But the little bugs don't understand Latin. I could swear that the great Ostendish sorcerer himself dispatched them to me. [*She scratches.*]

LAMORAL: Better than prayers... The archduke, your husband charged me with the task of passing this present on to you. It's a cute little bellows containing insecticide blessed by the Pope, before which the most Belgian of fleas succumb and drop straightway into a coma. The powder is perfumed and the bellows bears the Spanish coat of arms. It is called Salvator. If your majesty would permit me. I'll just powder very respectfully underneath, and these unworthy ass-bugs will flee top speed into the River Senne.

ISABELLA: Go right ahead, dear Lamoral, but bandage your eyes for there are aspects of my archducality that a gentleman ought not to suspect.

*Lamoral gets down on his knees. Noise. Lamoral gets back up. Enter Father Trullemans and the nobles of the court. Deep salamalecs.*

TRULLEMANS: Would Your Highnyness be kind enough to hear the very humble remonstrance of Milords the señors and señorkas present, all suffering from afflictions as the present look on their faces indicates.

ISABELLA: Speak, Father Trullemans, why do you hesitate?

TRULLEMANS: Because the request contains some very spicy items.

ISABELLA: Spicy — then they'll give me the shits. Go on my suckling pig.

TRULLEMANS: The aforesaid nobles, señors and señorkas, eachandeveryone the trusty and loving servant of your Highnyness remonstrate your Highnyness that they suffer in their marital dignity and might because their wives eachandeveryone noble and good Christians, out of devotion for your Highnyness, got it into their heads to imitate or better yet ape the very Catholic acts of Your Highnyness and that the aforementioned wives say they will not quit their chemyses as long as the siege of Ostend lasts and until such time as her Highnyness has judged meet to quit her gracious and Catholic chemyse. Remonstrate do the aforementioned husbands of Your Highnyness that as a result of the impediment to good marital functions, the nobles of Belgium being used to fulfilling the aforesaid marital functions in absolutely authentic biblical costume, which includes no chemyse in imitation of our original parents, thus find their marital authority and position mucho reduced, because they're forced to submit to their aforesaid wives' shenanigans, since the wives are taking refuge behind this vow in order to get out of their duties. Remonstrate do the aforesaid humiliated husbands that what is good and salutary for Her Highnyness in her lofty virtue may not work for more humble women, noble though they be, and that if her Highnyness by her sublime origins is of sweet odor, exempt from bodily infirmities, and if Her Highnyness by the grace of the Holy Ghost may live immaculate in her linen through all Eternity if she so pleases, the same does not hold for her too zealous subjects. Remonstrate the aforesaid husbands that because the siege is stretched beyond their patriotic desires, the sacred bonds of the sacred sacraments of marriage are beginning to go slack like old ribbons on account of the aforesaid symbolic and patriotic chemyse and that the aforesaid husbands are frustrated and quaver before the performance of the aforementioned marital functions and are afraid of being exposed, by their abstinence, to sin, since it is well-known that the nobles of Belgium are much inclined to the thing and practice it more frequently than the Spaniards. Implore do the aforesaid bitterly aggrieved husbands of Her Highnyness to order the aforesaid wives not to heedlessly imitate her and risk committing the sin of pride, or if it please Her Majesty to authorize the reopening of the bordellos and red-light district where the aforesaid husbands could find an outlet of their grief and regain the proper functioning of their humor, that is in numbered houses, hung with lanterns and partitioned off, the aforesaid husbands will find whores and ladies of ill repute whose particularity rests in wearing no chemyse whatever or if they have one, take it off willingly. Thus say the aforesaid suppliants to Her Highnyness, her very obedient and very melancholic servants...

*Silence. The nobles sigh.*

ISABELLA: My Lords, this is quite serious, and since your health is at stake, I am going to betake myself to write to King Phillip III and to the Holy Father on the subject of these venereal matters. Meanwhile, go piously to mass and make contributions for the churches. As for me, I shall leave the question pending and give the floor to the Reverend Father Trullemans who will dictate your conduct to you.

TRULLEMANS: I dare not venture too far, my lords. I needs must meditate long and hard on such a stiff affair, harumph. I think your wives to be quite vain, harumph, harumph. I think also that if your wives do not change their chemyse it's because they don't want to wash them, harumph, harumph. The only way to regain your marital authority is by wielding your sticks, milords. It never fails, harumph. And I find you quite childish, my lords, to wish to carry out the conjugal rites only in puris naturalibus when you can just as easily fulfill them dressed in a chemyse rolled up to the navel, not to mention fully dressed, harumph, harumph, so there. And what was the next thing? Reopen the bordellos? Wipe the thought from your minds, a decree has abolished them. Truly, in these provinces, there are no more whores, streetwalkers, harlots, ladies of ill repute or prostitutes, however you prefer to call them. A decree banished them, harumph. And if perchance, you happen on women without scruples with fire up their asses, it's bad for your eternal souls and must be confessed, harumph. But here's what I think, my lords: Be not too stubborn nor too domineering either. Far wiser to come to an understanding with your wives. I say, if you have great Belgian appetites for the amorous task, then the same holds for your wives who have the same attributes. And I suspect that if you keep being stubborn concerning this chemyse, you'll soon have enough horns on your heads to hang every living Spanish grandee's hat on, by which I mean, you will be cuckolded, a blessing I wish not on you, harumph, harumph.

*The nobles moan.*

ISABELLA: My little lords, I wished to offer you good words of comfort, but the eloquence of Father Trullemans has worked wonders. Yet will I add: you shall be cuckolds and that won't advance the siege of Ostend one wit. Your wives have taken a vow not to quit their chemyse, but they haven't taken a vow of chastity. Hasten to push the pestle, or else they will soon find other less noble gallants with massive battering rams who will bestow the sinful pleasure without remorse and without respite. Or else, belt up your females with steel of Toledo and take care not to lose the key. Or if you absolutely must remain chaste, notwithstanding the danger, use tapers dipped in vinegar, append relics to the instrument of sin, or simply do like the Spaniards, and drill a hole in a board. Go and torment me no further with these abominations.

*The nobles salute and exit. Trullemans item.*

Lamoral, what do these señorkas eat that their flies are thus full of such piggy ideas? Their torment is nothing next to mine. Goshdarnit: they are but cuckolds whereas I, I have bugs. Lamoral, wield your bellows. . .

LAMORAL: The wishes of Your Highnyness are my command.

*He performs the operation.*

## Tableau V

*In the tent of Captain Don Pacheco. The tent is red. Pacheco is loaded.*

OUTSIDE:  — Password, civvieo?
— No idea, sentinelo.
— Better come up with one or or else I'll grab ya by ya cadenza.
— Marzeedoatsandozeedoats.
— Okay, go oo-thray. And whadaya want?
— Eek-spay to Captain Pacheco.
— Take off your oot-bays and go on in.
— Please accept my ank-thays.

*In the tent, enter the Engineer Klabotsky.*

DON PACHECO:  Can't even drink my mulled wine in peace. Here's another one coming to sell me safety razors and medals of the Sacred Heart. The password, civvieo?

KLABOTSKY: Marzeedoatsandozeedoats, at your service.

DON PACHECO:  What a sweet language Castillian is! Have a seat?

KLABOTSKY: There's nothing to sit on, milord.

DON PACHECO:  Then sit on y'r thumb. You a noble?

*THE SIEGE OF OSTEND* 75

KLABOTSKY: 'course, but in Poland... noblyscky in Polscky!

DON PACHECO: Swellsky! You may talk to me, but not in Polishinsky.

KLABOTSKY: My lord Don Pacheco, luminous Captain of the valiant sword, you whose chronic exploits fill the echoes of the universe, I, inspired by my own genius and wishing to promote your fame...

DON PACHECO: Doodydamndidios! My fame, he says? What needs promoting is my rank-o, fucking civvie-o, my rank-o, you oink-oink, by which yo mean, stripe-os on my sleeve-os and a raise in pay-o for all the sipping mulled wine and listening to harmonicas I have to do.

KLABOTSKY: Captain, let's make a long story short. I'm an engineer.

DON PACHECO: Didn't you once invent a powder to lick the lice? [*heroic*] Lice, now there's the enemy!

KLABOTSKY: No, milord. My invention is in the equine family. Ever heard of the Siege of Troy?

DON PACHECO: I was there, my good man.

KLABOTSKY: Then you remember the famous horse?

DON PACHECO: By God, we stuffed ourselves on it at each and every meal.

KLABOTSKY: Impossible, it was made of wood.

DON PACHECO: Like I say. Wood. A saw-horse, and we even shit sawdust.

KLABOTSKY: A saw-horse, but much bigger. Hollow. And on wheels. That horse was actually a moving fortress.

DON PACHECO: From the sound of it, that horse was really a boat.

KLABOTSKY: Not at that point. It would have taken an engineer of my stripe to turn it into a boat. But it did take the city of Troy.

DON PACHECO: Long live the cavalry, hip-hip-hooray for that good old weapon on four legs which showers us with its dung!

KLABOTSKY: Are you listening to me? The city of Ostend must be taken. But not with another horse. That trick worked once, but it won't work a second time. So, the ingenious engineer has come up with this solution: this time the horse will be a fish. A gigantic fish. A sea serpent. Six hundred fathoms long.

DON PACHECO: Another boat?

KLABOTSKY: A boat in the shape of a horrifying and majestic hollow serpent, not on wheels this time but with oars. Filled with valiant Spaniards. The Ostenders are crazy about sea serpents. They'll see it floating adrift one fine morning and they'll go out to capture it, for they like big challenges. Once the serpent's brought into port, a thousand hidden Spaniards pour out of its flanks and swarm all over the place, killing everything in sight while the troops charge. Ostend is taken and the Spanish serpent goes down in history.

DON PACHECO: Sublimos!  Wonderful-lo! Splendididominos!

KLABOTSKY: And for that idea, señor caballero, have the goodness to advance me a few pesetas as my share of the booty from the victory.

DON PACHECO: With pleasure, Klabotsky! Turn around, amigo, and let me have a look-see at your butt-o.

*Klabotsky turns around.*

Here's a good down payment!

*He gives a formidable kick of the boot to Klabotsky's rear end. The engineer flies through the roof of the tent. The sentinel rushes in.*

SENTINEL: Captain! Alert! We're being bombarded with engineers.

DON PACHECO: Fucking imbecile, get back to your post! And if any more engineers come along, chuck them into the lime pit. If we listened to them we'd wind up winning the siege, and we've been ordered not to. Out, soldados, and leave me to drink my mulled wine in peace.

*The sentinel exits.*

## Tableau VI

*In Brusselos, in a room at the Inn of the Great Mirror, Mountain Street. Enter Don Juan de Bel-Hombre.*

DON JUAN: 'ods' bodkinos! So here we are in the ancient notorious inn, the Great Mirror on Mountain Street, adjoining the Chapel of Our Lady Saint Anne. I have a feeling the only mirrors in this inn are glass-covered wardrobe doors, there to rouse the ardor of lovers passing in the night like ships. [*He struts about flourishing his foil.*] What an excellentissima spot this Brusselos is, in spite of the fact that it schpritzes without let-up! At least there are buttocks to be found in profusion here in the capital of Brabant. Along with bordellos aplenty, cabarettos, and Mussel and French frito stands. And the whole thing goes unsupervised and uninspected by the alcaldes and alguazils of the city, who cast an indulgent eye on the gambols of the hefty mermaids of the River Senne. And what am I doing here? I am in the service of Her Dryness, the Infanta, who leaves me plenty of free time, since the noble zealot spends sixteen hours a day in churches that cater to her every silly whim. Hidalgos of my caliber don't like churches and don't waste their time hanging around vestries like vulgar friars. Hie thee, my divine Conchita, Baroness of Pierman, Lady of the Thick Bush, the Red Door, and the Great Isle, my adored mistress, item 47 in my calfskin-covered catalogue that lists all the great beauties. Better hasten or else I'll stroke my blade over your back and buttocks so you lose taste for rabbit for good!

*Enter Innkeeper.*

What does this wretch want of me? Have you come to announce the arrival of her coach?

INNKEEPER: Milord, I'm sad to say my pantry's fresh out of pâté of unicorn and Peloponnesian hydromel, but perhaps Your Honor will deign to make do with country blood sausage and a bottle of our fine Gueuze beer brewed before the siege?

DON JUAN: Both are excellent aphrodisiacs. Bring 'em. [*The Innkeeper exits.*] The belfry of Saint Nicholas is tolling three o'clock. The toad! How I love her. Dear Conchita, I met you at the Alcazar under the shimmering light of the oil-lamps. How beautiful you were with your great diamond combs casting out a thousand glimmers, and your padded behind swinging. Ha, Venus, the traps you set for us! Hasten, Conchita, for ever since the time I contracted the disease of the Indies, I have been subject to sudden fits of ardor. And the bordellos of coastal Flanders have nothing to offer but a barely digestible royal tumble. That forces all well-born gentlemen to push on to Bruges where the whores all wear habits, and make you show them a confession ticket before you're allowed to dip your tip and sing the asparagus. [*He emits a roar in Spanish.*] Come, Conchita, that I may throw you panting onto the musical featherbed. It will play the Carnival of Venus at just the right moment. [*There is a knocking. Conchita enters.*] My turd!

CONCHITA: My fiery yeoman!

DON JUAN: My little cellar rat!

CONCHITA: My littlish ticklish mustache!

DON JUAN: My little golden Spanish fly!

CONCHITA: My beautiful red stallion!

DON JUAN: My all-purpose baroness!

CONCHITA: My non-stop fuckating rover!

DON JUAN: Rover?! Stop right there! A thousand billion carambas. You do me wrong, my dear! In your hot delirium you call me by the grotesque nickname that's given to old chamber-pot emptying husbands and to those mongrel bow-wows of Brabant who lick each others' asses. Here, Rover! While throughout the Spanish empire on which the sun never snots, I am no other than Don Juan de Bel-Hombre de Villa Hermosa y Mecton de Miramar y Castel-Rodrigo de la Sierra Nevada, Grandee of Spain and Captain of Her Catholic Majesty's armies. Diosdamdominoes!

CONCHITA: Have pity on me, my love, I won't do it again! It's a little slippy-whippy because that's what I call Baron Pierman when he's feeling frisky.

DON JUAN: Carabijos, carambi de caramba de carambinos y carambollos. You've been cheating on me with your husband, that flat beer Baron de Burgonschie! My honor has been sullied!

CONCHITA: No, my yeoman, I swear, I'm speaking to you of the time before the Spanish occupation. The baron hasn't given me a roll in the hay nor laid a finger on me since the siege of Ostend began. We're fine, upstanding women who let ourselves be obliterated by grandees of Spain and no others. We noblewomen go for men of great stature only.

DON JUAN: So be it, I'll pretend to believe you and agree not to slit that seven-horned cuckold's throat. Prepare to be sacrificed on the altar of love which in this case is this padded mattress.

CONCHITA: Do you have another sadistic treat in store for me like last time?

DON JUAN: No, my pretty, I've been too busy thinking on military strategy, but on the way over here I saw some gallant dogs on Room For Only One Person Street who appeared to be experiencing a great deal of pleasure. Get down on all fours and let your tongue hang out a yard. The theologians teach that that position's forbidden, but you get six inches surplus thereby...

CONCHITA: And how many times do you plan to plunge your dagger of Toledo into my velvet sheath?

DON JUAN: No less than thirteen times which is my usual, but no more, since I've got a bigger one to joust on tonight. Ready? I'm gonna pull down my fly but my sombrero stays on my head for I am a grandee of Spain. Caramba! Remove your mound of Venus from out your panties for I can't commence the erotic combat until you've peeled down! Do you mark me, Baroness?

CONCHITA: Oh my lover, are you limpified thus, and is your pendant all shrunk? You don't love me anymore!

DON JUAN: Rest reassured, my adorèd one, Don Felipe will expand, for he is Spanish! All the same, I advise you to peel down if you want for me to cook you. What do I see? You grow pale?

CONCHITA: It's only the emotion. Ah, my gentle yeoman, might we not cook the tidbit and eat it without removing our finery? I assure you that people do do that. You have only to lift my petticoat up to my pupick, and you shall have all the field necessary to take your stand.

DON JUAN: Peel down, I say!

CONCHITA: I'd sooner die a thousand deaths! I'm religious, and I'm following the example of our gracious Infanta, model for all woman-kind. [*She cries.*] . . . It's all the Siege of Ostend's fault!

DON JUAN: I might have known! Yet another one who's taken the vow never more to quit her chemyse! Adios, unfortunate one, keep your ardor and your chemyse, while I hold onto my dart and dart off down Monkey Alley where there are merry wives enow, hot to trot, who have no more religion than is seemly for a woman.

CONCHITA: Cruel yeoman. . . here I am, consumed by amorous flames. . . and yet you refuse to extinguish me?

DON JUAN: A gentleman never refuses a woman. . . here you are, there you are.

*He slaps her.*

CONCHITA: Bastard! Gigolo! Pimp-o!

*She collapses.*

DON JUAN: And hand over fifty ducats for my transportation costs, if you don't want me to make a scandal and inform the poor Baron de Pierman, whom you've been cuckoldfucking non-stop.

CONCHITA: Here, take my purse, ingrate! *[Don Juan takes her purse and exits with a dignified air.]* Don Juan. Come back. It'll be a sacrilege, but I'll strip off my chemyse after all. Too late! *[She gets up and runs to the window.]* There he goes down Monkey Alley chasing after those chimpanzees. O Patriotism, the terrible things done in your name. . . Never, never, never!

*Enter Innkeeper.*

INNKEEPER: And here's the Gueuze beer and the black blood sausage you ordered!

*He exits.*

CONCHITA: I mean to stew myself in despair! *[She drinks.]* And this blood sausage! It pierces me to the heart! It stands for all the sensual pleasures lost. *[She eats the blood sausage.]* It's not bad. But Spanish sausage is better. Spanish sausage has the power to expand whereas the Belgian sausage just hangs. All the Belgians are good for is drinking, and after that, you can knock all you like, but nobody's home anymore.

## Tableau VII

*Ostend. The crypts of Falstaff's castle located on Army Plaza. Barrels serving as tables. Black hangings, candelabras, diabolical ornamentation. A large crowd is gathered, and it is carnival night.*

SIR JAIME: Milord devils, princes, dukes, marquis, counts, barons, and simple small fry of hell, I am well pleased with you, so into my fabulous paintings you'll go. And for centuries to come, whomsoever looks on them will get a voluptuous thrill. Just one look and they'll try to sell their souls. This shall I do, for it is written that I am painter of devils and not of angels. This sabbat night, as you know, coincides with the carnival of Ostend, which is the great holiday for all Knaves, the first carnival to be held since the siege began, and as you see, those cursèd Spaniards have not yet been able to take our fortress. Praised be you, devils, deviliteens, deviletons, and deviled eggs, not to mention devilettas of all sorts, smells and colors, leading off with imperial Lilith, who's here with us today and for whom I shall paint a beautiful violet mask. Lord devils, and you, maestros Astoroth, Asmodeus, Berit, and Belphegor, you look superb, and though academic, you sure can pack it away like krauts. Tonight we'll hold war council and after the mock funeral mass, we shall besport us in the joyful and obscene carnival of the Ostendish Knaves. How can I ever express my gratitude? Listen, when, three centuries from now, I make my coronation march into Brusselos, despite opposition from bands of house painters, students at the Academy and decorative theosophists, I shall lead you with great pomp to pump liquor down your throats at a certain inn known as Devil Under the Skin, where'll you'll feel right at home guzzling Stout and Kriek-Lambik beer. On me. This promised, I command you to salute the diplomatic Rhesus Monkey with tattooed enamel buttocks way up there on his pedestal, a delegate from mighty Lucifer whom protocal consigns to lower stories.

*All present salute the Rhesus Monkey who turns his ass to them.*

THE DEVILS: Long live the tubercular Rhesus Monkey with his galvanized ass. Hooey! Hooey!

THE RHESUS MONKEY: Sensational, Sir Jaime, your magician's costume suits you to a "t". Note, little devils, that the master has donned his great collár of the order of the Silver Flea.

THE DEVILS: Long live the Silver Flea and the Rhesus Monkey's eagle eye!

THE RHESUS MONKEY: Sir Jaime sure does make a terrific devil. I request that he deliver one of those beautiful speeches to which he alone has the recipe.

BISHOP DOM CANCRULOR: One moment! I, Dom Cancrulor, bishop in partibus of Diarrhea and of Wipeassopolis, I say it's time to eat. Where's the menu?

SIR JAIME: Your Lordship shall receive fricassee of smashed frog in three-in-one oil and spleen of seminarian marinated in blue-stocking juice. A very fine repast, better than a mixed Spanish grill or Congolese brains.

*The devils eat and drink.*

Milord Murmur of the Conservatory, during the banquet, why don't you turn the crank to the dropsical organ which'll harmoniously upchuck a little composition of mine, the Infernal Suite. It goes brilliantly with counterpoint around the hips.

THE RHESUS MONKEY: I'd rather hear the March of the Betrothal of the Crowned Sperloot accompanied by blasts from the counterbass.

SIR JAIME: We shall have my little suite, crapulous Rhesus. And here's what it consists of: The first part describes the entrance of the red devils stepping wittily on each others' tails, accompanied by skeletons, victims of electoral tetanus. The second part in various tones from the downy skin of nymphs' thighs, depicts a delicious idyll in which nubile witches lick each others' sheathes and rose petals, while hairless young sorcerers, Sistine-fashion, recite the little catechism which they hold in one hand, while with the other they subdue swooning witches with their dew. The third part is a spinning, tempestuous, swirling, maelstrom of garlanded incubi and succubi and multicolor clusters bristling with triple quavers, and dropping, along with billy-goats, down into the great ecstatic soup cauldron, pigmented with rusted out professors and ministerial mucus. And last but not least, the descent of the legions of horror onto the barbed wire boardwalk where they'll perform a dissection on the living cancerous bastard born of the loves of Pope Joan. Better listen, my music-loving devilettas, or else I'll take the lid off the plague jar...

*The organ plays. Sir Jaime beats out the rhythm. The devils get excited and gambol about. When it is over, copious applause.*

And now, milord devils, make your report to my noble Ostendish person on the Spanish rout.

BIFRONS: Master, see the waxen statue of Isabella in which we have encased a piece of infectious carrion, so that the damzel herself breaks out in green leprosy with black pustules. The wax has not yet turned purple. I propose that red-hot needles be stuck into her ticklish spots.

SIR JAIME: No, too many different sensations at one time. Have the Princely Rhesus Monkey clothe himself in all his vermin and fly non-stop to the palace in Brusselos and there lay down on the Infanta's canopy and make the eensy-teensy ones multiply. [*The Rhesus Monkey salutes and exits.*] And you, Crapitus?

CRAPITUS: As my name indicates, I have stunk up above, below, and everywhere, and the Spanish army's upchucking non-stop. I have gone copiously in the boots of the generals and the high command and in the military kitchen pots. The Spanish camp is barricaded, encircled, closed in, by infernal turds. The troops sink in them, eat them, inhale them, and in spite of all the incense they burn, the soldiers are dropping like flies. We've done our little best, there you are!

SIR JAIME: Victory defecatory! Just keep shitting

and you'll make it, devil Crapitus. And you, Israfel, you of the multiple disguises.

ISRAFEL: I'm another type altogether. Every night I loose my squadrons of professional vampires. They work wonders, howling, reeking havoc, and terrorizing. The enemy no longer sleeps and their arquebuses are dropping out of their hands.

SIR JAIME: Bravo! The dynamic werewolves are next on the agenda. And you Fifrelin?

FIFRELIN: Venerable Master, I have at my disposal a dozen certified vampires who dig up Spanish cadavers and slip them into the soup kettles. Which scares the enemy into thinking they'll be cooked alive or dead by my sidekick and friend Zozo.

SIR JAIME: What does Zozo do in his zozoatic zeal?

ZOZO: I've adapted the diabolical ray, which rots food from a distance, inflames corns on the soldiers' feet, and gives stomach aches. I also launch sneezing powder and clouds of itching powder through my blunderbuss.

SIR JAIME: And you Rotomago, premier prestidigitator?

ROTOMAGO: I put my little talents to work. Making apparitions is my specialty. I make comets appear before the enemy's eyes, fiery swords, luminous columns, dragons, and other incandescent phantasms. I make little volcanoes erupt, cause gaping holes in the terrain, asphyxiating fogs and meteor showers.

SIR JAIME: Your reputation's in the bag. And you, Clisteret, so resourceful?

CLISTERET: Me? I hand out candies which get the Spaniards all horny. They promptly commit the worst abominations imaginable, under the bewildered eye of their monks. Want to have a taste?

SIR JAIME: Thanks, but no. In the future, double the dose and give your candies to the monks as well. And the rest of you, Vociferan, Colodion, and Pruritan?

VOCIFERAN, COLODION, AND PRURITAN:
We're musical devils and prevent them from closing their eyes with our jazz instruments, our charmed roosters, and our cats in death throes.

SIR JAIME: That will do! Hear my orders. May all the Ostendish masks go garnish the ramparts and set off fireworks, while others shoot projectiles into the air which'll drop down on the enemy. And in celebration of carnival, chuck the twelve spying monks they just captured into the boiling wax and ask 'em if that turns 'em on. At midnight, have the multitudes of masks congregate on Army Plaza to hear and acclaim a smashing speech I plan to make on the Spanish ignominy. I shall also sing the praises of the masks and myself; don't worry, I won't make it a habit. And while we're waiting for our great funeral Te Deum, I invite you to my main tower on the Flemish Bluffs, which is a lighthouse and there we'll find the ceremonial accessories we need as well as the wooden-footed mandrakes and serpents in vats. I will cry you on the way long live Sir Jaime and his dazzling painting, in aspic and basil, and you Prospero, and you Crapolet, and you Sidol, and you Zigromar, you will keep a tight grip on the ropes that pull the stove along. And now, play the Dancing Procession of the Lice-Ridden Visionary Beggars on your hunting horn.

ALL THE DEVILS: Hip hip hooray! Long live Sir Jaime and his painting! Long live the Carnival of Ostend! Long live the lice-ridden beggars!

> *They parade out. The bishop upchucks into his miter. The tune of the Lice-Ridden Visionary Beggars on the hunting horn.*

## TABLEAU VIII[1]

> *The plain of Ostend beneath a beautiful sun, a company of Royal Pickers is lined up in size places. Standing in front of them an officerio holding up a little tree be-ribboned in the colors of Spain. Spinola in fancy dress uniform, laden with tinsel, strolls back and forth before the troops.*

SPINOLA: Quiet in the ranks or I'll impale you on your picks. Oh boy is it close! Is it ever close! And the ambassador still hasn't turned up! Gonzalez, no knee-knocking while holding the commemorative tree. You know it's in lousy shape as it is. We had to wrap wire around it to hold it together. Soldier Gomez, blow your nose! Corporal Sanchez, pull up your fly! Just because it's so close is no excuse to leave your fly open! So long as we're waiting for the ceremony to start, I'll just go ahead and make a little speech. Royal pickers, a picker is a military man who mans a pick. A certain number

---

1. Ghelderode eleminated this scene from the final version.

of these military men constitute a company of pickers whose motto is "He who rubs up against it, there shall he be pricked." A good picker pricks fast and hard, not too short or too long, with the pick held at 45 degree angle, and pricks time and again without let-up. [*The Pickers laugh.*] How dare you make fun of my noble discourse, you bunch of hard-tipped pricks? [*A trumpet is heard.*] 'Tenshun. Here comes the ambassador, Marquis de Miralobar, with his mechanical leg. If he marks us marking that his mechanical leg is in any way remarkable, then I'll let you have it. If what he marks is that you mark it not, then you shall all get cigarillos flor fina exquisitos from his plantations in Havana. Guard-hut! Pickos stiffos! [*The Pickers raise up their picks.*] You snot-picker solo horn-player, pick out the March of the Sharp-Pickers of Guadalquivir, otherwise known as the Regiment of the Pickshnozzes. [*The Hornplayer plays the march. Enter the ambassador, Marquis de Miralobar, who walks with a crutch.*] You are a thousand times welcome Excellency, and how's it swinging? A little close, don't you think?

MIRALOBAR: You said it, tootsie. [*He salutes the troops.*] Ah, the proud pickers! I like 'em long, supple, and sharp-pointed. Put them at ease.

SPINOLA: Guard-hut! Pickos-downos! [*The Pickers lay their weapons to rest.*] And you, horn solo, stop, for your brass instrument gives off unnecessary heat. Excellency, you have the floor. Sound the drums. [*Drums are heard.*] That's quite enough! Silence in the ranks. Corporal Sanchez, doodydammo, your zipper! If I've told you once...

MIRALOBAR: Let it be. My valliant Pickers, what a

beautiful day it is, this the first anniversary of the Siege of Ostend. It is due to the greatness of your picks that the renown of our weapons has never faltered. We are going to commemorate this anniversary by planting this little symbolic tree here, which shall offer shade and savory fruits, if it pleaseth God. I shall plant it and you will intone the royal anthem, which will express the good will of the troops and their appreciation for our highnesses, who bade me convey their compliments and congratulate you on how sharp you look. And in the future, wash yourselves well, hold your picks high, and in every spectacular struggle, prick your best, before and behind, pause not to catch your breath, and everyone will be happy.

SPINOLA: Guard-hut! Plant the tree! [*The officerio plants the tree.*] Sing! March!

THE PICKERS: [*In chorus, accompanied by the horn player.*]

It will grow, it will grow,
It will grow for it is Spanish. [*repeat*]

SPINOLA: And viva Hispania! And viva el rey! And viva the Ambassador!

PICKERS: And viva the Ambassador's cigarillos!

SPINOLA: Quiet creepos! And now, the first one who dares to pee on the commemorative tree will be strangulated by garroting, without let-up.

MIRALOBAR: Precisely General. Would it be indiscreet to ask you where I might perform a certain necessary function without risk of being executed?

## TABLEAU IX

*Bruges, in the crypt of Saint Babuijn. Torches and lanterns. Crucifix, tapers, skeletons, religious artifacts. At a long table sit the Hooded Brothers. In the pulpit, Father Trullemans.*

TRULLEMANS: Brothers, we are gathered together in this damp crypt on orders from King Philip the Third to judge a considerable detestable, possessed, horrifying, stinking, cankerous, impious, sacrilegious, heretical, damned miscreant— a Knave to make a long story short. . . and with our customary mildness. . .

THE HOODED BROTHERS: Where is he? Executioner? The instruments of torture. . . the molten lead. . . the pepper. . . the tongs, the ankle-boots. . . the cords. . . the wedge. . . the funnel. . . the bone saw. . . the ham machine. . . the portable stove. . . the pliers. . . the corkscrew. . .the sausage machine. . . the ass bellows. . . the hair remover. . . the brain remover. . . the brace. . . the bam-bam hammer. . . the holy water. . . the sulfuric acid. . . the stump. . . the conversion club. . . the boiler. . . the spiked plank. . . the wheel. . . the boiling oil. . . the head cheese grinder. . . the de-boner. . . the last sacraments. . . the coffin. . . Go and drag the great Knave here. Fetch the hooligan. . . Let's save his soul. . .

TRULLEMANS: My dearly beloved hooded brothers. . . Your zeal is touching, yet we will not have occasion to employ all those toys of penitence, not having been able to seize the culprit either dead or alive, and the inconceivable thing is that when we invited him to appear before us, he wasn't even polite enough to R. S. V. P.!

*The Hooded Brothers wail and cry.*

A HOODED BROTHER: Poor us. I believe I express the sentiment of all my brothers when I declare that this is intolerable. It's been three days now since we've saved any souls! And not one customer for our great auto-da-fe this Sunday. Not even a Jew. Shall we spruce up the mannequins of San Benito for the occasion? Verily, I say to you... religion is done for. Let us save the beautiful souls of children through the spectacle of our great auto-da-fes. Long live the clergy!

ALL: Long live the clergy...
Long live the clergy...
Long live the clergymen!

TRULLEMANS: May Heaven hear you! My brothers, before revealing the grounds for the trial, I will confess that I have carefully reread the noted works of Sire Jehan Bodin, with his Scourge of Demons and Sorcerers; Martin Antoine Del Rio, the wise Jesuit with his magic research; Pierre Delancre with his Treatise on the Inconstancy of Evil Angels and Demons; Jean Wierus, with his Pseudomonarchia Doemonum, and in conclusion, after having prayed to the Espírito Santo...

A HOODED BROTHER: Excuse me for interrupting you, my father, I believe I'm expressing the sentiment of my fellow brethren when I remark that this crypt contains thirteen barrels of brown beer. I am going to request the sacristan to serve it to us, since wearing a hood brings on both heat and thirst...

TRULLEMANS: Thus it shall be! Now then, I accuse! All Spain, all Christianity is growing tired with the way the Siege of Ostend is dragging on. All the military genius of the generals, all the Spanish heroism of the troops, all the churches built by our generous Infanta, all our prayers and mortifications have accomplished nothing and the people are abuzz with mockery; it gives the appearance of making progress, but it never gets anywhere. In point of fact the forts of Ostend are still standing! It would be surprising if it were otherwise since it is the demon himself who defends them... Stop drinking so much, you frocked hogs.

*The Hooded Brothers snicker and drink without respite.*

The demon say I, the Evil One, who is incarnated in the person of a most malevolent Englishman named Sir Jaime, endowed with every diabolical charm. He performs his marvels and somersaults with the help of an enchanted flute and a magic umbrella. He composes and delivers horrible, burlesque, cacophonic, pun-filled, seditious, anarchic, humoristic speeches, full of double and triple meanings and syntactical inventions which are surely the mark of the devil. He writes and plays abominable music which goes against all rules of harmony, of counterpoint and of fugue, filled with hidden fifths and octaves... music which fits right in with his speeches. He has morals beyond words, and lays with mermaids, fairies, and witches who embroider cushions for him. And when he praises women, he vaunts their halting gait, their crossed eyes, their ingrown nails, their warts, their scabby knees, all of which reveals his astonishing perversity. He has in his castle domesticated skeletons who serve him, dance and play the bagpipes when they aren't boxing with each other. In his paintings he depicts good Christians as nasty grimacing masks, equating them with the seven deadly sins. He claims to be familiar with all devils and denounces perfect parishioners as devils in disguise. He pretends to be able to identify them by their odor, their writing, or their way of salivating. With infernal inspiration he concocted strategies unworthy of a civilized peoples, such as bombardment with herrings and fecal inundation. He has organized the female warriors to lift up their skirts on the ramparts and show us their buttocks, which is the most underhanded trick of all. He endlessly draws and engraves satirical plates representing monks of the Inquisition administering torture, King Philip delightedly sniffing the roasted fat of heretics; the Infanta devoured by ferocious animals; the archduke dropping turds on the populace. And finally, makes fun of grandees, kings, princes, nobles, clergy, scholars, doctors, marshalls, and on the other hand glorifies the Knaves and lice-ridden beggars. And the worst of all his crimes is to represent himself in the aspect of persecuted Christ.

ALL: Get thee behind me Satan! Let's drink! Long live Trullemans! Down with the Knaves!

*They drink, belch, spit, and pitch back and forth.*

TRULLEMANS: When you've done spitting up all over your cowls, just let me know. I denounce that man. He is the Antichrist or surely a member of the family. He has laid waste to accepted poetry by inaugurating a new Mephistophelean style. He has overturned the laws of proper painting. He's a bachelor and never wants to have children. He presides over unseemly ceremonies in Falstaff's cellars. He caricatures and lampoons non-stop. He detests the human face created in the image of God. He harbors an overweening pride. He maintains that it is we that are destroying beauty, that we are torturers, spoilers, lewd, oinkers, lazy, deranged, profaners, impostors, jokers, tyrants, brutes, meddlers, charlatans, with Death and the shudder of hell at our heels, yes, and I can prove it to you too. Look at these engravings. Here is the triumph of Troquenada, here's the crowned skull of King Philip the Second sprouting worms. Here are clergymen with asses' ears and boars' groins. Here are mitered dogs sniffing each others' asses. And that's not all. He depicts these sins with an unbelievable wealth of precise details. And these are faces of people we all know... [*He brandishes the engravings.*]

THE HOODED BROTHERS: Let's see! Lust! Me first! Pass me my spectacles!

*They grab the engravings and drool over them.*

TRULLEMANS: And doody everywhere, epidemics, catastrophes, eccentricities! Howl out your indignation. .. cry for shame, but don't damage the engravings. And to top it off, have a look at this last one: The Entry of Christ into Brusselos... Woe unto us! Ah! If only we had him in our Catholic clutches!

THE HOODED BROTHERS: Wait your turn! Lust! Oh boy oh boy! Misericordia! Let's drink!

*They keep bumping into one another and redouble their drinking.*

TRULLEMANS: Verily, verily, it's the Devil's own work! We have done everything in our power to bring him to bay and capture him. First paternal exhortations; then we promised to buy a canvas at a reduced price if he consented to reform and renounce the error of his pictorial ways. Then the archduke, in order to coax him, offered to make him a baron and come to Brusselos to paint a large-scale portrait of him. I read you his response: "I refuse the piddling title of baron in light of the fact that every painter in Belgium gets the same title the minute they smear a canvas with three red cabbages, six fat cows, and twelve lard-colored boobs. And whereas I've had the title of English baron since the time of King Arthur who slept under a round table and wiped his ass with ermine. Whereas I'm ennobled by light and shades of color, and my opalescent coat of arms bears a real starfish on a background of foam, and I wear a diver's helmet with tangled algae all over it. And as for painting a portrait of Your Inquisitoriality, I refuse, since any painting of your archducal conceit would call for decomposed frog-green and I've banished that color from my prismatic palette. Still the subject tempted me. To have painted that pickle face of yours with strawberry preserves, as well as her Infanticide's anatomy in bronzed chemyse, what honor and what lust that would have meant!

THE HOODED BROTHERS: Lord, don't pardon him, he knows exactly what he's doing!

TRULLEMANS: That will do, my brothers. I'll propose to the Holy Father that Sir Jaime be solemnly excommunicated, that his hateful person be burned in effigy in the courtyard of the Academy of Art with all his paintings, that anyone who looks upon them, approves of them, or praises them, critics who don't vent all their detestation on them included, be hung without confession, that... the disgusting things!... they're all shitty-brokendown-drunkards. Give me back my engravings, you carcasses. [*He takes back his engravings.*] One day they'll be worth something. [*He blesses the Hooded Brothers.*] Go tank up in peace! [*He exits.*]

THE HOODED BROTHERS: [*drunk*] Long live Trullemans! More liquor! Long live Sir Jaime and his engravings! Down with the Academy! Long live the Seven Deadly Sins! The engravings! [*They collapse.*] He farted! Who farted? It stinks! More liquor!

*They vomit. One sole Hooded Brother remains standing. He drinks.*

THE LAST ONE: Verily, I say to you... he's one hell of a Knave! [*with effort.*] Down with the clergy!

*He collapses in his turn.*

## TABLEAU X

*The camp of Ostend, in a tent. Enter three doctors of the Spanish army, each carrying a chamber pot. They wear long robes. On their faces a mask of some bird of prey. They are also carrying saws, hammers, and huge instruments of butchery.*

DON POMMADOS: Milord doctors, we've got a horrifying epidemic on our hands. And what is it anyway, plague or cholera? Well, whatever it is, we'll wipe it out with this fantabulous ointment of my own invention.

DON PILLULOS: My learnéd colleague, it's not an epidemic say I, those soldiers are just a lot of loafers, and if epidemic there is, I'd call it phlegma militari maxima. Perhaps my pills...

DON CLYSTEROS: Most erudite of friends, I'm the oldest, and therefore the smartest. Neither ointment nor pills will do. The only thing that'll work is an enema, a syringe right up the troops' posterity. However, considering that there are but a mere two thousand casualties makes me wonder whether it's really an epidemic, or...

DON POMMADOS: What say the prophetic chamber pots?

DON PILLULOS: They say shit.

*They plunge their beaks into the chamber pots.*

DON CLYSTEROS: It sure doesn't smell like roses.

DON POMMADOS: Lilies neither.

DON PILLULOS: Nor the sweet smell of victory. Doctors, milords, these chamber pots are quite mute.

DON CLYSTEROS: Have you had a taste?

DON PILLULOS: Yes, two helpings. It tastes like herring.

DON POMMADOS: Curiosa! It really is an epidemic. The Ostenders bombarded us with herrings and the troops gobbled them up. So the herrings must have been poisoned.

*They set down the chamber pots.*

Let's not discard these chamber pots just yet. They may come in handy.

DON CLYSTEROS: It is an epidemic! Let's vote on it. [*They vote.*] Two votes against Don Pillulos's diagnosis. The majority wins and decrees that it most certainly is an epidemic.

DON PILLULOS: I won't argue, but I would like to call your attention to the fact that Spaniards are the only ones affected by this epidemic. The germ, Milords, is indeed noble. What shall we call this epidemic?

DON POMMADOS: The Flu. A vague and reassuring term. And due to its peculiar properties, it shall be Spanish Flu in honor of Spain!

DON PILLULOS: Science has taken a giant step forward into the virgin forest of knowledge. I propose to undertake an autopsy.

DON CLYSTEROS: With pleasure. Hey, there's a soldier passing by. Come in amigo.

*The Soldier, Romero, enters and comes to attention.*

DON CLYSTEROS: Are you sick?

ROMERO: No, Excellency, I'm on duty.

DON POMMADOS: Excuse me, but you are sick. Don't argue, or you'll get six days of violin practice. Let's try out my ointment!

DON PILLULOS: First my pills. Is he in fact sick or merely on duty? Let's do a diagnosis. Say 'Ah...'

ROMERO: AHHHHH.

DON POMMADOS: Excuse me, he has to try saying thirty three. Say thirty three.

ROMERO: Thirty three, thirty three...

DON CLYSTEROS: A certain twitching of the nose.

DON PILLULOS: Soldier, do you smell anything?

ROMERO: With all due respect, Excellency, I smell the odor of shit.

DON POMMADOS: Perfect! Undress.

*Romero undresses.*

DON CLYSTEROS: Twitching of the nose is a symptom of the epidemic. Ah, what do we have here? He hasn't washed his feet! Lie down soldier. We're going to undertake an autopsy.

ROMERO: But I'm not dead!

DON POMMADOS: What do you know? Who's the doctor here, you or us? The origin of the scourge is lodged in the head.

DON PILLULOS: In the stomach.

DON CLYSTEROS: Tut tut — in the large intestine.

*They rush Romero and cut him to pieces. The soldiers howls.*

ROMERO: Oh boy, oh boy... mommy! They're making boo-boos. I don't like it.

DON POMMADOS: Silence, my boy. It's in the interest of science and the Fatherland!

*Romero is dead and cut to bits.*

DON CLYSTEROS: Caramba! This soldier was in excellent health!

DON PILLULOS: It's possible. As it turns out, he didn't have the flu, but he might very well have caught it sooner or later.

DON POMMADOS: What shall we do with the parts of the patient? Glue them back together?

DON PILLULOS: Don't bother. I'll requisition the head for a tobacco pot, as a souvenir of the siege of Ostend.

DON CLYSTEROS: I'm taking the skin covering the balls and I'll make a cannister out of it as a souvenir of the siege of Ostend.

DON POMMADOS: What'll be left? I'll snatch the stomach and fashion a bagpipe out of it. Milords, bear in mind that the High Command is awaiting our report.

DON PILLULOS: We shall write them that the aforesaid epidemic is of noble origin and shall be called Spanish Flu in homage to our dearly beloved highnynesses and it has the property that one either dies of it or is cured of it.

DON POMMADOS: Perfect. Let us add that the soldados who neither die nor are cured are lazy-bonos who in case of relapse will be hung.

DON CLYSTEROS: As to remedies milords? Enemas.

DON PILLULOS: Pills.

DON POMMADOS: Ointment.

DON CLYSTEROS: Let's come to an agreement. Let us say that we very learnéd doctors Pillulos, Pommados, and Clysteros order simultaneously enemage, pillage, and ointmenting, with sea water and salted herring as preventive treatment. One may also administer final sacraments. I have spoken.

DON PILLULOS: Brava bravi. Milords, the real remedy is none of the above... [*He takes out a stone flask.*] It's here within this esoteric flask!

DON POMMADOS: We knew it all along, dear colleague. I have a little jug just like yours. It was invented by a very learnéd doctor from the University of Lightbeer.

*He takes out a flask.*

DON CLYSTEROS: [*He takes out a flask.*] You selfish fellows, you! Infallible medicine, milords, celestial pharmacopeia. May I add that in order for it to be effective, the flask's contents must be tossed down in one gulp. [He drinks.] Let's take off our beaks and drink. It'd be a fine state of affairs if we doctors were to fall ill...

*They swing it down.*

DON POMMADOS: Superb! Long live the great Doctor Lightbeer.

DON PILLULOS: Hurray for the Spanish Flu. Hurray for all lovers of medicine, mamma mía.

DON CLYSTEROS: This is a lot better than all our shitty enemas. Note, however, that this medication induces a thickening of the tongue and swaying of the kneecaps. Bibamus!

*They drink.*

THE THREE: And down the hatch in honor of Spanish medicine. One... two... three!

*They drink and drop at the same time, knocked senseless by the beer. A silence.*

CAPTAIN SANTA CRUZ: Soldier Romero — name de dios! [*He enters.*] Goddamn, he's kaput! And the three doctors have died from the epidemic. Hola, you good-for-nothings, I need three orderlies with the epidemic disposal wagon, and haul these Maccabees away to the garbage dump-o. And no grumbling or looking squeamish either.

## TABLEAU XI

*The Convent of Saint Schlongus, between Bruges and Ostend. Mother Scopelor is looking outside. Six young Beguines are kneeling down, their left eye fixed on heaven, their right hand on their navel.*

MOTHER SCOPELOR: Pray, sisters, go into trances. The Blessed Good Lord is dispatching me a vision in the form of a Spanish battalion that is even now heading straight for our sacred convent of Saint

Schlongus. At last our prayers are to be answered! Pray to great Saint Schlongus, girls, that the kind Spaniards tarry not and press on with springy step.

THE BEGUINES: Saint Schlongus, pray for us! Saint Schlongus whose voluminous, precious, and beneficent relic we guard with veneration, we are weary to tears of worshipping you for nought. In better days we were forever being raped by the soldiers each time once a piece, and that several times a week. Saint Schlongus, steer these Spaniards here, for they are criss-crossing the countryside and keep missing our convent, which they must mistake for a hardware store. Sure looks like the All-Mighty has not endowed them with the same attributes we adore in your famous relic. And, Saint Schlongus, see to it that Mother Scopelor doesn't practice too much ardor and pass them on to us afterwards, like so many drooping lemon peels.

MOTHER SCOPELOR: That will do, my lambs. May Saint Schlongus hear you! You will thus scream from fright, squeeze your legs tight together, tremble and wail: "We are but poor virgins and wish to remain so." [*Knocking on the door. The Beguines howl. Mother Scopelor opens up.*] My lordly officerios, we are but humble little French hens and doves, all quite Catholic and all quite stewed in our own juices, and you are very noble Spaniards, well-born and well intentioned, that's obvious. Enter and do us no harm.

*Don Juan appears.*

DON JUAN: Stay outside my soldados, and you Don Horace, keep them from getting impatient. I mean, make them keep their hands out of their pockets. Sister, this will only take a moment, just enough time to give your quarters the once-over, for we shall have to put up here, perhaps five minutes or perhaps five days, depending on the bobbins of the boginettas.

THE SIX BEGUINES: We cry you grace and mercy, Milord Captain, we are pristine and very prudish boginettas, eachandeveryone innocent, and we pray only to Saint Schlongus.

MOTHER SUPERIOR: My Lord, I'll vouch for them.

DON JUAN: We already know the canticle. There're only a half dozen of them? That's pretty meager, but you, good mama, you count as two. Now then, my lambs, if you're really as innocent as you say, I shall instruct you in the use of the shepherd's crook, and as for you, Mother Scopelor, you shall have a good solid swordfish to deal with. I am Don Juan!

SIX BEGUINES: It's Christmas! It's Christmas! It's Don Juan! Yo love you! Yo want you!

DON JUAN: Calm down my does, and take a number.

MOTHER SUPERIOR: Just one minute! Come into our chapel, illustrious Don Juan, that I might show you the grandiose relic of Saint Schlongus.

DON JUAN: The comparison doesn't scare me. But first permit me to gulp down a few of these pills from Herculaneum, which help to make a good showing at a joust of good Priapus.

*He enters the chapel accompanied by the six Beguines and Mother Scopelor.*

VOICES OF BEGUINES: Hallelujah! He puts Saint Schlongus to shame, he's met his match! A miracle! We'll cut it off, stuff it and put it in the reliquary! It's a regular museum piece! Hurrah! Hasten, Don Juan!

VOICE OF MOTHER SCOPELOR: Hasten, proud captain, the troops await. I with my experienced eye, can see that the troops are impatiently marking time and that their conviction is growing.

VOICE OF DON JUAN: But of course it is! It's Spanish, is it not?

*Various cries are heard. A carnage. After a moment Don Horace enters.*

DON HORACE: Aha, so that's it how it is! He sure knows how to do things, that Don Juan de Bel Hombre! How to appropriate rights to thighage, leggage, assage, and deflowerage, not to mention screwage! He is both Spanish and noble, but I, Don Horace of Antwerpia, I am no less noble and no less a swordsman. He has sullied my honor! [*He goes over to the keyhole.*] Caramba! See how well he slashes! Three of those chickadees already laid low, paws in the air, and the three survivors seem mighty comatose. It's all over! Mother Scopelor is the only one left. She's a more substantial tidbit. Corned-beefos! That boguina is hairy as a rodent! Excelsior! That's one for the books. It looks like a Roman battering ram breaking down an open door. His exploits, make me think of the heroes of old. Here he comes, withdrawing with dignity, leaving the field littered with cadavers.

*Don Juan appears.*

DON JUAN: That was quick! There you are Don Horace, if it please you to finish off the enemy.

DON HORACE: Thus it goes! Fie on these fuckeries, Milord! You've laid me low, and my honor bleeds. I don't want your left-overs, damme, I am cut to the quick. You leave me to cool my heels outside here while you stick it to 'em good inside. En garde!

*He draws his sword.*

DON JUAN: [*foil drawn*] Caramba! I'm going to put a dent in your sword, Milord. [*They fight. Enter Mother Scopelor.*]

MOTHER SCOPELOR: Oh heavens! What do I see? These yeomen doing each other harm. And we, sojourning inside to cross swords with them! Cease, O wretches. [*The Captains stop and sheathe their foils.*]

DON JUAN: So be it! Military duty calls. Good mama, allow me to introduce you to the valiant Don Horace here, who shall take up the battle where I left off, to be followed in short order by the bulk of the troop, which is girded for the assault. [*He exits.*]

DON HORACE: My pleasure!

*The six Beguines erupt onto the stage.*

THE SIX BEGUINES: Long live Don Horace. Yo love you!

DON HORACE: Come sisters, for the troops are peering in at the window, thus expressing their desire to assist at the service. Let us not leave these brave ones to languish.

*He enters the chapel followed by the Beguines and Mother Scopelor. Ruckus. Roars from the agonized sisters. Voices are heard.*

DON HORACE: That's that! Now, give me back my pants.

VOICES OF THE BEGUINES: No, you must stay and do it seven times in a row, that's the tradition.

VOICE OF DON HORACE: Mercy! My sword is warped. Give me back my pants.

*He appears in his shirt-tails. The Sisters and Mother Scopelor erupt onto the stage.*

MOTHER SCOPELOR: Long live the army of the streaming shirt-tails. He shan't have his pants back. See how he resembles Saint Schlongus on the day of his ascension. Tie him up and let's start in again.

DON HORACE: Help! I'll tell Sir Jaime on you, and the devils will pluck and pepper your figs for you. Soldados, deliver your captain from the hands of these demented sisters, they've got lightning up their asses.

*The soldiers break down the door and swarm through the convent.*

THE SOLDIERS: Caramba! [*They shove the Beguines about.*]

MOTHER SCOPELOR: Silence in the ranks. Here are your pants my yeoman. It's drafty in here and I don't want you catching a cold. Let's leave the troops to carry on and frolic. Come quick into my apartment, where I shall make a plaster cast of what you uphold in such soldierly style, so that a new Saint Schlongus may be sculpted when the war is over!

*They vanish. The Soldiers and Beguines hasten into the chapel.*

## TABLEAU XII

*The tent of General Spinola. Flags, palm trees, trophies. The day of Archduke Albert's patron saint. Spinola is surrounded by high-ranking officers. They are drinking port and have opened an umbrella, for it's raining right into the tent.*

SPINOLA: Caramba! See that señorkas, how it's raining and drenching everything. Our tent's turned into a bathtub. This perpetual pitter-patter's a pain. And on our beloved Archduke's saint day too. And he's not even here, as usual! Do you think I'm kidding? You're not yucking it up. I order you to yuck it up!

*All yuck it up.*

Go ahead, bust a gut laughing. Go ahead, Don Manuel, Don Lamoral, Don Pacheco, Don Salazar, Don Pachacrouto, Don Fonseca, and you Escudero, Pedro,

Fuentes, Venero, and so on by rank, dios damn it. Colonels, get those mouths open wide. And officerios ordinerios, pucker up your mouths like chicken asses. Don Mendoza — tell all the troops that they'd better yuck it up or I'll let them all have it.

*Don Mendoza salutes and exits.*

And bring me back that astrologer-major who's called Benévolo.

[*The troops can be heard yucking it up.*] Milords, this port tastes like rainwater. It won't bring on our statutory ration of drunkenness. Why don't we have fine English beers like those crumby Ostenders swill down? Water, water, everywhere, milords. This climate is an affront to our Spanish honor. We're being transformed into Flemish ducks and Sir Jaime will jump at the chance to point out that we're croaking in our swamp, which makes sense since we look a little more like smashed frogs every day. Yes my dear ones, we're all going to croak and all on account of this port, which is nothing but a vile bowel-squeezer. Let us die then, but let us die shouting "Long live Albert!"

ALL: Long live Albert!

SPINOLA: Ah, now it's schpritzing down twice as hard. Every time we cry long live Albert, it comes down a little harder. [*Gunshots are heard.*] What's the meaning of all that shooting? Do you mind? When I distinctly ordered a cut-back on fireworks!

DON LAMORAL: General, those are the cigarillos we passed out to the troops on the occasion of Saint

Albert's day. They're trick cigarillos that make a pop when you light them. It's just another of the great sorcerer's pranks over there in the enemy camp.

> *Don Mendoza returns, dragging Benévolo behind him, who's wearing an astrologer's robe and pointed hat, and taking refuge beneath an umbrella.*

DON MENDOZA: General, this here is the army astrologer, Don Benévolo.

SPINOLA: What news, charlatan! You had ordered splendid weather and 90 degrees in the shade for Saint Albert's day, and here it is raining cats and dogs on our nobility, poopydoodio. Astronomy's not turning out to be a very exact science, is it?

DON BENÉVOLO: Pardon me, General, astronomy has lost its precision here in these Belgiums. My planetary calculations are correct, for it's sunny throughout the entire world. It's only right here in Ostend that it's pissing down as if in spite!

SPINOLA: I order you to put a stop to the schpritz forthwith, and if the sun isn't shining down on the ranks in five minutes, I'm going to send you hard on to the gallows.

DON BENÉVOLO: I cry you mercy! I'll go rework my calculations and I'll get the sun back for you.

SPINOLA: Yes and sneak out from under the punishment. You do your calculations right here.

DON BENÉVOLO: I cry you grace milord; here's the truth of the matter. The sun was supposed to have been shining since dawn and sure enough, there it was, but at the very moment the Spanish artillery fired its first shot for Saint Albert's Day, I saw an ominous looking cloud sweeping across the North Sea. It puffed up and came to a stop directly over the camp. Grabbing hold of my telescope, I saw Sir Jaime on the ramparts shaking his magic umbrella at the cloud. Then the herring wives and masks all set to singing in unison the hymn to the Battle of Groeningen, the time when both Frenchmen and Flemings came back from the front with a gold coin in their boots. And they sang so off-key that the fateful cloud took the form of a gigantic frog which burst and let loose cascades of water... It is by witchcraft, I say, the witchcraft of the great Ostendish devil that we are now being drenched, re-drenched, hyper-drenched, and counter-drenched, enough to drown us, and I declare myself innocent of this wrong-doing and powerless against the spell.

SPINOLA: Thus you are useless to the army — let him be hanged!

*Mendoza exits with a crying Don Benévolo.*

It's turning out to be a nice day after all, milords, even though it got off to a bad start. And still we have a marvelous program in store. Read it Lamoral.

LAMORAL: First off, a hundred and one salutes of the cannon to entertain the troops. And then, a great procession of hooded figures expiating their sins and flagellating themselves for the troops' edification. And then, a general distribution of Alberto's stinkados cigarillos for the troops' gratification. This will be followed by a great and pious performance by the Teatro Nacional Popularo Española to give the troops food for thought. During the intermission, there will be Spanish dances with castanets and guitars featuring a great star from Barcelona. And we'll finish with a great bull fight. At noon, we shall assemble to hear a patriotic speech by the General and distribution of supplementary herrings. I would like to add that the troops have received the order to yuck it up like true patriots in honor of their dearly beloved Archduke.

*Hooting is heard.*

SPINOLA: What is the meaning of this clamor?

*Don Mendoza returns.*

DON MENDOZA: Milord, it's the troops enjoying themselves a bit too enthusiastically as they watch Don Benévolo croaking. But their pleasure notwithstanding, it seems that the troops are protesting against the exploding cigarillos and other scandalous incidents. They're calling for the hanging of the guilty parties.

SPINOLA: Let the guilty parties be brought here. We'll hang them so that the troops can have a really good laugh.

*Entrance of various characters, all soaking wet: a toreador, a young man, practically nude, wearing a belt of vine leaves and a wig, and a character disguised as a serpent.*

What is this, mardi gras? They're out of uniform!

Explain, Mendoza. And this sopping wet toreador?
Toreador, beware. I can see you've been up to no good.

DON MENDOZA: Milord General, the great bull fight was under way with this toreador, but there were no bulls to be found, since the only authentic ones are Spanish, and when we looked for one we found out there weren't any Spanish cows left in Flamenco country anymore, so we settled for a radical Flemish cow who, being phlegmish, didn't want any part of it. But then the cow took one look at the Spanish toreador and got so mad that the aforesaid toreador got the willies and high-tailed it out the exit beneath the jeers of the troops.

SPINOLA: And the cow?

DON MENDOZA: She was so angry, she had a stroke, and we gobbled her up to cover up the taste of herring. At this the soldados became so enraged themselves, that we had to throw them the hell into the Amigo Prison where they're devouring each other this very minute.

SPINOLA: This is disastrous for the troops' morale. Hang the toreador in his costume. That'll teach him to flee before a Flemish cow. He has forfeited his honor.

*The wailing toreador is dragged out.*

SPINOLA: What about this Apollo or Venus here, if you please, it's not so easy to tell which. And that serpent gulping back his saliva?

DON MENDOZA: Milord, this is a rather special situation. You shall now hear of very nice filth indeed...

SPINOLA: Unplug your ears, milord officerios, we're finally going to have the chance to yuck it up.

DON MENDOZA: Well then... The Nacional Teatro, which is very Catholic, was performing Adam and Eve or the Mystery of Lost Innocence by the celebrated Jef Casteleynos and as you know, women are not allowed to act for reasons of morality and their parts are played by young men. Thus, this young man was assigned the role of Eve. And when he appeared in his chaste nudity, it was with a morally acceptable belt of vine leaves. The troops yawned mightily, but respectfully, up until a couple of soldados remarked that Eve was pathetic, since she had a little bush garden growing on her belly where a chemyse ought to have been. Upon which Eve stepped out of character and replied that she didn't have the honor of being the Infanta Isabella, but, a pretty wench who could get along very nicely without a chemyse. Which is an affront to Her Highnyness. From that moment on the edifying performance turned into a circus and this serpent who now looks quite abashed, joined in and whispered all sorts of lewd things to Adam like this: Don't give it a second thought, old coconut, tickle the damsel. Which Adam did, thinking the line came from the Good Book. The tickling having achieved its intended effect, the stupefied public saw through the vine leaves that Eve belonged to the same sex as our fathers. The soldados got mad, calling out that she was phony merchandise and bombarded the theater with herrings.

SPINOLA: That's execrable. What happened to Adam?

DON MENDOZA: He high-tailed it out of there, and quite rightly too.

SPINOLA: Eve, why did you permit him to tickle you?

EVE: I like it Milord.

SPINOLA: It's unnatural, in view of the fact that Adam is a man as are you.

EVE: Not very, Milord. And anyway, I was so into my part that I thought I was a woman. It's the serpent's fault. He told me how pretty I was.

SERPENT: The whore, she's lying! I only meant to give the soldiers a good laugh because they schtupped me a little something to pull a few practical jokes.

SPINOLA: Drag them off to the scaffold — in costume!

DON MENDOZA: General, as for the serpent, that's simple enough, but Eve's not wearing any costume.

SPINOLA: Hang her the way she is then, and tell the hangman to tickle her good since she's so easily turned on.

*Eve and the Serpent howl with fright. They are taken away.*

Señors, let's drink some port. We've had enough hangings for one day! My boot-os are soaking wet. To the health of the Archduke.

*They drink. Fresh hooting.*

Go see what's going on, Mendoza. Bad day, Milords. It's only Ostenders yucking it up and at our expense to boot.

*Mendoza exits and comes back.*

DON MENDOZA: Señor, it's the Spanish dancer!

*Enter the dancer.*

SPINOLA: What's with her?

DON MENDOZA: Well, here goes. She was dancing the habanera and quite well too, only the troops booed at her, thinking it was just another drag act and insisted that the dancer lift up her skirts and prove that she wasn't a transvestite. The lovely child took offense and without the slightest regard for public opinion, let the troops see that she belonged to the same sex as our mothers. Without missing a beat the troops made an attempt to play at Doubting Thomas and the unhappy child put herself under the protection of the High Command. It's an affront to Spanish decorum.

SPINOLA: Only relatively speaking, when you consider that the troops have been looking at the same thing on the ramparts of Ostend all this time. Dry your tears, my pretty. You will dance before the colonels. What is your name?

THE DANCER: Cleo, my general.

SPINOLA: And you were born in Seville, Madrid, Barcelona, Toledo?

THE DANCER: On Good Samaritan Street in the slums of Brusselos, but I look Spanish. Probably because my father was Spanish. He met my mother selling mussels on Chapel Square.

SPINOLA: Name de didios! What a troubling memory comes to mind! When have I seen this face before? Milord officerios, kindly leave me alone with this artist so that I may interrogate her. I used to abide in that neighborhood in the old days.

*The officers protest.*

DON LAMORAL: General, it's a river outside!

SPINOLA: You have umbrellas, Milords. We'll all raise a glass of port to this goddess' health in just a little while.

DANCER: Port? Hot diggity!

*The officers go out groaning. Alone with the dancer, Spinola drops to his knees.*

SPINOLA: Señora, excuse me, I'd like to see your i. d. card.

DANCER: Don't be embarrassed, you old slob. Just tell me straight out what you really want. You're a dirty old man, just like all the rest. Well, be my guest, Saint Albert's Day comes but once a year! [*She rolls up her skirts.*] There's my i. d. with hair all around it!

SPINOLA: Caramba! You're my daughter!

*He falls down in a faint.*

DANCER: Good God and good night. Spinacheke! Who'd have ever thought that he'd be my papa!

*She dissolves in tears.*

## TABLEAU XIII

*The palace in Brusselos in the Saffron Salon of the Infanta.*

ISABELLA: Lord Dios, Saints Justine, Agatha, Caroline, Catherine, Leocadia, Scholastic, Babylas, Verhaege, Dagobert, Fruitful, Theodule, Sylvester...

FATHER TRULLEMANS: That's enough saints, Your Highness, the Court's full up!

ISABELLA: By all the saints, say I, is it to be today or tomorrow?

FATHER TRULLEMANS: With the ayde of the All-Mighty, it may very well be next year.

ISABELLA: What a blow to my honor. What a stinging pain in my privates!

FATHER TRULLEMANS: It is true, Highness, that as a good Christian you should wish decapitation on your worst enemy sooner than the torture of death by itching. You may get some relief by having another church built, but as for stamping out the great sorcerer, Sir Jaime, that's a whole 'nother pair of oil cans. We have excommunicated him, but that hasn't stopped him in the least. Even now he has written a new lampoon in which he claims that Her Highness was loaded with puss and overrun with vermin from birth and that this business with the chemyse is a farce, given that Her Highness is very much at home with dirt and not once in her life has she changed her chemyse.

ISABELLA: If you were not my sage and learnéd confessor, I'd have you skinned alive, since you seem to derive so much pleasure in announcing these infamies to me. Where are the officers who have come to report to us?

FATHER TRULLEMANS: Here they are, and I warn you that their reports are nothing to sneeze at.

*Enter Don Lamoral, Don Miramar, and Don Realgar, who salute.*

ISABELLA: Go right ahead with your little news items Hidalgos, while I say my Rosary.

DON REALGAR: The High Command wishes to inform Your Highness that the troops protest in regard to the herring. The army is in need of umbrellas and most of all, of pesetas.

ISABELLA: As for the umbrellas, I'll see to it.

DON REALGAR: It's schpritzing without let-up and not one of Heaven's blessings will advance the Siege, unless we're provided with boats, so we can navigate through the trenches, and unless admirals are appointed. Next, that the troops are fighting amongst themselves, which is making structural inroads. The Ostenders look on amusedly all the while. It goes without saying that the said Spanish troops are composed of Walloons, Germans, Brusselosers, Swiss, Moors and Visigoths and that these said mercenaries demand that they receive orders each in their own jargon and not in Spanish, which they don't understand in the first place. [*He bows.*]

ISABELLA: What ought we decide, Father Trullemans?

FATHER TRULLEMANS: That the troops be commanded in Latin.

ISABELLA: So do we order! And you Miramar?

DON MIRAMAR: The General Staff wishes to inform Your Highness that the army is suffering mightily from the swinish pranks of the Ostenders who've trained rats and sent them to putter through our rations, boots, tents, blunderbusses, munitions and all the rest, that is when they aren't eating Spaniards whole and leaving nothing but the bones behind. Then, that the aforementioned Ostenders have trained giant fleas and the army is scratching itself desperately to the great detriment of discipline.

ISABELLA: As for the rats, let the soldiers say prayers over them and eat them. It will be a change from herring, which we mustn't overdo. Also, send some furry cats to the High Command. As for the fleas, tell my generals that I find myself highly offended in view of the fact that I thought I was the only one to cultivate fleas by will celestial. The troops are forbidden from all unworthy scratching, so do we command. Is that all?

FATHER TRULLEMANS: Alas, Highness, here's the kicker. Concerning shameful things... which must be talked about nonetheless...

ISABELLA: I'll cover my Eustachian tubes. Read Miramar, and good diction now!

DON MIRAMAR: The High Command blushingly wishes to inform Your Highness that the troops have been living at their posts for close to two years without carnal commerce with women and that this has resulted in a scourge of contagious immorality, by which we mean a certain abominable sin that is spreading, whose very name is abominable and was the cause of the destruction of abominable Sodom.

ISABELLA: What's the meaning of this, Father Trullemans? I don't get it. Explain it to me and if need be, bring me a few guilty soldados, so I can see with my own eyes what all the fuss is about.

FATHER TRULLEMANS: What they're doing, Highness, exceeds all other horrors. They call each other señor and señorka and frequently set up little well matched-up houscholds and sleep together after the fashion of those nice, cute French musketeers.

ISABELLA: You mean to insinuate that the soldados have eachandeveryone turned into tush-fuckers?

FATHER TRULLEMANS: That's the word Highyness. In the name of honesty I should add that those who haven't turned into tush-fuckers have turned into tush-fuckees.

ISABELLA: Would you kindly explain the difference?

DON MIRAMAR: It's a question of temperament, Your Highness. If I had the same talent for drawing as Sir Jaime, I'd permit myself to depict the Spaniards in the exercise of their reprehensible fun.

FATHER TRULLEMANS: Or if Her Highness deigns to bow before the realism of this transgression, I could send for two monks.

ISABELLA: That would be very kind, but no! And what might be the remedy for this scourge of immorality?

FATHER TRULLEMANS: We're in a pretty pickle! Highness, the troops must drink their water and eat their herring. They must be kept busy, undertake repeated assaults on the enemy and the soldados must be kept from fraternizing, which is very difficult when one is trying to hold an army together. The wisest solution would be to take Ostend, for therein they will find mightily fat women to relieve their urgent need.

ISABELLA: Hallelujah! That's the right remedy. Let us seek out some mightily fat women. But such copulations would be sinful, I'll wager?

FATHER TRULLEMANS: Yes, but only relatively, in view of the fact that it's in the service of the triumph of Spanish might and Catholic power.

ISABELLA: Caramba! It occurs to me that two years ago I received a petition from some ladies of the nobility who, good Christian women that they were, wanted to strike out in groups for Ostend for the duration of the Siege in order to bring succor and care to our heroes. Order such patriotic dames as there are to embark post haste with charms and baggage in tow. If I had not taken the vow of chastity, I would to set the example myself. I was also forgetting that one of my little cousins, a Spanish prince, a very pretty boy who, as is his childish wont, dresses up as a young lady, lately proposed to me that he sojourn in the army where his hi-jinks might raise the troops' morale. He says he could solve the whole problem all by himself. Let's move on. And you, Lamoral, what news do you bear me of my husband?

DON LAMORAL: Highness, he's doing just fine. I come even now from having met him.

ISABELLA: What's that? Is he in Brusselos?

DON LAMORAL: Ostend, I was speaking of Ostend. He's learning how to shoot and the cannon is his favorite pastime. He asks for his umbrella and for flannel as well as his prayer book and pesetas with which to dispense gratuities to the artillery. Next, the High Command suggest that Her Highyness give urgent consideration as to what to do with Ostend once it's taken, which won't be long now.

ISABELLA: I have already said that we would build...

FATHER TRULLEMANS: It's all fine and good to

build churches. And yet, Highness, Ostend is a city situated right on the coast. An ideal place for extracting revenues for the Royal Treasury. The general of the Jesuits thinks that we might consider building a casino with gambling rooms there. There are also baths to reestablish, while of course safeguarding morality. For example, we might tolerate nought but foot baths. And in memory of our patriotic past, ass baths to commemorate laying the siege, with pain of hanging for one and all who would remove their breeches. The beach shall be supervised by alguazils to enforce the regulation. And then there's always trade in shrimps and mussels, with a large profit if we slap a tax on top of it, and the same goes for soap sold in the baths, and don't forget the kitty. Finally we could expel the Ostenders and replace them with Spaniards for the sake of morality and raise the price of food so high that the schleppy Belgians would come no more, save for their nobility. We could also arrange for a miracle to take place and for race tracks with taxes slapped on.

ISABELLA: We wish it so! Milords my Hidalgos, it's time for the holy offices. My congratulations to the Archduke and the army.

*She exits. The nobles bow.*

FATHER TRULLEMANS: Will you be spending the night here, my dear little Lords?

DON LAMORAL: Ah no, on account of the lice. But where can a person go in Brusselos where there are nought but churches? And what is there to do at the camp in Ostend where there are nought but umbrellas and tush-fuckers?

FATHER TRULLEMANS: Night is falling. Come my braves. Brusselos is a mighty fine city for those acquainted with it. You are proud Spaniards and I am a proud Brusseler. It's the hour when all valiant yeomen and crafty courtesans drop the language of the court and start speaking that of jugs and zippers.

DON REALGAR: But aren't you a man of the cloth, my Father?

FATHER TRULLEMANS: Rest assured, in the places where I'll be chaperoning you, a holy crucifix is always hanging on the wall.

DON MIRAMAR: And what about eternal salvation, my Father?

FATHER TRULLEMANS: We'll make up for it with a few invisible coins!

*They exit arm in arm.*

## TABLEAU XIV

*Ostend, in the tent of General Spinola.*

SPINOLA: What now? Lamoral, my deputy, we're holding war councils every morning now. What's the point of all these formalities? Send 'em all straight to the gallows, blessèd dios! Dismissed, milord deputy. I have to trim my beard.

LAMORAL: General, even so, you must hear the case, or else rumor of scandal will fly on the wings of slander right to the palace, and what will become of our promotions then?

SPINOLA: You should have said so before! Let us hear the case then.

LAMORAL: General, have you remarked that our troops have exhibited a fondness for bel-canto recently?

SPINOLA: Who the hell is this Bel-Canto person? Another tush-fucker I bet! Shove a stake the hell up his tush-hole!

LAMORAL: If you please, bel-canto, in Spanish, means singing!

SPINOLA: You should have said so before, amigo. Singing is good for the troops, it shows that morale is excellent, Lamoral.

LAMORAL: That remains to be seen. The song the troops are singing isn't the "Tantum Ergo" or "Venite Adoremus." or the royal march It isn't even the Herring Lullaby.

SPINOLA: Potdoodio, we are lost! Tell me the whole story, Lamoral, our honor is at stake.

LAMORAL: All right, you asked for it! They're singing a song about the Catholic and gracious chemyse.

SPINOLA: Caramba! The one belonging to our Catholic and gracious Infanta! Miserere nobis! Do you have a copy of the song?

LAMORAL: I had a hundred and fifty thousand confiscated. The verses aren't so terrific and the music's ordinary enough. But what it's trying to say, it says well. Would you like me to bring in the person who kicked the whole thing off?

SPINOLA: And the executioner?

*Lamoral shows in Casanova, followed by the Executioner.*

So you're a singer soldier, are you?

CASANOVA: Lead tenor, Excellency.

LAMORAL: Would you like to let us hear the couplets which you so wittily uttered with such success last night after curfew.

CASANOVA: With pleasure Excellency. I beg your indulgence. I'm a little hoarse, because they've been making me sing it from morn to night.

SPINOLA: Once more then. Off you go.

CASANOVA: Help me with the refrain. [*He sings.*]

Isabella swore to Jeez
Not to take off her chemyse,
And Duke Albert was quite grieved
And said now pretty-please...

Take the chemyse off this minute
There's fleas and crap all in it.
To eliminate those fumes
You'd better put on some perfume.

Refrain:
The Chemyse of Isabella
Got to have quite a smell-a,
And it's been that way for a while,
Never seen a chemyse so vile.

CHORUS:
Who in the world would think
A chemyse could make such a stink?

SPINOLA AND LAMORAL:
Who in the world would think
A chemyse could make such a stink?

SPINOLA: Why it's terrif! Continue, Casanova.

CASANOVA:
Isabella answered with ease,
I won't take off my chemyse.
No kisses 'twixt you and me,
And the Church will be quite pleased.

If the sanctity I exude
Doesn't put you in the mood,
And you think that it's too rotten,
Just stuff your nose with cotton.

The chemyse of Isabella, etc.

SPINOLA, LAMORAL, CASANOVA, EXECUTIONER AND CHORUS:[*Repeat the refrain.*]

*Casanova bows.*

SPINOLA: Splendid, Soldier Casanova! Are you the author?

CASANOVA: Your Honor, I have not the talent for't. The song was bombarded on us by the Ostenders. We got bundles of 'em dropped on our helmets. Then, up over the ramparts, they intoned the tune to teach it to us. As it was raining, we conn'd it to chase away the blues.

LAMORAL: That's what I thought! The ditty originated with the enemy, and it's Sir Jaime who made up the words and music. Damnation!

SPINOLA: We need to make an example of someone. Verdugo, hang this singer and nail the song to the gallows in plain sight of the whole army.

CASANOVA: Mercy. [*The Executioner drags Casanova off.*]

SPINOLA: Just between us Lamoral, that little tune's mighty funny.

*Fanfares are heard.*

Flip on rye! Since when do we have music played at military executions?

LAMORAL: If I hear aright, those are the Ostendish orphans on the ramparts making mincemeat of our honor by playing that delectable song.

SPINOLA: Have them pulverized and their instruments along with them. So order the artillery.

*Lamoral exits. The artillery begins to fire from the cannons. Lamoral comes back.*

LAMORAL: We're on the way, do you hear it?

SPINOLA: Yes but who's that who starts singing in the south whenever there's a pause in the singing from the north?

LAMORAL: Milord, those are the artiflows singing the song of Isabella while firing. Speaking of which, a letter's come from the Archduke.

SPINOLA: Let's have a look at it. "My trusty and dearly beloved Spinola: I'm having a rousing good time here in Brusselos where I heard a comic song being sung in the bordellos that I copied down just for you.

Isabella swore to Jeez

Not to take off her chemyse...

LAMORAL: [*reading*] And Duke Albert was quite grieved...

SPINOLA: [*reading*] And said now pretty-please...

LAMORAL: [*reading*] Take the chemyse off this minute...

SPINOLA: [*reading*] There's fleas and crap all in it...

LAMORAL: [*reading*] To eliminate those fumes...

SPINOLA AND LAMORAL: [*reading*] You'd better put on some perfume"

THE OSTENDISH ARTILLERY AND CHORAL SOCIETY:
The Chemyse of Isabella
Got to have quite a smell-a,
And it's been that way for a while,
Never seen a chemyse so vile.

THE WHOLE SPANISH ARMY:
Who in the world would think
A chemyse could make such a stink.

SPINOLA: And the Archduke concludes his letter, "General, my friend, if you happen upon some Spaniard occupied in singing this little jingle, hang him not, but rather give him a florin in my name, so great is my satisfaction at seeing my legitimate made an ass of." Alert! Unhang Casanova!

*Lamoral exits and comes back with Casanova.*

CASANOVA: The damage is done. I'll never sing again.

SPINOLA: Accept this florin, my dear soldado. I promote you to the rank of Captain for having raised the troops' morale with your head tones. High military spirits are sister to victory.

*He gives him the florin and embraces him.*

LAMORAL: Bravo. Viva Hispania! General, ask him to sing the unpublished version of the song. It seems that that one's so bad it would make a hog ejaculate! I've got the text in my pocket!

SPINOLA: So do I!

## TABLEAU XV

*At Brusselos in the great golden salon of the "Farting Jackass." Enter Archduke Albert, his face concealed beneath a mask. He is received by Aunt Rosie, ample patrona of the house of pleasure.*

ALBERT: Guess who I am, my big bubby, Alonzo, Gonzalo, Girálomo, or Manuel?

AUNT ROSIE: Well, my Yeoman, in the first place, you're Spanish, in the second you're married, and in the last, you're Archduke Albert, number two out of two, and my best client!

ALBERT: Fiddledeedee, I may be Pablo, Crístobal, or Báltazar but definitely not Albert. What a pleasant place this sweatbox is, for here palm trees grow and mirrors take the place of walls. My sweet little wasp, my little pat of butter, tell me what's become of Pepita, Marquita, Esperanza, and all the other goddesses revived from days of yore?

AUNT ROSIE: They're in the arms of Morpheus, but they'll snap out of it when they find out what high amorous nobility requests the pleasure of their company and offers them his flame of Toledo. They'll all go bathe in almond milk with bergamot and perfume their breath with jujube à l'amaryllis. So, what'll you have, caramel of my heart?

ALBERT: One of those potions which render one intrepid, for the siege has worn me out. Kriek Lambic beer, for example.

AUNT ROSIE: And how is the siege going?

ALBERT: Not bad, and you? Do they still play the viol d'amour here in your nunnery, and do they drink all those wonderfully hot spicy drinks?

AUNT ROSIE: Shut your mouth, my honey fly. No longer will you find Señorita Josefina, nor Señorita Perlamora, nor Señorita Schellrosalia, but ladies of high standing, all very noble, and even their bidets bear their coats of arms. They are masked in satin, so as not to give themselves away. And I can tell you that my boarders are women of super-high society, whose señorka husbands neglect them, and either come here to earn a little extra income or just for the fun of it. The poor dears are all on their lonesome at home and yeomen are all they've got to fill in the gap.

ALBERT: Godflippit-o! I'm going to meet my whole court here and my nobles cuckolded, one and all! Serves 'em right! But, my good dueña, do these gazelles at least take off their chemyses here?

AUNT ROSIE: This is the only place they do. The funniest part is that these noble señorka husbands put their trust in me and drop their codpieces right in front of their very own wives whom they don't recognize, and then they fricassee each other without the least reserve.

ALBERT: What a cuckoldrick paradox! I have a feeling then, that business is booming and that it's raining pesetas into your tiralira.

AUNT ROSIE: We can't complain. So long as the

siege keeps up and Isabella insists on sojourning in her undershirt. I've even had a chapel erected in honor of the great Saint Lawrence.

ALBERT: You must have started amassing your fortune quite a while ago.

AUNT ROSIE: It dates back to the glorious reign of Charles V, who deigned to inaugurate my house of wriggling and fuckeries. And all the big cheeses of Spain and the Lowlands have been bestowing their amity on me ever since. You'd be very surprised if you knew what characters of high standing show up here, under cover of the charming convention of the mask.

ALBERT: I believe it, dearie, my stuffed turkey — your chapel here's quite lovely! How I adore that player piano, the one that plays the tango, the seguedilla, and the bolero! Have you had a chance to fix the mechanical divan that's just like the one in Satyricon? And how is the Farting Jackass behaving himself? What do you say we crank up the old mechanical animal for my amusement? [*They walk over to admire the mechanical jackass.*]

AUNT ROSIE: All you have to do is shove a peseta in his trap and turn his tail three times. Listen to that!

> *Albert turns the tail. The jackass farts out the Spanish National Anthem. The Archduke salutes, and Aunt Rosie brushes away a furtive tear.*

Everybody's favorite! Ha, I forgot to mention the spiciest part. You'll get a kick out of my collection of etchings censored by the Holy Bazaar that were snuck in here from Ostend in a General's suitcase. He who made them is a most wondrous artist, well-versed in human merriment and obscenities. He drops in here quite often, not to besport himself, but because he loves the masks which he touches up. And while he's at it he teaches the ladies good manners and dancing and accompanies them on the recorder. Just between us, he shields me from demons, since he himself is the master of deviltry in cellars where not so white masses are held. Certain frolicsome men of the cloth turn up here too, but professional ethics forbid me to name them.

*Laughing and male voices are heard.*

ALBERT: Godflappit-o! The Graces seem to be waking up, but it sounds like they've acquired baritone voices. I'd wager that they have moustaches and spurs too!

AUNT ROSIE: Unh, unh, my lord, it's only the señors coming down from a performance of clandestine marionettes given by the poet, Don Miguel of the Blesséd Tree with an uncensored script and set designs by the Ostendish artist we were just talking about. But they might have gotten the urge to tickle the pussy-wusses in the hollow of their affections as they passed by their alcoves.

ALBERT: And what story is it that these libertine marionettes are performing, my padded guinea hen?

AUNT ROSIE: Now don't get upset, my marzipan piglet! It's a documentary about the Siege of Ostend, or, to be more precise, it's called "The Triumph of the Cacaphonic Banner," or " Isabella's Tasty Dishes."

ALBERT: Slipmefive-o! I'll be sure to attend the next showing, my scapularized matron.

AUNT ROSIE: As you think best, my little calve's liver.

*Enter three masked lords.*

DON JUAN: Potfreckit-o, I never knew the moon gave off so much heat.

DON HORACE: Jipdillit-o, my eversolovely nightingale birdie! How you flit through this grove!

SPINOLA: Sacramentos, I could proudly prick a majestic plume for my sombrero, the like of which has never before been snipped. [*noticing Albert*] And who's this individual standing there looking like a cross between a Belgian and a Moor wearing that paper maché snout the color of a pig's bladder?

AUNT ROSIE: Señorkas, this is a debonnaire aristocrat quivering with desire for fuckery, who's waiting his turn to take a ride, that is if there's any hay left in the mattress. He is Spanish, as you can tell by his fine red nose which comes fresh from the good nose-molder.

DON JUAN: ¿Se habla español? Stutter-o, stammer-o, talkshit?

ALBERT: So-so! What difference does it make, since

we're all nobles? Señor caballeros! I greet you. How are the little marionettes of the Siege of Ostend?

DON HORACE: Heroic and mightily noble, they're fine and growing. This Siege is of interest to you milord?

ALBERT: Passably. I am without news of my friend, the marquis of Spinola. I also have in my pocket a report from the intelligence services, better known as the secret cop outfit, on the subject of two highranking officerios, milords, Don Juan de Bel Hombre and milord Don Horace D'Antwerpia, two gadabouting men about town, whom we've totally lost track of. Have they been taken prisoner by the Ostenders or are they in the bordello as usual?

SPINOLA: Caramba! I'll transmit the message to Spinola. I often play tic-tac-toe with him in my apartment on Vanderiderodera Street.

DON JUAN: I'll tell Don Juan if I run into him. He's my cousin.

DON HORACE: I'll inform Don Horace if I see him. He's a buddy of mine.

AUNT ROSIE: Come on now. The drinks are on me. All you señorkas can get better acquainted over a Kriek-Lambic while waiting for the Beauties to come down to the salon. [*They drink.*] May the Kriek-Lambic deal gently with you, fair maskers. Only, no up-chucking on the carpets or on the ladies if you please!

ALBERT: Milord maskers, it would be neither very useful nor very wise to get too well acquainted.

SPINOLA: I agree! Can you imagine if a mask fell off and we beheld the sublime face of our most illustrious archduke?

ALBERT: Or that of our no less famous General Spinola! [*Great commotion and women's screams.*] The nymphs in great wooden clogs are scrambling down the grand staircase. Milords, beware. [*Enter a monk and priest, masked.*]

BR'ER KLETSAF: Yeomen, defend the Church! They're hot on our trail, the cows!

ALBERT: And how did the Church find its way 'neath these desecrated eaves, pray tell?

FATHER TRULLEMANS: We're spreading the gospel to these Magdalenes.

BR'ER KLETSAF: . . . and enjoining them to keep their chemyses on!

FATHER TRULLEMANS: And in their fury, the amazons pulled our robes up over our heads to see if we had tails with sap running through 'em.

BR'ER KLETSAF: And screamed: Sursum cauda and tried to tie a pan on 'em, the way they do to stray mutts.

AUNT ROSIE: Peace you little rascals! You got their dander up theologically, like the motherfuckers you are, and neglected to compensate them properly, just like all the other times.

*Enter all the señoritas, masked and in transparent chemyses.*

PAQUITA: After them! There they are, the old goats. Grab Trullemans there.

CONCHITA: Give us our pesetas, Br'er Kletsaf, or else we call the copperinos!

MARQUITA: And you, Don Horace, give me back that big diamond of mine that you requisitioned when I was about to swoon.

CARMENCITA: And you, Don Juan, you snatched my wedding ring in order to do a little blackymaily on me, just like always.

AUNT ROSIE: Leave personalities out of it my children. These señorkas are all right honorable nobles!

DON JUAN: Milords, they're defaming our honor. Ever faithful to my motto: Straight ahead! Caramba! Viva Hispania!

*He gives the women a thrashing, Don Horace does likewise, the two ecclesiasts as well. Great commotion. Albert cranks the jackass' tail, and it farts the Spanish national anthem.*

ALBERT: This is a downright ballsy free-for-all! I'm mightily pleased! Excelsior!

*Enter Sir Jaime, dressed in a great cloak and armed with an umbrella. He is costumed as Jupiter of Olympus with a silvery beard.*

SIR JAIME: Hahahaha! It's a carnage in the chicken coop and I can see these Spaniards with pusses like possums ruthlessly mistreating these maids of Eden with no regard for the gracious laws of Courtly Love. I'd like to see them thrown into the stocks frog-wise! By the tempestuous seagull and the lion of the silken tongue! [ *He cranks the mechanical music box which plays the March of Sperloot.* ] Long live the strapping Knaves! I'll rip the guts out of these puppet Yeomen! Glory to the fighting Sperloot!

SPINOLA: It's a Knave! And he's sullying the Honor of Spain! Let your swords see the light of day, heroes of the Siege of Ostend!

SIR JAIME: Milords, the real heroes of the Siege are the herrings! To the tourney, and may my wondrous parasol twirl 'round and about, so the fight may be brief. Bim-bam! Bim-bam! Bim-bam!

> *Fierce combat between Sir Jaime on the one side and Don Juan, Don Horace, and the two monks on the other. Sir Jaime knocks out all his adversaries, by striking them with his umbrella. They are laid out on the ground.*

THE SEÑORITAS: Long live the handsome snow-masked Knave, full of malice! Long live the avenging parasol. Down with the shredded Yeomen!

ALBERT: Well-played! But the Yeomen had the excuse as did the two monks, that they had just made sacrifice on Venus' altar. Milords, let's declare a truce.

> *The victims stand back up.*

I shall pay generously for the damages, compensation to these ladies, and a round of drinks for one and all.

ALL: Good fight. Let's make up. Long live both Knaves and Yeomen!

SIR JAIME: And may our beauteous Flanders live long in knavery and the great exterminating parasol too! Oh, my chipped masks, I'll repaint you good as new, spangled with lurid colors. I, sovereign of these climes, order these dryads and fauns be caressed to musical accompaniment and command that three-colored lanterns be hung from the horns sprouting from the Belgian husbands' heads, and I wish that the Spaniards be gobbled up by scorpions and the well-stuffed monks be drowned in the shit-filled River Senne. And long live the Blesséd Bordello and for she's a jolly good fellow to the great Whore Priestess who presides over it, adorned with religious relics. And long live the Jackass farting patriotic tremolos out its ass! And long live Her Dryness, with her dirty linen and all the royal lice! And on my perfluting flute, I shall play with unpleasant and shrill variations for the titillation of all my little bilingual devils of Brusselos! Excelsior! Let's dance the quadrille of pot-bellied, belly-buttoned aristocraticized I-don't-give-a-damnism!

*He plays the flute perched on a table. The Yeomen, the Churchmen, and the Señoritas dance, loosing savage cries. Aunt Rosie goes down the middle of the line. The Archduke climbs the Farting Jackass. Grand Finale.*

## TABLEAU XVI[1]

*War Council in the tent of General Spinola, surrounded by Colonels Don Pachacrouto and Don Ramollo Bombardos, plus the Executioner and scribe monk, Dom Faggo.*

SPINOLA: And there you have it, that's that! That's my opinion. And what is yours, my colonels?

THE COLONELS: And there you have it, that's our opinion too. Same as yours General.

SPINOLA: But I don't have any, Sacredios.

THE COLONELS: And there you have it, we don't either, sacredios, and that is our opinion: that opinion have we none, a thousand billion sacredios!

DOM FAGGO: Amen! [*He belches.*]

SPINOLA: Milord colonels and you Dom Faggo, listen up you Dom Pachacrouto and you Dom Ramollo Bombardos, you bunch of sons-of-bitch-os. Boy, this monk stinks bad! If he weren't such a good spy, I'd have half a mind to chuck him the hell onto the dungheap. Lead in the accused man. Do you know who it is? The unknown Spanish Soldier. Nya!

ALL: Nya! [*The Executioner exits and comes back with the Unknown Soldier.*]

SPINOLA: Shove him the hell down onto his knees, gentle Verdugo, and stick the iron pear the hell into his groin. And there you are. Answer soldier! Your name!

---

1. Ghelderode eliminated this scene from the final version.

DOM FAGGO: He doesn't have one, there you have it, no one knows it. Who is he? Gomez, Fernandez, Alvarez, Gonzalez. We'll never know. He's a soldier, there you have it! That's the way it is. They say that a cannon ball hit him in the noggin. So he's a hero, and there you have it!

SPINOLA: There's nought but heroes in all my great armies. Unknown Soldier, I order you to answer. This is the third and last time that you are appearing in contempt here before our council of your own sincere, free will. You were asked first graciously, then imperatively, to allow yourself to be killed by the enemy. Why didn't you die heroically at that point, as you were ordered to? He doesn't answer? Executioner, twist his toes.

DOM FAGGO: There you have it, he went over to the enemy, things didn't go the way they should, and he came back having lost all desire to die.

SPINOLA: You're really in for it this time, Unknown Soldier. You have refused to accept the honor of becoming the one and only glorious Unknown Soldier of the Siege of Ostend, as any other proud Spaniard would. You've lost out on the chance to become the object of future patriotic veneration by philanthropic, artistic, and recreational societies. But you shall be in spite of yourself. Answer. Do you or do you not accept? You have exactly ten minutes to place yourself in the Ostendish line of fire and fall on the field of honor. And if the Ostendish bullets don't finish you off, then the Spanish bullets will rectify the error. If you keep sticking to your guns, you shall be painlessly slain and buried with a great procession, a first class hearse, and Sunday service. Answer! My colonels, mark you? He makes no answer!

DOM FAGGO: Milords, he can't because we've stuck the iron pear into his mouth.

SPINOLA: Then remove the iron pear and let him speak.

SPINOLA: Milords — the cannonball which left him coo-coo rendered him dumb as well.

SPINOLA: Let him respond with hand signals to indicate that he understands us.

DOM FAGGO: Milords, he is tied up and he is deaf as well!

SPINOLA: Caramba! Let's face it, he's a con-artist! Judged and sentenced! The council declares that you are herewith promoted to the rank of Unknown Soldier from this day henceforth and commands that your solemn funeral services go forward at the expense of the State. My sincere congratulations! Verdugo, do your duty on the field of honor.

DOM FAGGO: I bless him in the name of the Father, etc. For God and Fatherland!

*The Executioner spits in his hands and strangles the soldier.*

THE EXECUTIONER: Crack! And now — shall we cook him, boil him, or serve him in Italian dressing?

SPINOLA: None of the above. Dress him up in his very best uniform and paint an ecstatic smile on his face. Milords, on your feet and hats off!

*They stand.*

There he lies, there you are, there you are, and we salute him.

[*with trembling voice*] Milords... we bow our heads... hearts contracted... before the remains... of this unknown hero... [*He cries.*] of the Siege of Ostend... His memory... will live on... never to perish... those who have piously died for the Fatherland... [*Sobs.*]... I've forgotten the rest... Viva Hispania! [*He covers the body with a flag.*]

THE COLONELS: Viva Hispania!

SPINOLA: Come, Milords. It's happy hour.

*They exit.*

## TABLEAU XVII

*On the plain before Ostend. The army is gathered. Numerous banners.*

SPINOLA: Now then, here we are, the twenty second of September, anno Domini 1604, and by the grace of God, the weather is excellent. See how resplendently the sun shines, made to order. Just sniff the rustling sea breeze.[*trumpets*] I have ordered trumpets, drums, and the whole fucking fanfare, according to the wishes of our Dryness, who wishes that Ostend be taken and dismantled before set of sun. It shall be thus, for I wish it too, and all of you wish it since this thing's been dragging on for quite a while now. To wit: officerios and soldados, we shall attempt the great final charge at five before the hour. And may glory and fame go before your standards. The m. p.'s will follow your columns and shoot at your paws if you don't keep marching according to regulations. And thus I cry: Viva Hispania.

THE WHOLE ARMY: Viva Hispania!

SPINOLA: Well then Milord graduates of the military academy, I attend on your most precious advice, which, in any case, I have no intention of following.

DON JUAN: General the sea air's done me good. You know also that we haven't yet broken out our stock of cannonballs, but that we've already ordered new ones. Let's keep right on bombarding and rebombarding or else our very Catholic suppliers will take it amiss and that'll be the end of our kickbacks.

DON HORACE: General, we've got to put a stop to this now since the common people are all saying that Ostend has long since disappeared from the military map. They say that this siege is nothing but a pretext for stirring up patriotic and fiscal enthusiasm and to give everyone something to talk about.

SPINOLA: Caramba! Well put. Well then, there you are. I'll toss this florin into the air. Tails, we take Ostend. Heads, we just keep on pretending to. [*Father Trullemans arrives.*] Here's Father Trullemans, just come down from Brusselos. His counsel will be decisive.

TRULLEMANS: Milords, Her Dryness bid me come and entreat you to put an end to the siege this very day, since she can't bear the agony of the chemyse one hour longer.

SPINOLA: And yet she's in the habit by now.

TRULLEMANS: Yes, but the little beasties that the specialists call crab-bus isabellensis are getting twice as fierce now. It's the little critters' mating season. If you are indeed gallant, you will comprehend and act accordingly.

SPINOLA: We are indeed gallant. Long live Her Dryness. Yoicks, to the crab-bus isabellensis! Yoicks, to the Ostenders! Charge!

THE WHOLE ARMY: Caramba!

SPINOLA: Artiflows, fire! Up and at 'em! Officerios and soldados, bestir yourselves. Play trumpets and play slide-trombones. Roll those drums. A hundred cigarillos to the first one into Ostend! [*The whole army roars and makes a rush for the city. Artillery fire and music.*] Ha! What heroes! They've got the devil up their asses. Milords, let us sing.

SPINOLA, DON JUAN, DON HORACE, TRULLEMANS: [*in chorus*]
It shall grow,
It shall grow,
It shall grow,
For it is Spanish!

TRULLEMANS: What's going to grow, if you don't mind?

DON JUAN: The crab-bus isabellensis.

TRULLEMANS: Laus Deo! Te Deum! Deo gratis! Ite mita est! A. M. D. G.! Look! They're inside-o the city!

DON HORACE: Where do you see a city? There's nothing left there but little scraps.

SPINOLA: What matter so long as the Spanish colors wave over the little scraps of what used to be one big scrap? Father Trullemans, go tell the Infanta that the siege has broken through and that she can change her linen with a clear conscience. Can you hear them bawling? Milords, let us prepare to enter the conquered city in triumph, and hang the great sorcerer sandwiched in between his flute and his umbrella as well as all the survivors. We will spare no one except the women of Ostend, whose stately buttocks exhibited on the ramparts leant so much charm to my days and my fieldglasses.

TRULLEMANS: And clear the field, for the monks are on their way with the architeks to build the fifty churches promised in commemoration of the victory. I shall burn up the road to Brusselos to announce the miracle. [*He goes off.*]

SPINOLA: Draw your great sabers, Milords, we shall now form the procession. Who goes there? It's Lamoral. What news, sonny?

LAMORAL: General, Ostend's in the bag. But in the interest of historical accuracy, I'm obliged to report that our soldiers encountered not the slightest resistance for the simple reason that there's not a soul left in the city. Neither Ostendish men, nor Ostendish women, nor Sir Jaime, nor devils nor sorcerers, not even herrings.

SPINOLA: Caramba... where are they?

LAMORAL: They've put to sea, sailing for Zeeland, drinking Schiedam and thumbing their noses at us from afar. As for pursuing them, you know as well as I that the troops can't swim.

SPINOLA: Caramba de caramba! We've been outwitted and on a grand scale too. Here we take a city that isn't being defended, because the garrison has turned heel and fled. Without delay go through all the surrounding villages, round up all the people that can be found and throw them the hell into Ostend so we've got a population to work with that'll acclaim us. Then we'll hang them. I say: let's get cracking!

LAMORAL: Alas, General, I'll bet five hundred thousand pesetas against one Pope's florin that you won't find a single Fleming within twenty leagues. It'd be smarter to write up a glorious communique in which we say anything we want.

DON JUAN: But, we better not report that the great mocking sorcerer has slipped out of our clutches.

SPINOLA: Too bad he got away! He was a real original, conshitting up their majesties thus. And he could have painted my portrait. Milords, let us puff up our chests, draw our swords and enter the city. And this evening we'll take a little turn around the beach and dip our toesies in the water. And I'll treat you to a banquet at which we'll have herring one last time. Viva Hispania!

ALL: Viva Hispania!

*They draw their swords and march towards Ostend.*

## TABLEAU VIII

*At the Palace of Brusselos in the Throne Room. Banners. Trophies. On the throne sits Isabella. At her side, Father Trullemans and Br'er Kletsaf. Numerous nobles.*

ISABELLA: And, trembling with emotion, I read the dispatch which tells me: "My darling Highness, your husband takes pleasure in informing you that the forts of Ostend have fallen, and thus we write this day, the twenty second of September with the ayde of God and all the Saints in Paradise. Your affectionate Albert." Hallelujah!

BR'ER KLETSAF: Hallelujah! Let the bells ring out, let the bells ring out!

*Churchbells are heard.*

TRULLEMANS: Gloria in excelsis! Let a hundred thousand candles be burnt at the parishioners' expense!

ISABELLA: And let a sumptuous cathedral be erected to celebrate the event. In execution of which we order that a tax be levied which shall be called the Victory Tax, and that the populace be authorized to pay it.

*The populace can be heard beneath the balcony.*

THE POPULACE: Long live the Siege of Ostend. Long live Isabella who's finally going to take off her chemyse. We all want to see the chemyse. It's Christmas. It's Christmas. Come out onto the balcony!

BR'ER KLETSAF: How the good people of Brusselos do love their sovereign!

*He closes the window.*

ISABELLA: Order that three hundred days of indulgence be bestowed on the populace, in execution of which my seventy-seven mendicant orders will take up a gigantic collection. [*Enter Albert with a parcel.*] Here's my archducal husband! Hail Caesar! Hail Alexander!

ALBERT: I'm late and a little wet since it's schpritzing on our victory. Madama, this here in the basket is for you.

ISABELLA: The keys and the privileges to the conquered city?

ALBERT: Er, no, my Dryness, the shrimps I promised you.

ISABELLA: Which I've been waiting for since July fifth Anno Domini 1601!

ALBERT: I swear by the Holy Trinity that they're fresh. Just smell them! [*Isabella smells them and staggers. The nobles hold their noses. Enter Spinola.*]

SPINOLA: All your Highnesses, I salute you. I'm as high as you.

ISABELLA: Sublimissimo generalissimo, I dub thee Marshallissimo. For you are the winnerissimo.

SPINOLA: Beg to differ, but Albert's responsible for the whole thing. If it had been up to me it would never have taken three years and three months!

ALBERT: No, you are, I tell you, or rather the cholera morbus, the Spanish flu, the flying diarrhea, the roving lice, the dead rats, the werewolves, the patrolling vampires, the exploding herrings, the tide, the wet feet, and Sir Jaime's devils are.

ISABELLA: Did you at least capture that great miscreant and rip him to pieces with four horses?

SPINOLA: He most opportunely flew the coop, Dryness, and in his castle, all we were able to find was a masterful turd on display, smoking in our honor. It seemed to be stretching out its arms to us. And it had a Spanish flag stuck in it, which, just between us, I found mighty funny...

TRULLEMANS: My children, this is not the time for criticisms and controversies, but for accolades, effusions, and generosity.

ISABELLA: That's well-put. Marquis de Spinola, I discern on you the plaque of my Order of the Blesséd Hood and the great devotional cross of my Order of the Window Shutters of the Temple of Jerusalem and put you in command over my Order of Weepy Seraphims and present you with an ammunition pouch emblazoned with the decoration of honor of my order of parochial merit.

SPINOLA: The only problem, Madama, is that I've got so many decorations all over my front side that there's no space left.

ALBERT: Why don't you stick some on your backside?

*Enter the decorated Yeomen and nobles of Brusselos.*

ALL: Long live Her Dryness and the good Archduke, and long live the Spanish Army!

ALBERT: Thank you, thank you, milord counts, barons, knights, squires. You shall have shrimp aplenty! Ostend's a mighty tummy-pleasing little dump, though unfortunately all that's left of it are tiny scraps.

ISABELLA: We'll glue them back together, that is if there's enough glue left after we've finished gluing the churches together.

THE ELDER OF THE NOBLES: Delicious Infanta, we the body and finest flower of the nobility will also build, not a church, for we don't have enough moolah for that, but a modest chapel, each chipping in a share in commemoration of this victory. At long last Providence has willed it that our wives take off their chemyses and wash their pussies, for which we are indeed grateful.

ISABELLA: Thank you, thank you, Señors and Señorkas, you shall be made grandees of Spain. Your wives have been good prudish Christians. Knowing that the males of my States are champing at the bit for the tournament signal, I shall not keep you languishing any longer, but herewith renounce my vow. And take full advantage of the bombardments to yourselves bombard to your hearts' content, so that the children seeded under the din of the bombardment may grow to be true soldiers for the greater glory of Spain. Father Trullemans, seek out the screen of prudery and let the thing be announced to the populace, who shall observe a moment of silence.

SPINOLA: I'm vamoosing. I'm going to pay a visit on Don Horace who's in prison for drunkenness and for insulting the alcaldes, and then I'll look in on Don Juan, who is in the hospital. He's been smitten by the disease of the Indies which he caught from ladies of the nobility. [*He exits.*]

BR'ER KLETSAF: [At the window.] It's Christmas! It's Christmas! Rejoice, good people, our ever-adorable Infanta is going to take off her chemyse and authorizes you to bring her soap.

THE POPULACE: And here's a scrub brush. . . and lime — and the back-scratcher, and water from the River Senne. . . and water from the River Maelbeek. Show us the chemyse. Long live the crapophonic chemyse!

TRULLEMANS: Here's the screen of prudery with the Holy Father's coat of arms. Silence, milords, the Infanta will now spring forth resplendent from her expiatory chemyse.

ISABELLA: [*disappearing behind the screen*] And to you My God, I offer up my sufferings, my chemyse, and all that it contains in exchange for pardon for the sins committed by the Spanish Army.

ALBERT: I want to watch.

TRULLEMANS: Pardon, milord. Only people of the church are admitted to so edifying a spectacle.

*He joins Isabella behind the screen.*

BR'ER KLETSAF: [*singing*] O-re-mus!

*Hammer blows are heard.*

ALBERT: What is that strange sound?

BR'ER KLETSAF: That, Milord? The chemyse has turned into mighty stiff armor and had to be split open with a hammer to deliver the Infanta from it. A miracle! It's Christmas! It's Christmas!

*All the nobles hold their noses.*

ALBERT: What a smell. Let incense be burned. Open the window. Aie! My lords, look what's galloping all over the carpets! What's the damned protocol for when an archduke's itching and he's got to scratch?

BR'ER KLETSAF: He abstains.

*The nobles murmur and stamp on the floor with their heels.*

ALBERT: Caramba! Just look at all these beasties! I decree the abolition of that ridiculous protocol for my own person as well as for the nobles. We've all of a sudden got beasties stinging us and sucking out our blue blood. Milords, in the face of such torment, make yourselves at home. [*He scratches himself. All the nobles scratch themselves.*] If worst comes to worst, give them all forks. [*Isabella appears in a nun's habit.*]

ISABELLA: What a deliverance! Oh, my husband, you may at last fulfill your conjugal duties after saying twenty Our Father's and fifty Hail Mary's. What do I see? What is the meaning of this ignoble scratching? Did I scratch myself, I, during three years and three months?

ALBERT: Alas, Madama, it's a test God is inflicting on us!

ISABELLA: That's very nice! The heroes of the Siege of Ostend! To tell the truth, milords, those beasties aren't as fat as all that. They're just barely the size of a Japanese beetle. But scratch away, I'm going to church to thank the Highest of the High.

*She exits.*

TRULLEMANS: [*following her out*] We of the church command the respect of such beasts. We're immune.

THE NOBLES: [*writhing and grimacing with pain*] Long—live—the—In—fan—ta—and—the—Ca—tho—lic—fleas.

*Churchbells. Cannon. Clamor without. Organs may be heard.*

ALBERT: Pray tell me, what do we do with the fragments of the chemyse?

BR'ER KLETSAF: Relics!

ELDER OF THE NOBLES: And what shall we do with our wives' chemyses?

ALBERT: Fashion banners of them and hang them from your castle beams, embroidering them with the festive caption "Siege of Ostend, 1601-1604," and may the multicolored standards arouse your sexual heroism! Milords, just one more moment. I see on our carpets the shrimp, which are rushing about at top speed pursued by the bugs. I propose to reward the populace of Brusselos, so valiant, whose fidelity is as bottomless as their purse. Toss these shrimps out to them. They deserve them, for my scruples forbid me from making you eat them. What are you gobbling up there Kletsaf?

BR'ER KLETSAF: It's not shrimp, milord, it's just a flea. [*He throws the shrimp out the window.*] A gift from the Archduke. A souvenir of Ostend!

THE POPULACE: Thank you! Long live the shrimp from the fish market! Long live the shrimp dating back to before the siege!

ALBERT: And now that all this is history, I must offer a historic word. Here goes. [*silence*] Milords: The Siege of Ostend...
[*short silence*]
Is now laid... to rest!

ALL: Viva Hispania! Le scratch! Scratchi! Scratcha! Caramba!

## FINAL SCENE

*'neath an old-gold sun in the Port of Flessingen in Walcheren. Upstage, little perforated towers and windmills, masts hung with bunting, Chinese lanterns, twirling sparklers, flying colors of both Knaves and Pirates. The Flessingen coat of arms is everywhere to be seen; it consists of a bottle in which the moon's face is enclosed. Men and women of Flessingen are on the dock and they each have a little jug hanging from their necks, from which they frequently tipple. Harmonious music is wafting in from the sea.*

ADMIRAL DE RUYTER: Hoist the great multicolored banner, for here they come. Bang on the bottles; shout out, in the great old Dutch tradition, and juggle juicy oranges. The Knave, Jaime of Sidney, Marquis of the Land-Fill, first class Grandee of Flanders, is pulling up on his flagship, the Love Skiff. This imposing ship bears a magnificent spread-eagled frog on its stern and the triumphant Sperloot on its poop, and all the signs of the zodiac on its sails with the great Ostendish coat of arms, which are the three keynotes, sol, fah, and do! Will you get a load of this, good people of Flessingen! They sure do look like they've had a fair wind from behind. All the jowled tritons tooting on trumpets and all the mermaids with mother of pearl mammaries singing off-key. Goddamn! They've really found their sea legs, these Ostenders, and I've got a feeling they're plastered in anticipation, judging from the way they're pitching poop to the prow, poopedydoo! And some are upchucking down into the hatchways, while others are climbing up the foremast and still others taunting the sperm-whales! But best of all's their astonishing English admiral, Sir Jaime, the brilliant victor of the Siege, playing the fine old tune, "Here's How We Fly the Coop" on his golden flute. Then come thirteen caravels with poetical names, bearing all the warriors and warriettas of the siege. Hurrah! Prepare cheese and tulips in their honor and especially the precious jugs that they can't get enough of. Ah! That admiral's top of the pile, he is. I'm jealous of him. And as for that skiff of his, I'm going to snitch it from 'im and stick it in a bottle. Fire off a ten-gun salute and have all the chimes of Walcheren ring out. Hang chimes off all the Dutch hats and windmills. The sea is silvery. Bright rays of light are fanning down from the sky's zenith, and the sun's smiling fit to burst, but not as much as me!

*Cannon fire. Chimes peel out. The people of Flessingen drink and shout for joy. The Love Skiff docks.*

THE PEOPLE OF FLESSINGEN: [*in unison*]

Long live Sir Jaime, the valiant Ostender.
Made a laughing-stock of the Spanish pretender.
Then here to Flessingen his way did wend,
For to wet his whistle and his spirits mend.

*The band plays the March of the Sperloot. All take off their hats and sing the tune, calling out Dutch expletives and throwing oranges. Sir Jaime steps down off the Love Skiff, wearing a plumed helmet, draped in his greatcoat embroidered with mermaids, planets, and devils, holding his imperial umbrella. He salutes and blows kisses.*

ADMIRAL DE RUYTER: Great battling lord, king of all the Sperloots, commander of the heroical herring maids, diabolical tactician, sarcastic musician, father of the heraldic frog, swordsman wielding his brush 'gainst-the-grain, epiccing poet, biting satirist, illustrious illustrator, tall-tale teller, avenger, virtuoso on both reed pipe and nose flute, pirouetter, Spaniard skinner, the terror of leafy cabbages and fleshy mounds of Venus, inspired bard of royal chemyses, impresario of lisping marionettes, multiplier of miraculous fishes, distributor of holy bread, metaphysical piper, rosy-heeled dance master, make-up artist for ugly mugs, painter of rotting skeleton faces and blotched nymphs, your head draped in conical rays, trapper of the North Wind, spitter of amber and foam bubbles, phosphorescent, snowy-bearded, coral crested, crowned with shells, with twelve golden spurs on your coat of arms and six thick-headed lions tinsel-helmeted on a soupy background of comatose rats — Greetings, greetings, greetings to you in the name of all the Zeelands, and I declare by the great Dutch motto, Luctor et Emergo, that this jug's gonna stay turned upside down, for you came, you ain't seen nothin' yet, and tonight we'll all be conquered, but not as much as the lousy Spaniards, goddamn cowards one and all who're dragging their tails between their legs with little pebbles in their bags, getting a proper Castilian tongue-lashing from salty Isabella, their mummified mother-in-law, positively crackling with evil-smelling church-going virtues, and I cry long live the legendary Knaves and the Siege of Ostend, and long live the astounding Sir Jaime, in honor of whom we have squeezed Her Highness the Moon into a Flessingen bottle!

**PEOPLE OF FLESSINGEN:** And long live the lethal, military herring, long love the sea-faring devils, long live the music-loving sailors and the music-making mermaids, long live the Moon in the bottle, long live the herring maids with rippling buttocks, long live the winking Flemish lion, and long live the Love Skiff that's been speeding along by slip-knots! Here be tulips and onions, cheese on its knees, and here are our hearts, so let's lap up the Moon's tears in honor of the great Sir Jaime standing now within our walls, ready to give the good town of Flessingen a new coat of paint!!

*Great clamor. All drink. Sir Jaime raises his umbrella. Silence falls. They gather around him with all the flags.*

**SIR JAIME:** Great Admiral de Ruyter shod in boots of Zeelandia, and all you rosy-cheeked citizens of philosophical Dutch Tulipies, Beeries, and Cheesies, shiny, glossy, flowery, and chubby, all so enticing all smelling so orangey and fishy, and you, my sperlooting Knaves, you, my tritons, my three-ton-trionic tritons and you my blackbuttered mermaids, I clutch you hyperbolically to my corset of Toledo and decorate you one and all and promise you the honest to goodness recipe for patriotic Flemish stew and Flemish chitlin's and also the recipe for witty, fairy-tale painting as opposed to puffed up, made-up grand masters of decorative fecality for the middle classes. Suck your baby bottles and when you're flushed and feeling good and poetical, then shall you look upon my noble paintings' bathed, sun-drenched ghostifications and a thousand and one corrosive images of the burlesque horror of patriotireligiomilitarknownothing-isabellgism. Be assured one and all that the gods have smiled on our voyage this historic day and that we took sweet pleasure in spitting into the shimmering waves. On our Skiff of Love surrounded by Flemish seagulls, we harpooned the ostracismic whale, and don't you know we sent scatological semaphores to the ill-bred Spaniards, standing forlornly on the Ostendish strand, mad as hell that they hadn't been able to bring back our Lordliness alive to roast me slowly under Isabella's schnozola. And here I am and here we are, knights and damsels, dressed to the nines, rising up out of our liquid fiefdom, rich with a billion starfish which we'll hand out to each and every one of you — it makes an excellent paste for fending off constipation of the brain. Here we honor the boundless air of Freedom and fried fish too, and it's not a moment too soon for me to breathe it, for the Spanish stench had got me down and kept me from painting. They say you're all peaceloving folk who mind your own beeswax. For this reason I have brought you bewildered, facetious, droll, satirical masks to ornament your knavish celebrations, replicas of our very own great artist Breughel. Hear me still: I say to my Knaves and Knavettes, you have waged war well, you are one and all noble, by Zeus, and grandees of Netherland, laden with doubloons, thanks to me. Stick plumes in your bonnets, place saucepans on your heads, and hoist yourselves up on your stilts and by this brush be dubbed barons, you are all made noble and bear your sea-lion-toothed coats-of-arms, dogfish eyeballs, evanescent codfish, fine-spun sea urchins, inspired crabs, cuttlefish bones, jellified jelly-fish, as well as marinated herring, stewed mussels, glazed sole, distinguished whitings... You have earned the privilege to fart higher than your asses, to bring forth babies with rabbit heads, to tie your dogs up with string sausages if you feel like it, and, as for the ladies, you have the sovereign right to do Jelly-Ass dancing, which is the opposite of Belly Dancing, and was brought back from the crusades by the soldiers of Von Kreep and Von Pruta. Then, you'll be free to erect a monument in my honor on condition that it's more wondrous than the one which was at Ostend, the one the cannonballs judiciously destroyed, the whole shmear along with an all-out banquet while we shmear our cares with Belgian sauce and bread pudding for dessert and a speech which I'll deliver. And to top off our inspired reforms: we decree that ass-wipe brown shall henceforth be known as the Color of Isabella and shall be employed in an esoteric spirit exclusively on the palettes of the common painters of Flanders, the flat kingdom, and all manner of centipedes, rodents, salivators, doody-eaters, and maggots of the Arts, Sciences, Letters, Government agencies and newspapers. We do decree that, be they virgins or not, the girls and women of Flanders will no longer wear opaque chemyses nor coats of mail, nor camisoles with ex-votos sewn into them, but airy, translucent, extra-short chemyses, made of lace, gauze, and tulle, lavishly perfumed, musked, be-ribboned, and be-flowered for the pleasure of our painterly stares. We do decree that the following shall fall into disgrace and be banished from our luminous shores and dunes and beaches unto perpetuity: all people of the church, all finks, inquisitors, vivisectors, torturers, architeks, moralists in underwear and moralists with pruning shears, cockaroach-eaters, squinty-eyed peeping toms, beasts of ink and holy water, stainers, erotic gorillas, national guardsmen, phallic pirouetters, and other holy asses who by nit-picking means, keep Art and Love from turning Love into an Art and Art into Love. We do decree that all contemporaries shall wear brightly colored sham masks representing noble virtues, smiles of angels, sweet faces of fairies and good genies in order that they no longer sport such offensive hog faces, owl profiles, and others in the likeness of jackals, turtles, rabbits, scorpions or sharks. And we do decree this great carnival to be perpetual and obligatory, and we shall determine all its aesthetic, orchestric, and dynamic rules. And lastly, we do decree that all monuments such as Academies, Schools, Temples of Finance, Theaters, Armories, Scholarly Associations, and other houses of ill repute shall bear above their entrance ways the emblem of the universal, frogiddy smash-up, and that the aforementioned frog shall be painted on Parliament and that all politicians shall have to tattoo it onto their left buttock so they can be told apart from honest people. Thus ordered in our territories of Zeeland by us, Don Jaime the Scamp, Lord of Sidney, Marquis of the Land-Fill, and other celebrated meadows where the nasty-faced crab-apple grows alongside the nationalist dandelion, the nourishing turnip, and the humble violet. And now, you there, masked with loveliness and downright rosy with happiness, so are you each and every one Flessingated, inflamed, entuliped, encheesed, enknaved, excommunicated, exhilarated, lewdified, admiralized, heroified, I wish to charm and excite you all with the Great Waltz of Love which is the beginning of a world-wide fraternity of Knaves and Knavettes who're waiting their turns for their kamasutric wedding ceremonies on orange colored quilts!

*He picks up his flute, climbs up onto a barrel and plays the Great Waltz of Love. Knaves and Knavettes, Men and Women of Flessingen, Tritons and Mermaids dance wildly, while Admirale de Ruyter fills one of his boots with*

*Schiedam and empties it in one swig. The sun is setting magnificently, illuminating this touching tableau.*

**AND THUS ENDS THE SIEGE OF OSTEND.**

*The Actor Makes His Exit*
Théâtre Royale du Parc, Brussels 1982
Bernard de Coster, Dircetor
photgraph by Nicole Hellyn

# *THE ACTOR MAKES HIS EXIT*
A Play in Three Acts

Translated by:
**David Willinger and Gilbert Darbouze**

Characters:

Renatus
Jean-Jacques
Fago [Otherwise Known as Fagoti]
Amanda
Gus
Rosa
Head Angel
Four Angels
Actors

## ACT ONE

## IT'S COLD BACKSTAGE

*The curtain is down, laden with shadows, lit feebly by the worklight. Jean-Jacques paces the proscenium, his hat pushed back on his head and his overcoat collar up. He is leafing through a script, listening to the hollow voices that take turns speaking behind the curtain, where a rehearsal is taking place.*

ROSA'S VOICE: [*rolling her "r's"*] Have mercy, my lor-r-r-d!

JEAN-JACQUES: Lord!

ROSA'S VOICE: [*high-flown*] I was in a very abyss and your-r-r for-r-rm and your-r-r face had dissapear-r-red... [*Coughs.*] At the start, falling in love is like... [*groping for the right words*] when you feel a cold coming on..

JEAN-JACQUES: "Love in the beginning is like an illness!" No ad libbing. The scales are... The heart is... and so forth.

ROSA'S VOICE: Love's fever causes your hands to tremble. You start smelling strange odors...

JEAN-JACQUES: [*yelling*] How stupid! Stop this instant...

ROSA: [*Who has stuck her head through the parted curtain.*] What did you say?

JEAN-JACQUES: I didn't mean you, miss. I was saying that the script is stupid.

ROSA: [*Coming all the way out from behind the curtain and going over to Jean-Jacques. She is costumed as a young noblewoman of the Middle Ages.*] I think so too. What should I do about it?

JEAN-JACQUES: Cut all the literary crap. In the beginning love is like an illness! [*He makes a face.*] Is that true, Rosa?

ROSA: I don't know anymore, Jean-Jacques. My first one started out on a park bench. [*Vulgar laugh. Jean-Jacques does not laugh*] So, should I cut it?

JEAN-JACQUES: Yes, cut all that love stuff. We'll simplify it: the king accuses you of cuckolding him, and you haughtily retort... Well, what would you say?

ROSA: I'd say, honey, don't get bent out of shape...

JEAN-JACQUES: Really? In a play? What you'd say is: Milord, have mercy on me. Then there'd be a silence. I am guilty. Another silence. I shall wait.

ROSA: [*all on one breath*] Milord have mercy on me I'm guilty I shall wait. [*She moves toward the curtain*] It's freezing in here! [*and disappears.*]

JEAN-JACQUES: And the king answers in character, like a classical cuckold. Got that Gus?

GUS'S VOICE: Yeah! [*declamatory*] Wretched woman! You're waiting for me... You... you... you... For me to... Yadadadada... I command you to confess his name to me.

ROSA'S VOICE: I shall proclaim it to the universe!

*A silence. Jean-Jacques is perplexed. He waits. Then, finally:*

JEAN-JACQUES: And then? Well, where is he? Scene seven: he enters and stammers: "I am here!"

GUS'S VOICE: Not here. He was just a little while ago. [*Calls:*] Renatus? Yoo-hoo!

JEAN-JACQUES: And with these people... these lines... this emptiness... in this damp we're supposed to create an illusion, an illusion! What a business! That does it. Raise the curtain!

GUS'S VOICE: Curtain?

*The curtain rises painfully, in slow jerky motions, taking with it all the darkness which weighed it down, revealing the rest of the stage, bathed in a harsh, meager light, pouring down from the battens. Odds and ends of scenery are dimly seen upstage. Downstage, in the half-light, a table loaded with clothing and suitcases, and also a candelabra which is emitting gloomy light. The actors are huddling around the flames: Gus, a sort of story-book duke, smoking a pipe; Rosa who is putting her own coat on over her period costume; three others, further back, who are imprecisely moving and gesticulating. The dusty emptiness which reigns throughout suggests a ship's hold or an auction hall. But a large, bluish tin moon, suspended over the pallid expanse, indicates that we are in a theater.*

JEAN-JACQUES: Boy, it's cold!

GUS: You said it! It's icy. What the hell should we do?

JEAN-JACQUES: The rehearsal's going lousy.

GUS: They always do. But on opening night, everything falls into place!

JEAN-JACQUES: How come?

ROSA: Because we shiver our way through rehearsals, while on opening night there's always lots of animal heat!

GUS: That's for sure! And besides, it's dark in here. And the acoustics are lousy. It's a well-known fact, actors are always cold. There's bound to be a draught somewhere. The dressing rooms, in the wings, on the docks, the trains, the furnished rooms. It's only in the summer that we can lean back and live the life of Riley.

JEAN-JACQUES: But where's Renatus?

GUS: Probably down with the porter, trying to keep warm. He is the most frozen one in the whole cast. [*He looks at Jean-Jacques.*] You're different, you're aflame with the sacred fire as they say.

JEAN-JACQUES: Excuse me, but I requested this rehearsal for the express purpose of running the entrance in scene seven. "I am here!" And he isn't here! Besides. .. It's true, that entrance is just a vulgar stage effect, but when that strange boy Renatus does it, then it's very moving. Why didn't he ever try his hand at the circus? He's a born clown, don't you think?

GUS: Yes, and I should have been a stockholder.

JEAN-JACQUES: [*joking*] Well thanks to me, you've been crowned king.

GUS: And a cuckold at that!

ROSA: Everything's always so tragic in the theater. In real life, it's always much simpler. Ask the blonde. She'll tell you.

JEAN-JACQUES: The saint, you mean? Is she coming?

GUS: Did you really write this play, or did you dream it? The saint doesn't enter until Act Two. Come on!

JEAN-JACQUES: Renatus is the one we need.

ROSA: [*who has been listening*] I think he's coming now.

JEAN-JACQUES: Let's pick up where we left off.

GUS: I command you to confess his name to me!

ROSA: I'll proclaim it to the unive-r-r-rse!

*Silence. They wait. The author and the two actors face upstage. A Chaplinesque little man arrives rapidly, shoulders hunched over, moving sideways as if were afraid of getting clobbered.*

FAGO: I am here! [*He greets everyone politely.*] A thousand pardons for being so late.

*He is answered by laughing. Fago seems put out. He fades into the shadows.*

FAGO: Really, I'm terribly sorry. There was a funeral this afternoon.

JEAN-JACQUES: And did it make you think of the play you were supposed to be rehearsing? Order up a first-class, hm?

FAGO: Oh, sir! I'm a prompter, and you're absolutely right to remind me of the fact. The least I can do is be prompt. I'm always prompt to blow out the candles at church. I'm a sexton too, you know.

JEAN-JACQUES: But isn't this your profession?

FAGO: Theater? Sure. In the old days I used to act, back when mimes were in demand. Once again, a thousand pardons.

*He promptly vanishes into the prompter's box.*

JEAN-JACQUES: Hey, guy! Don't bother. [*He leans over toward the box*] He's evaporated! [*and comes back over to the actors.*] You can all go now. Tomorrow, everyone in place. [*to Rosa*] And if you happen to see that blonde, tell her. . .

ROSA: To read the call-board.

JEAN-JACQUES: Thank you my dear.

> *Silence. The actors prepare to leave the stage.*
> *Gus winks and comes over to the playwright.*

GUS: By the way, my dear Maestro. . . [*the others are listening attentively*] Did you know that they cut the passionate love scene?

JEAN-JACQUES: Who did? And why?

GUS: Who? The producers. Why? For reasons of morality. Have you considered the newspapers? We're in a very high-minded back-water, the county seat. They also cut the saint's song which, it seems, was too suggestive. . .

JEAN-JACQUES: [*choking*] Is that all?

GUS: Wait. . . And the stage business in Act Three where the saint kisses the severed head. . . They just sliced it away!

> *The actors enjoy Jean-Jacques's discomfiture.*
> *The latter reacts.*

JEAN-JACQUES: What will be left of my play if this keeps up?

GUS: There's still plenty. We'll glue all the pieces back together. No one has any real appreciation for theater in this country.

ROSA: [*who is going off with the actors*] You coming Gus?

GUS: Water from the john or holy water, what difference does it make? If I were a playwright, you know what I'd rub in the audience's face? Mustard, my dear maestro, or else, just plain shit. Mustard costs money!

JEAN-JACQUES: So they say. [*He waves goodbye to the actors, who are joined by Gus, and comes back downstage. The five actors re-group upstage and become fuzzy, blending in with the gathering darkness. Their talking becomes a far-off drone. Jean-Jacques seems absorbed in a downcast reverie. He sits down on top of the prompter's box, his back to the auditorium, hunched over, seeming discouraged. During this pause, someone enters, creeping out from behind the stage left wings. No one has seen the entrance, or rather, apparition of this skinny, famished-looking young actor whose face is bony and wan, his hat floppy, his coat too long, covering a nonexistent scarecrow body. Like a soggy dog, he waits timorously in the corner, gazing into the middle distance. Jean-Jacques suddenly stands up and leans over into the prompter's box.*] You inside there? Why are you pinching my leg?

> *An arm stretches from the box and points to the apparition.*

FAGO'S VOICE: The condemned man!

JEAN-JACQUES: Renatus?

RENATUS: [*feebly, not moving*] I am here!

JEAN-JACQUES: [*Goes over to the actor and brings him into the light.*] Quit horsing around. What did you say?

RENATUS: I am here!

> *The actors turn to watch this incident from far off, and then resume their conversation.*

JEAN-JACQUES: So you are! But too late, the rehearsal's over and done with. What's wrong?

RENATUS: I'm cold.

JEAN-JACQUES: Yes, it's deadly here in this theater. Don't stay. You've got no business here anyway. Just tell me where you've been hiding out.

RENATUS: [*talking fast, in fits and starts*] A place where it's as cold as this and worse! Here at least there's wood, canvas, and cables. Where I've just been, nothing but stones. It felt good being there. And there are precious few places where I feel good. [*He grabs hold of Jean-Jacques's hands.*] You're an artist, you must understand.

JEAN-JACQUES: Your hands are burning up. Once and for all, tell me where you were.

RENATUS: What difference does it make? I'm here as the part requires! No, listen. I just saw an incredible performance. You never know what wind it is that blows you this way or that. I was in an indescribable state of mind. [*with just a shade of rancor*] Anyway, whatever's happening to me now is your doing, since you wrote my part. This time you've condemned me to death. And tomorrow night, I'll be put to death!

JEAN-JACQUES: Are you starting in on that again? Why are always giving me digs like that? Why do you think my poor, painstaking creations turn into cruel and threatening realities? If you keep this up, I'll wind up believing it too. [*friendly*] We've all got our idiosyncrasies, Renatus. Don't alienate the one person in the world who understands you. Tell me where you were just now.

RENATUS: A funeral. Whose, I have no idea. There was the church, gaping open wide, and that marvelous catafalque, emerging from clouds of incense. And the organs, splitting open like sluice-gates and loosing their violet waters of death! The theater can't compete with all that. Then...

JEAN-JACQUES: Then?

*He anxiously approaches Renatus, who is staggering.*

RENATUS: The incense... I know a priest who faints every time he gets a whiff of it, he loves it so much. [*He forces a smile.*] There are certain lines of work that are dangerous, and should be declared off limits to certain people.

*He falls. The author grabs hold of him and helps him slip gently down to the ground.*

JEAN-JACQUES: Hey there! Everybody! [*The actors come over and gather round Renatus.*] I could see that fainting spell coming on. What should we do?

GUS: Just wait for it to pass.

ROSA: This isn't the first time. [*She leans over him.*] He hit bottom. But now he's coming to. Feeling any better, Renatus?

RENATUS: [*Has already regained consciousness and is lifted back to his feet, assisted by the actors.*] Where am I?

GUS: At the New Lyric, old pal.

*The actors are bubbling over with laughter, but then contain themselves. They straggle off indifferently, leaving the stage entirely.*

JEAN-JACQUES: You're at the theater. Friend? Are you with me?

RENATUS: [*rejecting the playwright's helping hand*] Always in the theater! I've acted every passion under the sun, suffered, passed out. I'll even die here at some playwright's say-so...

JEAN-JACQUES: Well now the playwright's advising you to go straight to bed! You seem so weak. Who are you looking for?

RENATUS: The saint. She ought to be here at my side in my hour of need.

JEAN-JACQUES: [*exasperated*] She's not coming today. Sit down. [*He forces the actor down into a Gothic armchair.*] Why on earth do you insist on going to funerals? Are you trying to torment all of us now that you've tormented yourself to the absolute limit? Your nerves are shot, but mine aren't any better really. Well? Where did you get that obsession that you're the most wretched creature on earth? We're all in the same boat! Tell me straight: are you going on tomorrow or not?

RENATUS: [*sheepishly*] How could I not go on? It's my destiny.

JEAN-JACQUES: You will go on then? Good. So now, go home. I won't take no for an answer. You haven't stopped shivering since you got here.

RENATUS: I'm cold, it's true! I myself. Theaters and churches aren't the only cold places in the world. You get a move on and don't worry about me, Mister Jacques. I'll get a rest right here.

JEAN-JACQUES: I'm waiting for someone. [*He goes a little ways off, as though annoyed, and goes to sit on the edge of the table. A silence. Renatus, curled up in the armchair, has closed his eyes. The playwright finds the silence difficult to take and comes back.*] What are you dreaming of?

RENATUS: I wasn't dreaming. I was listening. To the silence of the empty theater. Full of rats.

JEAN-JACQUES: [*roused*] The silence! 's hard to get the sound to bounce in this pit! You can hurl the most beautiful words out into it, you can toss diamonds out into it, and still they fall flat. I've never been able to get this pit to come alive. Since the time when men first began to suffer under the tyranny of silence, not a sound that's come out of their mouths has been audible. How many simply stood there like deaf-mutes, clenching and unclenching their impotent hands? Only a few have broken through, and they were reviled! Me too, I thought. I once considered myself a great lyric poet, and I turned out to be nothing but a big blowhard! All I ever chucked into the pit was soiled paper, paper smeared with my brains! I know that now. Anyway, I'm throwing in the towel. [*serious*] Do you get me, Renatus? I'm throwing in the towel.

RENATUS: You're right. Nobody ever heard a thing you had to say. You gave more than anyone ever asked you to. [*ironically*] You offered what no one ever wanted!

JEAN-JACQUES: [*who hasn't been listening to the answer*] No talent, just a lot of courage! I have no talent, do I?

RENATUS: Yes you've got talent, unbounded, ill-starred talent. And the courage that goes with bad luck. You may be throwing in the towel, but it's a little late in the day for that. The evil deed is done.

JEAN-JACQUES: What evil? It's high time someone explained to me. . .

RENATUS: I consider your work destructive, even

though it's hardly ever performed, and then to empty houses. Even though it remains inaccessible to most. But for certain impressionable people, your work is harmful. Those that you've contaminated don't blame you for it. I'm one of them. The fact is that I was susceptible to the contagion. I was an unhappy man like yourself, and you tore my ignorance of the human condition away from me. It was you who revealed it to me!

JEAN-JACQUES: How was I supposed to know? I never wished to demonstrate or reveal anything to anyone. Ever since man first began to babble speeches, has the theater ever revealed or explained a blessed thing? [*miffed*] It's true, I'm incapable of being happy myself, but I never meant to rob anyone of their happiness!

RENATUS: What does it matter to you now, since you're giving up writing anyway? [*He utters a fragile laugh.*] We're not as responsible as society would have us be, or else we'd have to turn back the hands of time and curse the strange foetuses we began as!

JEAN-JACQUES: [*laughing too*] Funny idea... [*and looking at Renatus*] Your teeth are chattering. [*He covers him up with a velvet curtain.*] Put that over you. It's utter madness, hanging around here in this freezer!

RENATUS: Thanks. I'm staying, but I'm not waiting for anyone. Not even our sister, the saint.

JEAN-JACQUES: [*taking out his watch*] Time's flying.

RENATUS: People who care most about time are ones who are dying or infatuated. You're not infatuated, are you? I'd be very surprised, since there's very little space devoted to love in your plays!

JEAN-JACQUES: [*amused*] There are women in them nonetheless.

RENATUS: Yes but what kind of women! And characters die too often in those plays of yours, my dear playwright.

JEAN-JACQUES: Don't you think there's enough love in them? I'm beginning to understand, even if it's a little too late!

RENATUS: You're really not going to write anymore? So this is the last time I'm going to have to die in the third act? I can't believe it! The last will be the best and for good and all, since this time, my head gets chopped off! For having slept with the queen! Is there no hope of reprieve?

JEAN-JACQUES: Don't talk to me about the scaffold. What a touching scene it is though. The saint, who has succeeded in persuading you to repent your crime, and as she kneels alongside the executioner's block, she cradles your sliced-off head and gives it one tender kiss! [*carried away*] What I intend this to mean is that you fell in love with her while you were in jail and that that kiss, more profane than sacred, is all the compensation you get for bowing to divine justice.

RENATUS: That blonde girl, a saint? If you say so! But what's so heroic about kissing a dead skull except for all the disgust you have to choke back? [*as though to himself*] It was the only kiss from a woman I ever hoped to obtain.

JEAN-JACQUES: You rave with great lucidity, but you're raving nonetheless, Renatus. Can you tell the difference between reality and illusion?

RENATUS: What? These shadowy forms all around me are a theater. I'm babbling, and I know it too. I am an actor who specializes in agonies in three acts. And you, Master, you are a troubled playwright who's giving up his craft.

JEAN-JACQUES: May I?

RENATUS: Go right ahead. The fairy tread I hear is coming for you.

*A female silhouette is moving about upstage. Jean-Jacques rushes over and brings the woman back downstage.*

JEAN-JACQUES: Good evening. I'm surprised you made it!

AMANDA: Oh, I was in the neighborhood. It certainly is cold out tonight! Before we go one step further, tell me what brought me here.

JEAN-JACQUES: Oh, we just come here out of habit.

AMANDA: Are you alone?

JEAN-JACQUES: Renatus is here...

AMANDA: [*moving towards Renatus*] Is he sick?

RENATUS: Hovering between life and death. My soul is wavering. Don't trouble yourself, ma'am, tonight you're no one in particular. But tomorrow you'll be back, as a saint.

AMANDA: Why is the kid treating me this way?

*Jean-Jacques makes a vague gesture. Renatus stirs, his voice ascorbic.*

RENATUS: At that point the pity which the playwright implants in your heart and which, by the way, I don't give a hoot about, will gush out over the audience. Whatever you are, a saint or an ordinary woman, you have the kind of heart that lets you shed sincere, abundant tears over the imaginary misfortunes suffered by imaginary beings, and all the while you're being lasciviously sprinkled with the blood that's shooting from an executed criminal's neck. Your supplications on the scaffold are hymns in praise of the executioner...

AMANDA: Sometimes! What else?

JEAN-JACQUES: Leave him be, Amanda, he's suffering. Can't you see that he's talking about your part in the play?

AMANDA: If he's sick, why aren't you taking care of him?

JEAN-JACQUES: He turned down my help. [*He draws Amanda off to one side.*] Come. There's something I've been meaning to tell you.

AMANDA: Since when?

JEAN-JACQUES: For some time now.

> *He looks over toward Renatus to see if he is being observed, but the latter has pulled the curtain back up over himself and is sleeping or pretending to sleep. Jean-Jacques is about to speak when the woman prevents him.*

AMANDA: Yes, yes. I can guess. A woman knows what it means when a man asks to speak to her. But you? Whole seasons have gone by and you haven't deigned to notice my existence, except to insult me! And all of a sudden, the ice is supposed to break between us just because I happen to have been cast in your play and we're thrown up against each other? [*She shivers.*] Ice, that's the word all right. [*mocking*] So have you something to tell me worth listening to?

JEAN-JACQUES: I think so. I've had the opportunity to admire you in silence, and I pretended to be mean so my real feelings wouldn't show. I was timidly waiting for a chance movement, the very chance which thrusts you toward me now. That's the plain truth. Will you hear me out, Amanda?

AMANDA: First you listen to me, Mister Poet. In the past your silences and haughty manner would have made quite an impression on me. But I was young then. Since that time I've learned that men, no matter who they are or seem to be, have nothing to say to you which doesn't eventually lead to one particular body part over which they make a great fuss and are more than a little proud. You can wrap the old part up in all the literary terms you like, but it won't make the tid-bit any more appetizing!

> *She bursts out in a forced laugh, trying to seem vulgar.*

JEAN-JACQUES: Amanda, I've rid myself of any illusion that I'm a writer. You see before you a man like any other, a naked man...

AMANDA: In this cold weather?

JEAN-JACQUES: Morally naked... [*humbly*] Before I leave the theater for good, I wanted to get rid of this awkwardness, this distance, this inexpressible whatever it is that stands between us. Don't get me wrong. It's all my fault. I've given women lines to speak in my plays, but I don't know how to talk to women. And what I wanted to say at this crucial moment has nothing to do with sex, nothing...

AMANDA: [*disappointed*] Oh?

JEAN-JACQUES: I'm seeing you tonight for the first time... and the last.

AMANDA: You've seen me so often, yet looked so little. You've seen me in so many costumes, and even without any in my dressing room! You ought to have explained all this to me in my dressing room. I wouldn't have heard a word you said, and that would have been far better. But that would have been too simple, wouldn't it? [*She stifles a muffled laugh.*] Or is it because you've been seeing me dressed up as a nun lately that you got all... I don't know how to put it.

JEAN-JACQUES: [*stunned*] Who knows?

AMANDA: A fine bit of charity, wouldn't you say? [*hissing*] You must have lots of vices, and none of them commonplace either!

RENATUS: [*Taking the two of them by surprise, as they had forgotten he was there.*] The main thing about him is his imagination Saint Amanda -- oops -- I mean Saint Catherine. We have to be nice to playwrights. And if ours here ever loses his head, pick it up for him.

JEAN-JACQUES: [*mastering his chagrin*] Are you sure I can't get you anything? [*He goes over to the armchair.*] Would you like me to get you a hot drink?

RENATUS: It wouldn't do any good, thank you.

AMANDA: [*moving away upstage*] 'Bye now, fellas. You're not going to lure me here again. Assignations in theaters!

JEAN-JACQUES: Let's go somewhere else...

*He is on the point of following her.*

RENATUS: Farewell sister! It'd be a pretty good joke if I wasn't here when they called places tomorrow! All the great traditions would vanish on the spot.

JEAN-JACQUES: [*who has caught up with the woman*] Are you mad at me?

AMANDA: Why don't you stay with your friend? I've got a feeling that he's in this fix on account of you.

JEAN-JACQUES: [*furious*] What? You too?

AMANDA: I'm not accusing you of anything, Mister Tragic Playwright... [*raising her voice*] I only know that you have a strong influence over that poor, little fellow, and even though you weren't deliberately trying to be a murderer or a sadist, you've sown some pretty morbid seeds in his mind.

JEAN-JACQUES: Did you think that up all by yourself?

AMANDA: No, these are things I've been sensing, a bit confusedly maybe, but I'd been meaning to talk about... [*She goes out suddenly.*] And anyway, why don't you just drop dead!

JEAN-JACQUES: Bitch!

> *He sets off after Amanda and vanishes. A long silence. Renatus listens, his head the only thing moving.*

RENATUS: Thunder? A rehearsal perhaps? Jean-Jacques please don't write plays like that... "Drop dead..." "Bitch!..." And so the dialogue goes. Jean-Jacques why don't you write plays about men who are cold instead, about men who are scared, about men who're losing faith in God... [*He calls out.*] Jean-

Jacques? [*Then waits.*] He no longer exists, wiped out with one flick of the pen! [*He calls out.*] Amanda. [*A moment, and then:*] Renatus? [*He waits, gets up from his armchair, and wrapped in his curtain, raises his hand.*] I am here! [*He walks up to the table where the candles are still burning.*] What luxury! Are we holding a wake over someone who died? It can't be. Not for me anyway. Not yet. I may have already received my sentence, but the road to the scaffold is a long one! [*a little laugh*] These playwrights think they're so clever. [*He confidently goes stage right, where the properties are piled up.*] And the nerve of them! They say: The theater revolves around me! Well you're wrong, my dear fellows! You're never alone in a theater, you never know who's lurking! Death, for example, who takes up so much space in the theater. How would plays ever end without it! But I know how to throw it off the scent! I'm an expert! I sniff it out wherever it may be. Death was there in church just now, spying on me from behind a pillar. It was trailing me just a couple of minutes ago, thinking I had dozed off, it was spying on me crouching in the prompter's box. Hey! Maybe it's planning to sneak up on me now as I'm sitting in this armchair. Death's as inept as any playwright piecing his plots together! [*Sneezing can be heard.*] There it is! [*He feverishly rummages through the heap of properties and pulls an oblong bag out of it, which he drags along the forestage back to the armchair. Out of breath, stands back up again satisfied.*] Do you understand? The person in this bag was the actor known as Renatus. He perished on stage, by the executioner's hand. Made of flesh though he was, he was reduced to rags and straw. Is there a man alive who wouldn't know him if they saw him? [*He pulls out the body which is in the bag, a mannequin dressed in ancient period costume, exactly Renatus's size and face. The latter holds his replica upright and speaks to it.*] What's up, old man? Still got your head glued on straight? They stuck it on with pins I see. A head's a delicate thing! [*He sits the mannequin in the armchair and covers him over with the curtain, which he pulls from his own body, leaving the face uncovered. In the fuzzy lighting, the mannequin appears to be the spitting image of Renatus asleep. The actor steps back and rubs his hands.*] Keep up your courage! The hour draws nigh, but since the play's so lousy, you'll only have one performance to die in. [*He kisses the mannequin's forehead.*] Brother, pardon me for the trick. I'm fleeing from danger. I'm cheating Death. Let it come and fear it not. It's not all it's cracked up to be. Death's a scruffy character who couldn't scare a fly. Shifty, dusty. [*He goes rapidly over to the heap of properties, dragging the sack after him.*] Farewell Renatus, I'm too tired to carry on in this vein. I'm nothing but a stage prop, made of rags and stuffing, a nameless thing in a sack...

*He lays down in the middle of the props and covers himself over completely with the sack. He pulls some drapes over him and stops moving to the point that no one could ever guess that there was someone hidden in that corner of the stage. Silence reigns. But not for long, since a guitar is heard ringing out. And after a bit, upstage, appears a white form, spinning 'round in time to the music. It's Fago, diminutive and dainty, dressed as the classic Pierrot, his face made up in clown white and playing the guitar. He has put his overcoat over his white costume. On reaching the table, the mime comes to a standstill, leaning towards the candles.*

FAGO: Please? In the name of the Father... [*He blows out a candle.*] ... the Son... [*Blows out a second one.*] and the Holy Spirit... [*The third.*]

RENATUS'S VOICE: Amen.

*Fago starts and, leaving the last candle burning, inspects the stage. Then, noticing the armchair, moves toward what he thinks is Renatus.*

FAGO: Oh, you're here too! For a minute I forgot I'm not the only one who likes to haunt the theater after working hours. You have my full sympathy, gentle comrade, yes, yes. For don't we have a certain mania in common? [*He gives the mannequin a salute.*] We know so much about each other, don't we? That's why we've teamed up. [*protesting*] You don't have to apologize. Dear Renatus, admit it... this is a crucial moment. I am no longer Fago the sacristan, nor Fago the prompter. I am the mime Fagoti, who once upon a time was famous. The mime Fagoti! Many grown up children can still remember clapping for him. [*He offers another salute.*] I'm not the least bit surprised to find you sitting here like that, dear Renatus. I was there watching you in the church a little while back, while you were in delirium over the funeral services. What's so great about all these manias and flights of fancy? They don't last long, and once they're through, people like you and me drop right through the trap-door. [*confidentially*] Better watch out! You're mad in that you take theatrical illusions for real, and then you think life's realities are imaginary. My own madness comes from when my mother was pregnant and used to stare at the moon, confusing it with her belly. That's how I became Pierrot! And the moon? It's still shinning, and I'm the only one who loves it. I stole it and hid it in this theater in spite of the fact that we don't perform fairy tale plays here anymore. No we live in a century stripped of fantasy. Fagoti's moon. I'll show it to you. [*He trots off right into the wings. The zinc disk, suspended above lights up and becomes the moon, dispensing a dull light. Fago returns.*] What do you say to that, dear Renatus?

RENATUS' VOICE: Lit like a cemetery!

FAGO: Are you a ventriloquist too? You're down here talking but I hear your voice coming from back over there! Lit like... what did you say? For a pantomime, good Lord, yes! I love it. Ah! How I do love the moon! But my love is chaste, you surely see that. [*He takes off his overcoat.*] Now pay attention, and I'll do my act just for you. Oh yes! And it will make you smile. And laugh... oh no. For pantomime is a very serious art form. And you couldn't laugh anyway, you're always playing those tear-jerking parts. Pierrot is a very strange character. Moon-struck. Well, anyway, you'll smile, and you'll have have had the good fortune to see the last living mime in action. [*He softens.*] One morning they'll come in and find me rolled up in a corner. And public opinion will blaze forth: Scandal! The sacristan was really a mime! He wore black in church and white in the theater! [*He adjusts his guitar and scratches out a little ballad.*] I shall evoke Venice during carnival time. Madmen, madwomen, masks, daggers, stars... Silence. Silence reigns supreme!

*He moves forward, swaying, miming discouragement.*

RENATUS'S VOICE: How sad he is! How sad he is!

*Fago, his act interrupted, stops, puts down his guitar, and after an incensed look at the mannequin, continues. He sighs, taps his heart. Renatus's voice comments:*

Cardiac condition? Me too....

*Fago makes traditional mime gesture of despair. He is resolved and draws a dagger from his blouse. Intent on suicide, he contemplates the blade. Renatus warns:*

Watch out, Pierrot!

*Fago, furious, pockets the dagger, and goes over to the mannequin.*

FAGO: Will you shut up? You rascal! Or I'll turn into Harlequin and beat you with a stick!

*The pile of stage props moves. Objects fall. Fago turns around, terrified. And Renatus, spectral, rises laboriously from the curtains and sacks. Fago's fear turns to pity, and the mime, dismayed, rushes over to the actor.*

Ho, ho! You joker! That's not very nice. He was hiding all along!

RENATUS: My dear mime, you're not supposed to talk! You're betraying your craft.

*He moves out onto the stage and staggers. Fago supports him and leads him over to the armchair, trying to act cheerful.*

FAGO: That was quite a trick you pulled! [*He points at the mannequin.*] That's you over there! And you're someone else.

RENATUS: I am someone else. [*He salutes the mannequin.*] Best regards!

FAGO: [*worried and trying to put an end to the game*] Renatus? You're trembling. Playing jokes isn't supposed to make you tremble. Will you come along?

*He tries to lead the actor off.*

RENATUS: Are you crying old man? Is this mime actually crying on account of me?

FAGO: [*choking back his tears*] Yes, it grieves me to see you this way... you, a real artist.

RENATUS: Not anymore I'm not. I gave it all up.

FAGO: [*Fago puts his overcoat over Renatus's shoulders, and drags him toward offstage left.*] Come along and warm yourself up downstairs at the porter's station. And then I'll take you home.

RENATUS: [*Lets himself be pulled along, without paying attention, but seems lit up with joy.*] Someone's actually crying for me? While I'm still alive! And not the saint, but a Pierrot, a real Pierrot! That's better than a thousand hands clapping for my farewell performance. ..

*He tries to greet an imaginary audience, but practically drops down to his knees. Fago catches him and resolutely drags him off.*

FAGO: Do as I say now!

> *But Renatus resists and takes a step toward the table. With one finger, he points to the candle, which is still lit. Fago rapidly blows it out. Then the mime and the actor vanish, lurching, into the gathered darkness. Their steps can be heard dying out, and the creaking of a metal door which closes after them. The theater is an abandoned polar expanse beneath the blue light which pours out from the lunar disc. It is a phantom theater. After a long moment, a shadow bursts forth and flailing about in the void, comes downstage, and bumps into the scenery.*

JEAN-JACQUES: Light! Is anybody there? [*He comes closer.*] Hm? Renatus? Are you sleeping? [*He makes it over to the armchair.*] You still pretending to be dead? I'm sorry for leaving you all alone... but that little bitch... Anyway, we cleared things up. And how about you, kid? Feeling any better? Wanna come along? We'll go get something to drink. [*He grabs the mannequin by the shoulder. The head comes off and rolls away.*] Hunh? [*He leaps back, but pulls himself together.*] Nitwit! [ *He emits a forced laugh.*] That's not a very good joke. [*He picks up the head.*] You couldn't have been all that sick, since you were strong enough to play practical jokes on me! I'm glad 'cause I had... [*He tosses the head into the flies, with a vigorous shot.*] a sinking feeling that...

> *He then exits hastily, as if scared, his hands flailing about like those of a blind man.*

## ACT TWO

## ILLUSION IS STILL ON THE BILL

*The room of a poor person. Upstage, a little bed. Above it, hanging on the wall, photographs, palm leaves and wreathes, things yellowed with age. Alongside the bed, a chair. Stage left, a window with its shade drawn. Whatever little light it allows to filter in is insufficient to drive away the shadows accumulated in this room. Afternoon light, October, under a rainy sky. There is a door stage right and close by a screen which sections off a refuge in the too empty room. This screen hides a table loaded with dishes as well as an old armchair. As the curtain raises, the bed is occupied by Renatus. All we see of him is a shock of hair against the whiteness of the sheet and the outline of his wasted body. He barely moves. Jean-Jacques and Fago downstage. They have not removed their overcoats and hats.*

JEAN-JACQUES: What did he just say?

FAGO: Nothing.

JEAN-JACQUES: Do you think he's getting worse?

FAGO: The doctor I sent for treated him like an object.

JEAN-JACQUES: And what did he say?

FAGO: He shrugged his shoulders.

JEAN-JACQUES: But still, he must have said something to you before he left.

FAGO: Yes, that I owed him ten francs.

JEAN-JACQUES: What else? What's he got. . .?

FAGO: My dear sir — why, what of, when and how a man dies, only interests those who aren't dying themselves. Sure, we can try to help. But no one really needs any help in passing over.

JEAN-JACQUES: Is this the right time to be philosophizing? Why won't you tell me who took him home last night.

FAGO: I found him all alone in a fever, shivering in the theater. I brought him back, laid him down, and watched over him. He fell into a deep sleep, and only snaps out of it from time to time. But then he doesn't seem to be entirely in his right mind. [*a silence*] It's very nice of you to come over and spell me. If I didn't have things to do over at the church, I wouldn't leave him. But I'll be back pretty soon. I think he's better off now that he can't recognize you. . .

JEAN-JACQUES: I don't understand.

FAGO: I'm sorry, sir. It's just that in his delirium, he's been re-playing all his old parts. If he sees you, all the old hobgoblins will rear their ugly heads.

JEAN-JACQUES: I didn't think he was that far-gone. What should I do for him?

FAGO: Just wait for me to get back. Are you scared?

JEAN-JACQUES: I don't like being all alone with sick people, especially one you think is dying.

FAGO: Oh, sir! [*He pulls Jean-Jacques away from the bed.*] Don't keep on like that. He's asleep. He's nice and calm, but... [*He puts one finger over his mouth.*] You've written so many plays where Death appears and where Death keeps coming back. Far more than usual where Death wins in the end! And yet you're scared?

JEAN-JACQUES: Yes. If it were a stranger maybe... But, him... Renatus? Did someone knock?

*He gives a start and goes to the bed.*

FAGO: I didn't hear anything. [*He goes toward the bed and pulls the sheet down, uncovering the sick man's face.*] What is it you want, dear child?

JEAN-JACQUES: His eyes are open. Do you think he was listening to us?

FAGO: Why don't you talk to him after all? Your voice and your presence may reassure him.

JEAN-JACQUES: [*playfully*] Good evening Renatus! A little under the weather, are we? I dropped by to see how you were doing.

RENATUS: [*sitting up and leaning on his elbow, staring out into the void*] I am here!

*He drops back down and turns his back on his two friends in a sulk.*

FAGO: [*pulling the sheets back up*] Yes indeed, you are here! [*He walks away from the bed.*] There he is! Playing all his old parts over again. That's all his young life consists of: a patchwork of parts he's played. He's reverting back to childhood. First he'll be a little boy, and then he'll cease to exist altogether, and go back to what he was before he was born: nothing. [*He now gives a start. For this time someone really has knocked at the door. Fago goes stage right on tiptoe, opens up and draws aside.*] Come in, ma'am. [*A woman enters. Fago scrutinizes her, then recognizes her.*] Well, well, Miss Amanda? [*He greets her.*] I'll be back within the hour. [*And exits.*]

JEAN-JACQUES: [*going over to the woman*] You? How did you know I was here?

AMANDA: [*who remains on the threshold*] They told me at the theater.

JEAN-JACQUES: That was nice.

AMANDA: I didn't come to see you. [*Jean-Jacques makes a resentful gesture. Embarrassed silence.*] So your play isn't opening tonight after all?

JEAN-JACQUES: Obviously not. [*He indicates the bed.*] Did they warn you about this?

AMANDA: More or less. [*in a low voice*] I sensed it as I was coming up the stairs.

JEAN-JACQUES: What? [*in a low voice*] Death? Can you really do that?

AMANDA: Even dogs can.

*She utters a little laugh, which she then stifles.*

JEAN-JACQUES: Watch it! [*next to her*] Don't laugh while you're here. Or else, go outside.

*Renatus has turned around in his bed, as though attentive. The woman starts determinedly for the door.*

AMANDA: Tragic as usual? Well, I'm going. It's raining out, and I like that. Something told me I should come. Now, I have a feeling I'd be better off going somewhere else. [*silence*] I'm never welcome anywhere.

JEAN-JACQUES: [*Apologetically brings her back.*] I'm sorry. You've got as much right to be here as I do.

AMANDA: [*placated*] I'm the one who should apologize.

JEAN-JACQUES: I don't understand. . .

AMANDA: For the way I left you last night.

JEAN-JACQUES: Woman scratches, man hits. The theater has ruined both of us. [*A silence*] I'd greatly appreciate it if you stayed. But promise me not to laugh anymore.

AMANDA: I swear. [*Her face is contorted, as she is seized by an irrepressible laugh. She contains it.*] Just because I laugh doesn't mean that I feel great.

*They have taken refuge in the nook formed by the screen and are rendered invisible to the sick man. Jean-Jacques stays standing. Amanda seats herself in the armchair, takes out a script, and starts reading absent-mindedly. The silence displeases the playwright.*

JEAN-JACQUES: What are you reading?

AMANDA: My part.

JEAN-JACQUES: That play's not going on. It'll never be performed. [*He grabs the script out of Amanda's hands and tears it up.*] It's worse than a bad play. It's a bad deed. [*short silence*] ...or so it seems.

AMANDA: Suit yourself. [*She yawns.*] What shall we do while we wait, then, stare at each other?

JEAN-JACQUES: We'll hold our peace.

AMANDA: Well, before we start I'm going to have a look at our patient. Do you think he'll mistake me for the saint?

JEAN-JACQUES: [*keeping her from getting up*] Don't go! There's no need for such a kind deed. He has enough phantoms haunting him as it is.

AMANDA: Whatever you say.

*She settles into the armchair and sinks into a stubborn daydream, ignoring the playwright. She has taken something out of her right pocket and wound it around her right hand. Jean-Jacques is intrigued by the object. He eventually leans over toward her hand.*

JEAN-JACQUES: Are those rosary beads? Is that for real?

AMANDA: What makes you think that?

*She turns her head away and seems to be dozing off, but her hand moves at times, rolling the beads. Jean-Jacques, not moving, seems hypnotized by the hand, which may be moving in prayer or simply mechanically. Silence hovers over them, thick and heavy like the light, saturated in shadow. Day is already coming to an end and as time goes by, the playwright and actress in the corner become no more than two indistinct forms. Not all of their attitudes and gestures are distinguishable, not all of what they say audible. Meanwhile, in the bedroom, Renatus stealthily rises, resting his elbows on the bed, and sways, now to the right, now to the left, his thin mask-like face straining toward the screen. His eyes are shining in their sockets. He rubs his forehead, as though he had just made a discovery. Then he leans out of the bed and addresses someone who might be under the floorboards or under the couch, only he knows which...*

RENATUS: Doctor? You can come out now. The spies have hidden themselves away in the spy hole and behind that screen. No, it's not spies, they're actors in fact, come to get me and make me go on no matter what it costs me. Listen, they're rehearsing. You can hear them every now and then. They're pretending to rehearse.

AMANDA: Why are you staring at my hands?

JEAN-JACQUES: They're beautiful.

AMANDA: A compliment... coming from you?

JEAN-JACQUES: There won't be any others, don't worry. You have very expressive hands. Tonight I have a sense of what a powerful artist you are.

AMANDA: That'll be enough of that.

RENATUS: Ahah! It's a couple over there! They're rehearsing a love story, as usual, a nasty story. Turn the bolster over and all you ever uncover is hate. Turn it over again and there's love! And everyone's happy! Me too doctor. You're my witness. I've stopped being an actor! You forbid me to act didn't you, on account of my weak heart? But no one's asking me what I want to do. They want me to go on! Come out doctor, there's no need for you to keep hiding. They can't see you, any more than they see me. Come out, for if you forsake me, they'll take me prisoner. They'll drag me onstage and hand me over to the executioner. Of course they already have a mannequin who looks just like me, but that won't satisfy them. They won't rest until they have a real live execution, till the audience screams: Enough! Curtain! And boom, my head'll roll down the steps, do, si, la, sol, fa, me, re, do. But they're not as clever as they think! Maybe they've blocked off the entrance, but they're forgetting to shut the window... the space... They're rehearsing so they've lost track of what time it is. They'll just keep rehearsing on and on and nothing'll come out but words, words... Don't you think? Just listen...

AMANDA: Stop pestering me. You can see I'm praying.

JEAN-JACQUES: Your hands may be praying, but how about your soul? I'm to thank for this religious zeal. Didn't I write that part and those hymns all for you? What difference does it make if the soul remains unaffected so long as the hands...

AMANDA: All this praying is warming them up...

JEAN-JACQUES: [*Who has come over to the woman and sat down on the arm of her chair.*] Mine are rather chilly. Give me your hands to hold.

AMANDA: I give nothing away. You'll have to take them. [*Jean-Jacques takes the actress' hands.*] But don't hurt them.

RENATUS: I'm thirsty Doctor, I'm warm, warm at last. I need cold liquids. I'm in pain too, dull pain, everywhere and nowhere. You must know that, you're so knowledgeable. Your sermons, the way you wink your eye... all most effective medicine? You keep me laughing. Don't be scared, I won't give you away. Don't forget to open the window at the right moment. [*shaking his fist at the floor*] Charlatan! Leaving a condemned man, whose seconds are numbered, alone without any help, with the curtain going up at eight. You were the only one I could depend on! [*He shakes his head.*] I must have been dreaming. There's no doctor here. [*He reflects.*] There was a doctor before though! And how about the one who's hiding? [*He bends over and pulls some cloth out from under the bed.*] I've got you! Come out of there. [*He keeps yanking at it stubbornly.*] The spies have fallen asleep in the middle of their parts, and anyway, there's a wall between us, a fragile scrim to keep the angels from going over to their side — like the Great Wall of China, did you realize that? [*He grows furious.*] Come out, or I'll tell everyone that you're nothing but a grease-painted impostor, and... no... I'll let the world know that you don't exist at all! [*He drops back down, worn out. Then, a swaying form rises by his bed, which despite its appearance as a specter made of smoke, is a character. The chiaroscuro lighting facilitates this character's believability. For Renatus, it is a living being, and objectively it may be one too, since it behaves as though it were.*] Doctor, it's you! So that's how you do it, hiding under a sick man's bed and spying on him just like all the others! Listening to my pit-a-pat! Even so, I'm glad, reassured...

> *And Renatus bends over to greet the character his fever has brought to life, dressed like a doctor out of the plays of Molière: doctor's robe, wig, spectacles, pointed hat, although to the naked eye these details aren't readily apparent. There is a hint that, beneath his stage robes he is dressed as a Pierrot. And when, from time to time his face becomes visible, it is the white-faced one of the mime, Fagoti. He is perhaps addressing, responding*

*to the invalid, as his gestures and his facial movements show, even though he cannot be heard. The doctor actually returns the patient's greetings, and starts in on a long harangue. And Renatus listens, awe-struck, his mouth open like a child watching a clown. Jean-Jacques and Amanda speak through this silence.*

JEAN-JACQUES: Shall we sign a peace treaty then?

AMANDA: Why... Were we enemies?

JEAN-JACQUES: Antagonists. It's a law. You detested my silence and reserve. I didn't mean to seem like I looked down on you. Please try to understand that it's just modesty on my part.

AMANDA: I hated... In fact women are horrified by anything unexpressed, withheld and unstated... [*Jean-Jacques is now holding the woman's hands.*] Do you really need both my hands? What'll you take next?

JEAN-JACQUES: Nothing.

AMANDA: I knew you'd say "nothing." Anyone else would have left me without a comeback. He'd say, "And you, what would you like me to take?" [*She pauses.*] No one would ever guess that you were such a skillful playwright. [*She pauses.*] Your hands are talking, though, and what are they saying?

JEAN-JACQUES: That they're rich...

AMANDA: Faint heart never won fair lady, as they

say... [*Her teeth can be seen glinting in the darkness. But the glimmer promptly vanishes.*] Ah! You're crushing my rosary.

RENATUS: Hurray, Doctor... Diaforus? No, you're not, you were just imitating him... Doctor Fagotus... what is it?

AMANDA: I just heard someone talking...

JEAN-JACQUES: I didn't say anything. Who'd be talking here?

RENATUS: Don't talk so loud, doctor. The actors'll hear you. Whisper it in my ear. That's the way. What an honor! Those great men are worried about me? Yes, it's true, I did them justice. Who did you say? Calderón? Hmm!... And Goldoni? And Ben Jonson too? I thought they were long dead. No? That's true actually, in the world of the theater, the past and the present are all the same. You must be telling the truth, they must really have come. And how about Jean-Jacques, the most recent one to date? Hasn't come? Does he know I'm sick, or has he guessed that I'm only pretending to be sick to escape from that plot he wrote? He's pretending to believe me, for, deep down, he's totally indifferent now. He's spent years trying to get out of the theater. He's lost his love for it anyway. And what do I stand to lose anyway, pretending to be sick or even dying? [*The doctor retorts and shakes the invalid's wrist.*] What? That I might have really come down with something from pretending too hard? That's not the way people really die. You're a specialist. I want you to know that there are certain deadly illnesses that doctors are totally unaware of. Say, it's too dark in here. It's hurting me. The walls are closing in, the ceiling's coming down, the floor is rising, and I'm suffocating. I'll wind up between four planks of wood. Won't you take care of me? [*The doctor makes cabalistic gestures, and as though at his command, a yellow light floods the room, coming in through the window — a streetlamp that has just come on in the street.*] Well! Dawn? Down on the forestage, please! That's just what we needed. Keep going. Make doves fly out of your sleeves, they'll show the way as they fly off. Oh! The faces you're making. . . I'm resigned to them. Do whatever you have to, it's part of your job as an actor. . . But take into account that I've been cold all my life. Today, for the first time, I'm not cold anymore, I'm hot. . . I'm being cured. The only thing, I'm so thirsty! I could drink the liquid out of your watery eyes. [*The doctor listens to Renatus's chest.*] Breathe? I'm trying, but you're leaning on me so hard. Make a sound? Yes. . . [*He cries out.*] Ah!

*He stops moving. The doctor is as though reabsorbed into the darkness.*

JEAN-JACQUES: [*who has instantly gotten up at the scream*] I heard something. It must be our friend.

AMANDA: Go take a look. You're too far from your friend and too close to me.

*Jean-Jacques emerges from the nook and takes a few steps into the bedroom. As Renatus isn't moving and seems to be sleeping peacefully, he goes back.*

JEAN-JACQUES: He must be running a temperature.

AMANDA: Yeah, like you.

JEAN-JACQUES: Shall I turn on the light? There's a lamp right here.

AMANDA: Can't you see enough as it is?

RENATUS: [*Stands up and exhorts the doctor who has reappeared at the bedstead, after the false alarm.*] Let's pick up where we left off... what're the results of the autopsy? My heart? Defective? Go find me one that works! This heart has never loved anyway! Though I must concede that it has never tired of throbbing. But, I want to hear what you think of it. [*Doctor Fagotus starts a pompous speech that gets peremptorily cut off by the invalid.*] I get it! If it isn't the heart, then it must be the lungs, you're telling me, or it's the stomach, or it's the head. Do I have a choice? [*He makes a movement of sawing.*] Is the best cure to saw it off? Why not simply chop it off or better yet, remove it with a flick of the finger. It's only hanging on by a pin. Doctor, there's been a misunderstanding. I'm only made of rags stuffed with straw. Be serious. [*He listens and nods his head.*] Keep away from theaters you say? Fine... Playwrights? Fine... No more daydreaming? Fine... Purge myself? And in Latin yet. Fine, fine. And finally, go far, far away. This very instant? Fine. Come to think of it, many people die because they haven't changed the scenery or their costume soon enough, like animals that don't shed their fur or their skin. How profound. And what else? That I'm in danger? You read it in the printed wallpaper on the wall, but I got there first... Destiny writes its decrees wherever it can. But I've seen it all in advance, and the worst part is that my doctor's going to make me die to punish me for pretending to be sick. Who's the butt of the joke? [*He shakes his head.*] No priest, no! I'd only make my confession to an archbishop, one wearing beautiful colors. Fie on those friar's robes they've got in the costume shop! Besides, I believe in God, and I was a monk, and a saint one time. I played Saint Francis, talking to the birds and shedding real tears. No, don't call the sacristan. He moonlights as a mime too, a performer, and the church doesn't put much stock in him. Leave me to my unhappiness.

*Worn out, he lays his head on his arm, and the doctor's silhouette recedes.*

AMANDA: It's so dark. I hadn't realized that you were so close to me!

JEAN-JACQUES: Children are scared of the dark... now you see why.

AMANDA: Children don't sneak up on you and lay their hands on you.

JEAN-JACQUES: Excuse me... I was just dozing off...

AMANDA: Your hands are wide awake.

JEAN-JACQUES: And dreaming I was caressing you.

AMANDA: Could you tell if I was blushing here in the dark?

JEAN-JACQUES: But now I'm awake.

AMANDA: That's too bad. I'm falling asleep.

JEAN-JACQUES: Well, what if you were dreaming that someone was caressing you?

AMANDA: I'd do my best not to wake up too quickly.

> *She laughs low and deep, and sinks into Jean-Jacques's arms. Thus intertwined, they move very little and seem to be engaged in a very slow and silent combat. Meanwhile Renatus, on his bed, has sat back up and drawn the shadow of the doctor to him once again.*

RENATUS: Doctor? Let's get moving, the actors are losing their patience and the performance is about to start. All the extras and sword carriers'll be running all over the place. We've got to throw them off track. I absolutely must get out of here before they come. Do you understand what a crucial moment this is? I'm not sick anymore. Would a sick man be trying to get out of his bed and his room, come on! My will? A dramatic monologue. I bequeath my appearances, the appearances which were my real self. And tell the actors to watch out for the insidious draughts which waft through all theaters, those never-ending blasts which seep into your tubular bones, your hollow bones. Okay? And tell them to forget me. My life was a series of roles, I was nothing, I never really existed. Considering that, could they ever believe I was dead or gone? No, don't tell them. They're too wrapped up in their own lives. They're rehearsing. Doctor? Are you still listening to me? You're looking over to their corner! Yes, I can hear them just as well as you: the action is rushing along, drawing to its end. Are you really that interested in those people, those stoolies? Aren't you one of them, a spy, no? You're an actor, aren't you, a doctor out of a comedy? How could I ever have put my trust in you? [*He throws off the covers. The doctor has gone over to the screen and, hazy as he already was, been absorbed into the darkness of the screen which dominates that corner. He has already disappeared, the screen swallowing him up like an ink stain on blotting paper.*] Farewell. I'll get out of this situation without your help. And do you really exist anyway? Have you ever existed? Appearance, same thing, appearance! The window, now that exists. There's the door... [*He is now sitting on the edge of his bed. He is dressed in a long white shirt. Looks toward the screen, where he anticipates danger. He becomes motionless, only his hands still in motion, as if they were spinning cloth. He cranes his neck and goes on talking weakly.*] They've all betrayed me. I'm so alone, I'm so alone! In every play, in every situation. And just when the playwright offers you a tiny bit of help when you need it most, the actress blows her entrance. What a lie! The theater keeps right on going. Keep rehearsing right up until the end of the world. I've never played your parts at all!

*He seems to be shrinking into himself, bent over toward the ground. There is moving behind the screen. Creaking. The shadows of the man and woman briskly separate and stand up, then join together again. They seem to be in a panic within the tight space allotted to them. Their voices are panicked as are their gestures, even though what they do and say is extremely precise.*

AMANDA: Stop. Well, what are you waiting for?

JEAN-JACQUES: I'm scared. What were we doing?

AMANDA: Do you take pleasure in torturing me? Have you had your fill of me?

JEAN-JACQUES: I'm scared of myself.

AMANDA: . . .of running after the saint! I give in. . .

JEAN-JACQUES: Here. . .

AMANDA: Where are we?

JEAN-JACQUES: You're giving yourself to me?

AMANDA: No, I've had it.

*A silent commotion like someone dropping into the armchair, a white gleam rising up that is made of cloth or flesh. Renatus has stood up once more, his arms outstretched.*

RENATUS: What agony! What is it they're acting that sounds so eternal and so sad? Any second now they'll cry out. . .

JEAN-JACQUES: [*in an unrecognizable voice*] Ah! Little saint. . .

AMANDA: [*gasping*] At last!

RENATUS: [*tottering toward the yellow brightness at the window*] I'm suffocating. It's stifling, it's swelling up, it's going to explode. They're coming. I'm getting out of here. [*He grabs hold of the curtain.*] I'm finished. The room is burning up. Help! [*His jaws clamped together, still managing to come out with:*] My God... have mercy... have mercy on your creatures!

*And gently collapses which, however, produces a loud noise, so total was the silence just at the instant. In the nook, everything goes haywire. The screen comes crashing down.*

JEAN-JACQUES: What's going on?

AMANDA: Don't stop.

JEAN-JACQUES: Renatus?

*Jean-Jacques's shadow struggles to extricate itself from Amanda's shadow, which is clinging to it. The man finally extricates himself violently.*

AMANDA: Bastard!

JEAN-JACQUES: [*Moves into the bedroom.*] Matches! The bed's empty.

AMANDA: What? Is it over?

JEAN-JACQUES: [*Arrives in front of the window.*] Renatus! [*He utters a hoarse shout.*] Yes, it's all over.

AMANDA: What? [*A scream.*] There's a man here...

FAGO: [*Coming in and bumping into the woman.*] Where's the light?

JEAN-JACQUES: Fago? Turn on the light.

FAGO: But... what the hell are you two doing? [*He strikes a match and lights a lamp which is on the table. Shadows dance over the walls, then grow still.*] I've come too late.

JEAN-JACQUES: All of sudden... just fell... I didn't hear a thing.

AMANDA: [*coming over to the two men*] What happened to him?

FAGO: I was just wondering the same thing. What happened to him? [*He is leaning over the body.*] Renatus? [silence] Help me. He's so heavy now.

*With Jean-Jacques's help, he lifts Renatus and carries him over to the bed. Amanda gets shoved to the side in the process. She recoils with a movement of revulsion. Jean-Jacques recoils as well.*

JEAN-JACQUES: [*distraught*] Is that death? Is that the way we die?

AMANDA: [*taking Jean-Jacques's arm.*] Come.

*Amanda receives a rapid blow to the face. She staggers backward and drops into the armchair, uttering an animal cry. Outside, a similar cry answers. The door opens. A woman rushes in carrying a package.*

ROSA: I knew it! [*She lets the package fall. Pieces of*

*fruit roll on the ground. Rosa turns back toward the door.*] Don't come in! [ *But she is pushed back inside. Colliding, Gus and several other men enter carrying little packages. They seem bewildered, and turn in place. Fago comes toward them.*]

FAGO: [*feverishly, pushing the actors out the door*] Gentlemen, ladies. . . one moment. . . You're all most kind. Take off your hats. You can see him in just a little while. Wait on the landing. And a scrap of prayer, if you don't mind, a little scrap of prayer. . .

GUS: [*who has finally understood*] You mean. . .? [*He throws his hat to one end of the room.*] Dammit. . . Dammit. . . [*His voice tightens.*] For God's sake!

## ACT THREE

## THE TWILIGHT COMEDY

*The October mists have set in. Even though it's barely dusk, the streetlamps are already on in this remote suburb at what seems like the end of the world, shrouded in fog. Along the upstage plane runs a white wall, lined with tar along the bottom — a wall the artist Eugène Laermans would have loved; trees and crucifixes peek over the cemetery wall, which, stage left, is flanked by a pillar and part of an iron gate. Downstage, one isolated streetlamp, whose flame licks the vapors which are rolling toward it. Downstage right, the ochre façade of a short little house, of which the entrance alone is visible. It's a pub, whose sign reads; "WELL-BEING." Against the facade rests a bench, a table, and at the far end, a wrought iron stand displaying ceramic wreaths encrusted with pearls. Both the setting and the characters look blurry through the fog. But as the scene progresses, the October mists disperse; the unobstructed streetlamp will emit a golden sphere of light; the night, once fallen, will be violet and sumptuously studded with stars.*

*Someone approaches through the fog. It's Jean-Jacques, wearing a top-hat to which he has tied a piece of black crepe, whose tails run down his back. He is clothed in a sort of very long cape, which makes him look like a character out of the time of Dickens. Black-gloved with a white tie.*

JEAN-JACQUES: I'm in limbo. A godforsaken place, that's for sure... overrun with nettles... the whole city's refuse burning over the smoldering woodpiles. Just like the unrelenting fire I chucked all my scripts into. Ita est! [*He leans against the lamppost, speaks to it.*] You're on fire and you blaze, but you give no heat. I'm a lot like you. [*He makes for the house.*] Heck of a place! The dead, the peddlers, stray dogs and rag-pickers who've chosen to inhabit this cursed land wouldn't say any different. Far from the long arm of the law and the men that make it! [*He reads the sign.*] Well-Being? So be it... Hello in there, service! [*He sits down on the bench. An obsequious little man comes out of the pub, a napkin over his arm, and fusses over Jean-Jacques. It is Fago. He is now dressed up as a waiter.*]

FAGO: Well, well! The fog is lovely to look at, but it's not very good for your health sir. Don't stay out here, sir, unless you happen to be an artist by nature.

JEAN-JACQUES: But I'm not an artist, not for all the tea in China. [*He recognizes Fago.*] You?

FAGO: My dear maestro!

JEAN-JACQUES: Oh! I know. I know who you think you're talking to. But you're wrong. He's my doppleganger.

FAGO: You're not an artist, you say? The crepe hanging off your hat gives away the fact that you're a playwright. I guess you've come here to bury your friend Renatus, who's just passed away.

JEAN-JACQUES: What if I am the man you're referring to? I'm still no playwright. It's over. And you, Fago? First you're sacristan, then a prompter, then a wretched mime — and now I find you've been promoted to waiter in a cafe!

FAGO: Presto-chango! In his life a man plays many parts. We change because we think it'll be more fun, but then when we do change, we don't enjoy it at all. Life is really a series of lives, one linked to the one that follows.

JEAN-JACQUES: Were you drawn here by the color of that wall, staring out at us like a mime, with a face as pallid as your own?

FAGO: Sir, would you like something to write with?

JEAN-JACQUES: No. Give me some of that alcohol that gives you that sense of well-being. The same kind you serve to the gravediggers. [*Fago disappears inside.*] Something to write with. What did he mean by that? Write what? For whom? To whom? To Renatus, the actor? Moved without leaving a forwarding address. Whatever confused explanation — it'd be in vain, and anyway, it's too late. How could I tell him that I wasn't always his most devoted friend? Or that during his final hours on earth I was holding somebody else's hands, not his? That's enough creative writing now. Stop it. The ultimate vanity! [*Fago returns carrying a glass and bottle.*] Waiter, what advice do you have for someone who's full of remorse?

FAGO: [*serving*] I'd advise him to have something to drink. Are you by any chance that someone? If you are, then later on this evening you'll find yourself staggering along that wall confessing out loud. And plaster angels will be there to hear your confession. [*mysteriously*] Do you. . . believe in anything?

JEAN-JACQUES: That's just the sort of question I'd expect from a sacristan! Do I believe? The important thing's to believe that you believe in something. [*somber*] He. . . Renatus. . .

FAGO: Did believe, yes. He's in Heaven.

JEAN-JACQUES: If only you were telling the truth! What a comfort it would be if I knew for sure that he'd been able to forget all his pain on earth, that he's happy, or something of the kind. . .

FAGO: Sir, you can rest assured he is. Doesn't the law of charity command us to assume that glory awaits even the basest scoundrel?

JEAN-JACQUES: Hooray! [*He drinks. Fago grabs the bottle and takes a swig from it.*] Let's hope that helps. [*But Fago has his ears peeled, the bottle suspended in air.*] What's that you're listening to?

FAGO: The funeral procession.

JEAN-JACQUES: The cart must have gotten stuck in the mud.

FAGO: I hear the horse's hooves. What a strange horse, hip-hopping its way back from a funeral.

JEAN-JACQUES: Well? Where's the procession now?

FAGO: It's almost here. Oh dear, there's the cart.

JEAN-JACQUES: That's real. And we're in the clouds.

FAGO: You're not dreaming, sir.

JEAN-JACQUES: I hear the horse. I'm not dreaming. [*He has gotten to his feet.*]

FAGO: Get a hold of yourself! You used to be so cool and calm!

JEAN-JACQUES: I still am, but I just can't accept what's happened. Sad, I'm so sad.

FAGO: Give me twenty cents.

JEAN-JACQUES: I had no idea a person could be so sad.

FAGO: Twenty cents to give voice to that sadness? [*He holds out his hand.*]

JEAN-JACQUES: [*Mechanically hands him a coin.*] Here they are.

FAGO: You're doing a good deed. You're lending some class to your friend's miserable burial. The silence was too much to bear. [*He goes into the pub.*]

JEAN-JACQUES: Too much to bear...

> *He takes a couple of steps to the left and comes to a standstill, craning his neck. A hoarse*

*churchbell rings feebly. Horses' hooves are heard pounding the pavement, then stopping. Upstage, by the iron gate, thronging shadows can now be made out. These shadows slowly separate and merge together, sliding, stooped over, following an imaginary coffin, that is being carried to within the cemetery walls. Jean-Jacques has taken off his top-hat. Just then the shadows merge with the fog, and a musical plaint pierces the silence and hovers majestically. As though dropping down from Heaven, music swells: an aria from Bach's Suite in D for strings. Jean-Jacques has given a start. Fago reappears in the doorway. Jean-Jacques takes out a handkerchief and is about to wipe his eyes, when he feels himself being observed by Fago. He pockets the handkerchief. Fago has come upon him in time to catch the gesture, walks over to the playwright, looks into his face, and, with his serving cloth, dries the tears he finds there. Jean-Jacques gently pushes the waiter away. This pantomime ends just as the musical lament starts to die off. The two men's voices quiver when they speak.*

JEAN-JACQUES: They're at the grave. I really ought to go over, but I get dizzy standing over grave sites.

FAGO: You'll go sometime, tomorrow. . . or never. What difference does it make since you've already done your crying?

JEAN-JACQUES: Who? Me?

FAGO: I know. . . it was the music. It gets to you. [*The*

*music soars once more, further off, as if flying over another space. Fago starts sobbing, but gets a hold of himself quickly.*] That's how... I wrapped him in the shroud... found in his trunk... how odd... And I made him up. [*his throat dry*] He was smiling! [*taking the playwright's hand*] Now that, sir, was a pure person...

JEAN-JACQUES: And he was right here in our midst.

FAGO: And we couldn't see him. Cry for him as I do. There's no shame in it. And you shall hear...

JEAN-JACQUES: What?

FAGO: The sound, come on now! The dirt being tossed in... and going ftump!

JEAN-JACQUES: So that's death, is it?

FAGO: Yes, that shovelfull of dirt, that shovelfull they dump on top of your guts.

*The music is over. Silence. The two listen. Nothing...*

JEAN-JACQUES: Well, where's the ftump?

*But instead of the expected sound, there comes a solemn voice which starts declaiming emphatically from the cemetery.*

GUS'S VOICE: Dear comrades... The painful chore of bidding farewell to our unfortunate companion falls to me, he who, before his time, has come down off the stage which his genius brought to life. The audience misunderstood him, and... let's admit it?... so did we. But even so, we loved him. [*A woman's scream interrupts the speech.*] Shut up, Rosa! [*And the orator starts up again, unsure of himself.*] We loved you for your youth, your modesty, your honesty. [*Once again, the woman shrieks. Gus starts to stammer.*] Well. Pardon us. If we don't understand ourselves well enough, it's because life doesn't make much sense, but our hearts are with you, old man, with or without wreathes. Let us hope that you'll have a bit more luck on the other side of the curtain, hm? We won't forget you. And may these few flowers... [*He hiccups.*] Farewell my dear fellow... [*His voice fades out, to be succeeded by an ensemble of noses being blown and childish wails. During the speech, Jean-Jacques has turned his back on Fago, and Fago has been looking at his back, shaken with tremors. As the speech comes to an end, the playwright turns around, revealing a face convulsed with laughter.*]

FAGO: Are you laughing?

JEAN-JACQUES: I can't control it... [*He is still trying to suppress the laughter.*] It's just a nervous reaction.

FAGO: [*siezed by uncontrollable laughter in his turn*] This is ridiculous... Stop it... [*He gives the playwright a couple of shoves.*] Did you hear what... he said?

JEAN-JACQUES: [*shoving him back, which makes the two men look like two clowns bullying each other*] Stop it yourself. What a ridiculous speech...

FAGO: [Gets a grip on himself and shakes the playwright.] Sir, watch out! [Jean-Jacques finally stops laughing and stands there panting.] The ftump!

JEAN-JACQUES: Yes, of course... [He comes back to himself.] Nothing...

[a silence] We must have missed it... [an angry gesture] We're despicable.

FAGO: It's only human. They'll all be coming out of the cemetery. What will we look like to them?

JEAN-JACQUES: No different from them. [trying to retain Fago, who is heading toward the pub] Where are you going?

FAGO: To put on another record.

[He disappears. Twilight descends.]

JEAN-JACQUES: You make a mighty strange philanthropist! [The waiter has already returned carrying a lantern that he attaches to the facade of the pub which gives off a circle of red light.] This would make a perfect beacon to light the way for shipwrecked sailors.

FAGO: That's a thought. The survivors take a head count just before leaving the cemetery. Just take a look at those shadows in distress. The only thing that keeps them here are the soles of their shoes sticking to the planet's surface! Come along to the Well-Being, good souls!

[The music strikes up again, echoing through space, rhythmic and light this time: Schubert's Military March. The shadows which were grouped stage left in the fog, seem to sway to its rhythm, like cattle on a pontoon. They gesticulate, their stretched-out arms pointing toward the pub. Then the shadows start moving and come prudently closer, taking on the substance of men. One begins to recognize Gus, Rosa, and other actors, who are trying hard not to fall into a military cadence. They arrive at the establishment and come to a stop, dejected looking. Fago greets them at the very instant a locomotive howls in the vicinity. This lengthy eruption of interweaving strains sends shivers up the actors' spines, especially when the music comes to a stop for no good reason.]

FAGO: Good evening, ladies, gentlemen!

GUS: Should we go in? [recognizing Jean-Jacques] Here's the playwright! [resuming his lugubrious voice] It's terrible, hm?

JEAN-JACQUES: [in the same tone] Dreadful!

ROSA: Ah! I'm glad you're upset too... and that you came...

JEAN-JACQUES: I was behind you the whole time. [a silence] Well, anyway, there's nothing to say. Nothing...

GUS: Nothing... [a silence] And the fog's so thick you could tear a piece of it off with your teeth! Can I treat you to a drink inside?

JEAN-JACQUES: It'd be a pleasure. I'll be with you in a second. [*Gus and the men go into the pub, preceded by Fago. The playwright holds Rosa behind.*] Have you been crying a lot?

ROSA: Sure. But I would have cried a lot more if you hadn't come. He loved you. You've been crying too, admit it.

JEAN-JACQUES: Yes. [*Rosa squeezes Jean-Jacques's hand and goes in. Alone, the playwright vacillates between going in or staying out. He stays. He sits down on the bench and talks to himself.*] I cried, but not the same way as you. I'll still be crying when you've totally forgotten that he ever lived and died. When I'm old, I'm sure I'll cry because I didn't cry enough earlier in my life. You don't require these tears of me. Renatus, you understand me just as I finally understand you. Everything about animals and dead people is simple, in silence. That's why I have nothing to say to you, Renatus, just like when you were alive. We were very far apart at times, sometimes very close. Nothing has changed. Are you far away? It doesn't feel like you are. There's a wall separating us, and when it comes right down to it, what's a wall![*He takes his head in his hands and sits there drained. The silence is not absolute. Faint gusts of waltz music and laughing spill out onto the street from inside the pub. Night falls. The street lamp gets somewhat brighter, although the fog remains just as dense. The gate to the cemetery is now closed. Jean-Jacques, in the halo of the lantern hanging on the wall, seems safe and sound, on the edge of the void created by the fog. Not for long, however. He sniffs the air.*] I smell something. Things I smell afflicting me. Old rotting bouquets of flowers? The countryside in the fall? Or else the smoke from the logs that are consuming my manuscripts? [*attentively*] Is it the fog I smell? Is it the cemetery? A smell, no, perfume... The clouds, the graves, do they have a perfume we don't know about? Does Death smell of musk? [*From stage right, a limp form glides along the wall. It is moving toward the streetlamp. It is a woman, bareheaded and dressed in a raincoat, under which one can make out brightly colored clothes, apparently a theatrical costume. Her face is heavily made-up. She comes to a stop in the luminous circle and goes no further. Jean-Jacques, intrigued, cranes his neck.*] Musk. And sulfuric ether. If this creature isn't Death, then it must either be Illness or Charity, worse than Death and Illness. [*He rubs his eyes.*] The hallucinations that can come out at you from of the fog!

*The woman coughs to draw attention to herself and, standing directly in the streetlamp's glow, lifts her skirts and pulls her stockings up quite high, revealing impeccable legs and thighs.*

I was wrong. It's Love. And what a condition she's in, too! [*He greets her.*] Good evening, Saint Amanda!

AMANDA: [*Feigning surprise, covers up her undergarments and walks spryly over to the table.*] Or Saint Hair-on-the-Ass. [*She grabs the bottle of alcohol and drinks out of it, holding it by the neck, then drops down onto the bench alongside the playwright.*] Better late than... [*with a hoarse laugh*] Is it over? Is he buried?

JEAN-JACQUES: What's wrong, young lady? [*silence*] What brings you here? Some extreme distress, a morbid wish? There's no one here.

AMANDA: The fog...

JEAN-JACQUES: And me in the fog, I'm nobody anymore. And the dead. And you, who are nothing, walking through a bad dream.

AMANDA: Are you trying to be mean? And here you haven't even slept with me!

JEAN-JACQUES: No. I'm alone. And you're alone. You can't be mean when you're alone. Even tied to each other the way we were, do we ever stop being alone? I feel sorry for you. Do you have a fever?

AMANDA: I don't know. I'm disgusted. Not with you. With everything. Ever since that poor kid fell out of bed, I've been sleeping, a sleep the like of which I've never had.

JEAN-JACQUES: Your eyes are astonishing. You're in a trance, dark and perilous, but a trance all the same. ..

AMANDA: It's the ether I take. I slept, I didn't sleep, I forgot what day it was, what time it was, the dead man. Where do you think I just was? The closed theater. I had a dream in my dressing room, no, not a dream. You were sewing Renatus's head back on. And then you saw me. You soaked my clothes in gasoline, you started to ignite them and burn me up, purify me. I tore the burning clothes off and put on the costume for my part. [*She opens her raincoat.*] The saint's costume. And then... [*She seems to come to.*] Shit! That's none of your business anymore!

JEAN-JACQUES: No, and I'm going to pretend I never heard all the little secrets you just told me. The only part of you I'll hold onto will be your face this evening, not beautiful, no, but unforgettable.

AMANDA: You mistook me for a prostitute.

JEAN-JACQUES: My dear, you were an apparition. Just let it go at that.

AMANDA: [*rising to her feet*] I have a feeling that this is goodbye. The whole thing must have been a big mistake.

JEAN-JACQUES: What do you want? Words, caresses, passion?

AMANDA: You could have given me any of that stuff, I wouldn't have taken any of it in. You don't know how to give or take. Goodbye. [*She changes her mind.*] Give me twenty francs? [*In silence, the playwright gives her the money. Amanda takes it and throws it far away. She mumbles humbly.*] Thanks honey.

> *And goes into the pub without a second glance. The door to the pub stays open, and the street is thus illuminated; yelling and laughing spill out in a sudden gust; they are acclaiming the entrance of the most recently arrived guest. Jean-Jacques, as though assailed by the light and sound, stands up and is about to take flight. He hides behind the stand full of wreathes. Someone comes out of the cabaret, reeling, a glass in hand. It is Gus, looking for something.*

GUS: Hey, playwright? We've got a full house! Are you coming in or not? [*He doesn't see anyone.*] I guess the playwright doesn't fit in with the rest of us! Aren't you thirsty, playwright! [*He takes a couple of steps toward the wall.*] Life is beautiful, life is. . . [*He drinks.*] To you, Renatus! [*And he throws the empty glass over the wall.*] From all your pals!

> *He goes back in, laughing stupidly. Once the door is closed, the ruckus subsides and the night grows silent once more. All the same, the fog is swiftly dissipating, and the streetlamp glows freely. The wall shines forth, yellow ochre under a dark blue sky. The countryside no longer seems so sinister, in spite of the outlines of crucifixes. Jean-Jacques leaves his refuge and stops under the streetlamp. He is about to take off, regretfully so it seems, for he glances at the cabaret where joy, vulgar perhaps, but joy nonetheless, reigns supreme.*

JEAN-JACQUES: Life. . . how did he put it, life is. . . And the choir would answer from the cemetery. . .

A VOICE: Beautiful!

JEAN-JACQUES: [*who hasn't heard*] Anyway, what the hell difference does it make if life is this of life is that?

> *He tips his top-hat, in the direction of the cabaret. He starts to go off stage left, but a head enveloped in white pops up over the cemetery wall.*

THE HEAD: Peekaboo!

JEAN-JACQUES: Good evening! [*He turns toward the cabaret, thinking that the call came from there. Behind the wall the head rises and a form wrapped in a bed sheet painfully hoists itself up, then sits on the top of the wall, its legs dangling in space. Jean-Jacques, disconcerted, doesn't know what to do. Then the ghost tosses an object in the playwright's direction. Sound of a glass breaking against the pavement. The playwright looks into the air.*] A falling star? Seven years' bad luck! [*He bends over and moves his hand through the debris.*] Those amateurs. I'm going to... [*At last, he sees the ghost.*] Oh, it's you? Well, come down off of there.

THE GHOST: Calm down sir.

JEAN-JACQUES: There are rules and regulations governing cemeteries.

THE GHOST: Help me to get around them, sir.

JEAN-JACQUES: How?

THE GHOST: By asking me to come down off this wall and join you.

JEAN-JACQUES: Stay within the prescribed limits, you're just fine up there on your perch.

THE GHOST: I accept your humor, but do me a favor and come over here by me. Come sit by my side.

JEAN-JACQUES: How persistent... Come... That wall doesn't interest me... [*The ghost jumps spryly down onto the pavement and goes over to Jean-Jacques, who backs up a little.*] What do you want, ghost?

THE GHOST: [*greeting him, without uncovering his face*] Just a little word with you. You put yourself outside of time, since you stopped writing.

JEAN-JACQUES: When I did write, nobody paid any attention. Now that I've stopped writing, even the dead are informed of the fact! So?

THE GHOST: So, I have the great honor of saluting you. Don't be scared. My name is Ghost. I know, ghosts aren't really welcome. And they've gone out of style, even though the theater made great use of them back in the old days. But we shall make a comeback, sir. Styles come and go, but ghosts are here to stay. But you, sir, who have passed so much of your life in your imagination, you who've created so many imaginary entities out of disgust for the real ones, you of all people must love ghosts, or at any rate not hate them. Are you going to chase me away?

JEAN-JACQUES: [*greeting him*] Since you seem to know me so well anyway, I must confess that I do love ghosts, since I've never been able to know love in any normal fashion. As your divine power of intuition is telling you, I am... I was a playwright who wrote of bygone times. And I put ghosts in my plays, even at the risk of displeasing the audience. Because ghosts speak with voices from the beyond which work so well on stage. And then too, I'm at home with the subject. What is it you're trying to make me see? Are you hoping to be restored to your former state? Do you want me to compose a prayer for you? A poem? An epitaph? Or else are you planning to divulge the location of some hidden treasure? In that case, I'll call you Fortunatus, the gentle ghost of October. Fortunatus, for he who's lost his name.

THE GHOST: Fortunatus is fine! [*a silence*] Poets are so lacking in intuition! They sing like blind men and because they're blind they sing! [*He falls prey to an internal struggle, which is revealed through his hands clasping.*] Sir, dear sir... Are you still capable of being astonished?

JEAN-JACQUES: [*inspecting the ghost more closely*] That voice. Those mannerisms...

THE GHOST: Allow me to introduce myself. [*He takes several steps back, removes his shroud, and returns.*] Here I am! [*He stands there humbly, his arms open wide. Jean-Jacques makes a gesture of revulsion, then one of ardor. He hugs the ghost in a prolonged embrace.*]

JEAN-JACQUES: Renatus... forgive me... Renatus.

*Renatus gently extricates himself. He seems thinner and more insubstantial than ever, decked out in a ridiculous costume, a little jacket that is too tight, checked trousers, hunter's cap, elastic booties, and gloves.*

RENATUS: What have I got to forgive you for, old friend? Everything's become clear as can be, now that we've been divided from each other by a wall of darkness. You blame yourself for not having loved me well enough? Nobody on earth knows how to love right. You're not a monster. You're like me, a weak impassioned man. We don't owe each other anything.

JEAN-JACQUES: What anguish I've gone through, and now what release! What you say matters so little, your very insults would make me mad with joy. You are real, realer than you ever were before. Speak again. Where have you come from? Where are you going? What do you know? You're not going to vanish into thin air, are you?

RENATUS: Haunted man. I have nothing of any importance to tell. You ought to write a play about death, about an actor making his exit; it'll be your very last one. Listen. This is why I was coming — they're hot on my trail, and this isn't the first time a dead man's asked a living being to help him. Hunted down! The dead are generally naked or else wrapped in a winding sheet. Which calls attention to them. But goodhearted Fago dressed me up in this costume, so I can go unnoticed, or practically...

JEAN-JACQUES: Oh yes, I remember that costume. It's from the part I wrote just for you, the simpleton They're after you? That's absurd.

RENATUS: And logical, implacably logical, like a well-ordered dream. Maybe we're both dreaming, the same dream at the same time. But I'm not sure of it. Yes, my old friend, I'm wondering aimlessly between heaven and earth. I'm a rebel in my own way.

JEAN-JACQUES: Has your soul been condemned?

RENATUS: No, chosen! Specially chosen, since I actually was a saint. Onstage for a couple of nights, do you remember? You wrote the play. A saint like they don't make 'em anymore. How could I have known? I was only acting. But because of that I've been grouped with a tiny number of the elect! But [*in a low voice*] I resist the powerful suction drawing me upward, I want no part of that warm breeze, I am not fit for that happiness. If only, on taking leave of life, I had been able to walk straight up to Jesus and say to him, here I am! But alas, that's not the way it was. It's impossible to explain. That's why they're hunting me down.

JEAN-JACQUES: The angels?

RENATUS: Those feathered pains in the neck. If only I could get to some neutral space, get to limbo, a free-floating nebula, anywhere those angels' magnetic pull has no effect. The universe is full of prompter's boxes and stage wings. If only I could get rid of all my remaining earthly weight and density, that would do the trick. Where can I hide?

JEAN-JACQUES: If I understand you correctly, you don't want happiness but you don't want unhappiness either. You just want not to exist.

RENATUS: If possible, absolutely. I can tell what you're about to suggest, that I hide in your house. Your life would become impossible, my friend, you couldn't put up with me. Even though I think that you could be more heroic in my behalf as a friend than if we loved each other... Don't deny it. You wouldn't betray me, you only want to have me die all over again. Just help me tonight, and swear never to tell anyone that this happened.

JEAN-JACQUES: Can others see you as I do?

RENATUS: No, they have no eyes. None of them can. [*Sound emerges from the cabaret. Renatus takes fright.*] All the same, I'll go hide behind something. They'll leave...

> *Presto, he takes his place behind the stand loaded with wreathes. The door to the pub opens with some commotion. A stream of light. Yelling and laughing. The actors appear, arms waving, with Gus dragging them along, all drunk.*

GUS: And we're off, nitwits! Who'd have the gall to imply that we've been drinking? Let's all go back to town. And I'll spring for a round of pig's feet. To the city!

ONE OF THE ACTORS: Down with Maccabees! Long live the Well-Being!

ROSA: [*Crying and laughing at the same time, addresses the playwright, who is watching this little band's approach.*] 's not our fault, Jean-Jacques...

GUS: [*pointing at Jean-Jacques*] Just look at that drunk! He's coming with us.

ANOTHER ACTOR: Let him be, he's thinking. He's an artis'!

GUS: And what does that make us, aren't we artis'? We've all got the stamp of genius, goddamit, genius, no less!

ROSA: Gussie baby, don't yell like that in front of a cemetery.

GUS: I don't give a damn, it's on the other side of the wall...

AMANDA: [*Also drunk, but who has stayed in the background, moves toward the playwright.*] Excuse them. They just buried Renatus.

ONE OF THE ACTORS: What of it? We're crying for him, aren't we?

GUS: Renatus? Damn straight we're crying for him. [*bellowing*] Hey there, Renatus! Greetings!

ROSA: Quiet, there're cops down the road, I saw their hats.

GUS: Down with the cops! See you later, Renatus, as late as humanly possible! [*He takes off his hat.*] Life is beautiful! [*And he goes out left singing:*] When you're dead, you're screwed, They stick you in a big coffin...

THE OTHERS AND ROSA: [*following him out, singing:*] And the worms chew up your asshole.

*The singing and yelling fade into the night. Amanda, who has stayed after, walks past in front of Jean-Jacques, in the light of the streetlamp and grasps his hand without stopping.*

AMANDA: Good night!

JEAN-JACQUES: [*Hat off, bows and kisses her hand.*] My respects.

*And Amanda goes out like a grande dame making an exit. Still other voices, very close, but dispersed. And silence. Fago has come and stationed himself on the threshold of the cabaret.*

FAGO: Good night! Whatever life is, beautiful or not, they've got it! But they'd better hold onto it tight! [*He laughs and takes a few steps into the street.*] I thought there was a customer. [*He sniffs the air and looks at the stand.*] Who's there? Would the gentlemen care for anything? [*He goes behind the stand and brings Renatus, who is bursting with laughter, out from behind it.*] Dear little dead fellow, I had a feeling... [*He hugs Renatus.*] Everything okay?

RENATUS: Not really. Who mentioned cops just now?

FAGO: [*moving toward the cemetery wall*] I'll survey the surroundings. Fear not, Renatus, I know all about your dilemma. Mimes know all the tricks. They're really old angels who've lost their wings.

JEAN-JACQUES: [*Has come back over to Renatus.*] How despicable those actors were!

RENATUS: They were real, burning with life... I like them just the way they are.

FAGO: [*coming back*] Danger! There's a patrol out. If you want, Renatus, this vent leads to the beer cellar. It's a good hiding place since celestial beings can't abide strong odors. [*He is in the doorway.*] I'm going back inside. I used to be a sacristan, so I have no wish to cross paths with those guys. [*gestures of friendship*] Good luck!

*He disappears. Now the door is closed again, the light has diminished. And it's now extremely dark. Renatus is frantic.*

RENATUS: It's not that those patrollers are quick or clever or anything like that. But still, I've got to get away from them.

JEAN-JACQUES: Out there in the graves? No. [*The merciless lasso of a search-light hits the cemetery wall, then the front of the pub. Renatus and Jean-Jacques come downstage, barely escaping the luminous trap.*] You see?

RENATUS: I feel faint. I'm still too physical. What should we do?

JEAN-JACQUES: Don't lose heart. How about the vent? Or better yet, this prompter's box. . .

*He points to the prompter's box.*

RENATUS: What? A prompter's box in the middle of the street, in front of a cemetery?

JEAN-JACQUES: Yes, it's surprising. . . but since it's there. . . I hear the pounding of boots. [*He helps Renatus slip into the box.*] See that? We haven't completely lost the magical powers we got from doing theater. Poof, you're gone!

RENATUS: [*disappearing into the box*] Bye now!

JEAN-JACQUES: How simple he still is! Such souls should never die and set out on their own. He'll get himself into trouble! [*He makes for the pub.*] I'll go keep an eye on things from inside. Angels would never go into a bar. [*But a stream of violent red light freezes him in place and blinds him. The light vanishes abruptly. A patrol enters from stage left. Four slender, athletic angels, wearing grey overcoats. Belted in metal, helmeted in silver, they have bronze wings and wear military squadron numbers. Their faces are barely visible, but they are handsome and commonplace, all cut from the same mold. A green lamp shines out from each forehead and the tip of each wing. They are led in by the head angel, his helmet decorated with purple plumes. He is bigger than the others. The two angels who follow him carry portable search lights. The last is transporting a narrow golden ladder, the top so high that it vanishes from view up above. The patrol comes to a stop on command. Jean-Jacques has recovered his sight and scrutinizes the intruders, not put off in the least.*] They look pretty mean! What do you want?

HEAD ANGEL: He known as Jean-Jacques.

JEAN-JACQUES: Present! What do you want?

HEAD ANGEL: Have you happened to run into anyone?

JEAN-JACQUES: A lost dog. Are you looking for someone?

HEAD ANGEL: Particulars: twenty six years old, vaudevillian style clothes, pronounced pallor, distinguished by a voice which sounds like it comes from beyond the grave...

JEAN-JACQUES: Haven't seen him.

HEAD ANGEL: Well, he certainly sounds sure of himself! [*To the angels.*] You, comb the cemetery; you check out the high road that goes toward the country; you with the ladder, stay put. . .

*Two angels go off, the third remaining to the side. The Head Angel moves over to Jean-Jacques, who recoils with marked disgust and goes and sits on top of the prompter's box. After a silence. . .*

JEAN-JACQUES: You don't have a very pretty job to do, do you?

HEAD ANGEL: [*Shrugs his shoulders and turns around toward the ladder carrier, speaking loud enough to be heard by the playwright.*] It won't be long before we nab that parasite. [*As if he was announcing a theory.*] It is interesting to note that, similar to killers who inevitably return to the scene of the crime, people of erratic nature, hobos, and other non-conformists return to the places where they have lived. We shall therefore have to keep an eye on theaters and theater people, and we certainly won't leave out playwrights.

JEAN-JACQUES: I know what you're trying to say, masked angel!

HEAD ANGEL: [*moving toward the playwright, conciliatory*] Let's get right to the point. Where is he? There were two of you here just a moment ago. If you help us with our difficult and, I confess, not very appealing task, you'll be able to avoid headaches.

You're surely aware of the reprisals we mete out. They may be indirect and mysterious, but that makes them no less cruel or effective. No one's ever got out of them with their reason intact.

JEAN-JACQUES: You'd be doing me a tremendous favor by taking any I've got left.

HEAD ANGEL: [*raising his voice*] I'm not fooling around here. Time is of the essence.

JEAN-JACQUES: [*same tone of voice*] So? You expect me to rat on somebody? I may be baroque, I may be unsavory, and totally out of my mind at times, but one thing I am is loyal and I refuse to act as your stoolie. It's not worthy of a man. Is it my fault if you don't have what it takes to find him yourselves? [*mocking*] I always thought that angels were supposed to sing before the throne of God, in glory, with lyre and cymbals!

HEAD ANGEL: That remark leaves me cold, coming from you. You're a poet or something, aren't you?

JEAN-JACQUES: That's right! But you, are you really an angel? [*He bursts out laughing.*] All your paraphernalia notwithstanding, you're just a bunch of cops, do you hear me?

HEAD ANGEL: I dare you to say that again.

*He moves in on him, menacingly, a billy club in hand.*

JEAN-JACQUES: [who is backing up in order to grab the bottle that had been left on the table] I didn't make myself clear. Did I say cops? Well I meant pigs!

*The Head Angel springs forward, his billy club raised. The playwright eludes the blow and smashes the bottle against the angel's helmet. The latter registers the blow and sways under its impact, but soon recovers. He locks the playwright in his grip, but the playwright holds his own. The fight continues in silence. The angel carrying the ladder turns on his search light and illuminates the wrestlers who are rolling on the pavement. Then he whistles three times. Other whistles respond from quite nearby. The fight starts to get dirty, the playwright seeming to be getting the worst of it. Then two arms reach out of the prompter's box, and Renatus's head appears.*

RENATUS: Stop! I don't want this... not this... I'm turning myself in. [*He comes out of the box. The combatants stop fighting and get up off the ground, stupefied. A silence. Renatus is standing, trembling from head to toe. He stammers.*] Beat me instead. But don't ask me any questions.

HEAD ANGEL: Fall in!

JEAN-JACQUES: [*hugging Renatus*] What have you done my poor fellow?

RENATUS: Don't be pig-headed. I'd come to the end of my road. Just consider it a suicide.

HEAD ANGEL: [*to the two who are re-entering*] Fall in! We've got him! Hold up the ladder! [*to Jean-Jacques*] Let's leave it at that for the moment. We'll meet again some other time. The universe is smaller than you think.

*The two angels grab Renatus and push him toward the ladder which the third angel is holding inclined upwards.*

JEAN-JACQUES: Poor Renatus.

RENATUS: Farewell... Your friendship can't help me anymore. I was doomed... I have a feeling that we'll never see each other again. It doesn't matter. You loved me. And you fought for me. Thank you.

JEAN-JACQUES: [*Squeezes Renatus's hand and turns away, his face contorted.*] Farewell for all eternity.

HEAD ANGEL: Up you go! [*Renatus gets on the ladder and climbs up clumsily. The angel who goes up behind him, pushes him none too gently.*] Faster!

*And Renatus climbs, struggling against dizziness. The second angel goes up. Then the third. The moon has risen over the cemetery— a fairy-tale moon, scarlet, giving off an eerie light. Jean-Jacques, his nose in the air, woefully watches them climbing. Fago has just appeared in the doorway to the pub, and observes the scene without being fazed in the least. Renatus is on the point of disappearing up above. He cries out in a child-like voice.*

RENATUS: Jean-Jacques?

JEAN-JACQUES: Renatus!

*He gently waves his hat in a sign of farewell. The Head Angel mounts the ladder, pulling up the rear. Renatus has vanished. One by one, the angels vanish. And the ladder is rolled back up towards the vast expanse, enriched by moon and stars. In the midst of a solemn silence, the actor's voice whimpers from very far off.*

VOICE OF RENATUS: Jean-Jacques?

*It is over. The playwright puts his hat back on. Fago continues looking up at the sky.*

JEAN-JACQUES: It's so painful. Ah! If it were simply a matter of dying! And how cold, how cold it is beneath the stars!

FAGO: Splendid, the firmament!

JEAN-JACQUES: [*to the waiter*] Yes Fago, but even if you stood watching it till the end of time, would you ever find the key to the mystery?

FAGO: [*snapping out of it, or more exactly, falling off the moon he's been looking at so amorously*] Sir... I don't understand you. The key to the mystery? Don't you know that mysteries have no doors?

*He resumes his contemplation. Jean-Jacques exits slowly.*

**CURTAIN**

# TRANSFIGURATION IN THE CIRCUS

translated by:
**David Willinger and Luc Deneulin**

Characters:

The Ringmaster
Luna
Mister Clown
August
Dudule
Babylas
Casimir
Piccolo

*The band plays a muted, leisurely march. Then, electric buzzers sound. The Ringmaster runs in, preoccupied.*

RINGMASTER: Number Five! Mister Clown, King of the Clowns, in an act shown here for the first time! Hey there! Mister Clown! To the ring! I trust the distinguished audience will excuse me! Mister Clown! Ah, these prima donnas! Hey there, all clowns, to the ring! August! Dudule! Babylas! Casimir! Piccolo! Orchestra, quiet! [*The band stops playing.*] What's the meaning of this? No more clowns! What will become of me?! Will the distinguished audience be able to survive without clowns? Mister Clown, one last time, are you going to start your act or aren't you? I'm losing my patience! [*He posts himself before one of the entrances. Mister Clown appears from the opposite entrance and mockingly takes a position behind the Ringmaster. On seeing Mister Clown enter, the Bandleader strikes up the quiet march. The Ringmaster roars:*] Orchestra, quiet! [*The music stops.*] I'm going to refund their money! [*to the audience*] You see me in a desperate situation... ladies and gentleman, for who could ever take the place of Mister Clown?! And yet, he can't be that far away! [*cupping his hands like a megaphone*] Mister Clow-o-o-own!

MISTER CLOWN: [*imitating him*] Mister Clo-o-o-o-own!

RINGMASTER: [*stupefied*] There you are! Where were you?

MISTER CLOWN: Where you were!

RINGMASTER: I was here!

MISTER CLOWN: Me too!

RINGMASTER: Don't try to be funny!

MISTER CLOWN: Fine, fine! I'll just be on my way!

RINGMASTER: I mean... go ahead, be funny! Start your act!

MISTER CLOWN: Why?

RINGMASTER: It's your turn!

MISTER CLOWN: It's my turn? I heard that there was somebody acting the fool in the ring so I didn't think my turn had come yet!

RINGMASTER: You're the fool! Are you going to start or not?

MISTER CLOWN: I can't be a clown tonight.

RINGMASTER: Why?

MISTER CLOWN: Because I feel so happy!

RINGMASTER: And what have you got to be so happy about?

MISTER CLOWN: That I will never work again!

RINGMASTER: You'll never work again? What about your act?

MISTER CLOWN: Well, here goes: "Mister Clown doesn't want to work anymore!"

RINGMASTER: Then who's going to entertain the honorable audience?

MISTER CLOWN: You!

RINGMASTER: Me?

MISTER CLOWN: Yes! You are going to be the fool!

RINGMASTER: Oh no, that's not my line of work! I could never handle that!

MISTER CLOWN: Just be yourself, and it'll go fine!

RINGMASTER: I refuse!

MISTER CLOWN: I'll make you!

RINGMASTER: I'd like to see you try!

MISTER CLOWN: Look! [*He draws a dubious looking horse pistol from his pocket.*]

RINGMASTER: [*terrified*] Mister Clown... My dear Mister Clown, what's the meaning of this?

MISTER CLOWN: I'm going to kill you! And I sincerely hope you're not going to keep refusing to act the fool after this little warning!

RINGMASTER: Your gun isn't loaded!

MISTER CLOWN: That's true! How do you load it? [*He takes out a cap.*]

RINGMASTER: [*grabbing the gun and the cap*] You grasp the cartridge between the thumb and the index finger. You put it in the thingamajig. That's it!

MISTER CLOWN: And what if you want kill someone, then what do you do?

RINGMASTER: You'll see! You aim at the victim. [*He takes aim at Mister Clown*] At the heart? At the head? At the stomach? Where would you like?

MISTER CLOWN: I have to give it some thought! And then?

RINGMASTER: Then you count. One!

MISTER CLOWN: I understand! Two! Four! [*He looks around him.*] Where's the victim?

RINGMASTER: [fiddling with the trigger] Hmm! Funny gun!

MISTER CLOWN: The real problem's with people who don't know how to count! Give it here! [*He takes the gun and aims it at the Ringmaster.*] I've given it some thought and... it will be in the stomach! Count please?

RINGMASTER: Five... six... seven... eight...

MISTER CLOWN: Keep going! [*He pockets the gun.*]

RINGMASTER: Nine... ten... eleven... twelve... thirteen... Aren't you going to kill me?

MISTER CLOWN: When you're done counting! Are there a lot more numbers in arithmetic?

RINGMASTER: Quite a few. Twenty five... twenty six... I think I made a mistake! Would it be alright if I start over? One... two... three! [*Gun goes off in Mister Clown's pants, and he drops dead.*]

MISTER CLOWN: [*on the ground*] Stop counting please!

RINGMASTER: And now are you going to work?

MISTER CLOWN: I'm dead!

RINGMASTER: [*to the band*] Then strike up a funeral march!

MISTER CLOWN: [*Takes advantage of the Ringmaster's back being turned by slipping the reloaded gun into the pocket of his morning coat, then lies back down.*] Not too sad with the funeral march now, Mister Conductor. I have a soft heart!

RINGMASTER: [*to Mister Clown, sententious*] Now you see what happens?!

MISTER CLOWN: [*to the band*] Stop! [*sitting up*] Mister Ringmaster, I have been duly punished! By the way, what was the fatal number that brought about my death?

RINGMASTER: Three! [*Gun goes off in the Ringmaster's pocket, and he falls down dead.*]

MISTER CLOWN: [*standing up, to the band*] Keep the funeral march going! [*to the Ringmaster*] Now I see what happens! [*He runs to one of the entrance ways to the circus.*] Babylas! Dudule! Casimir! Piccolo! August!

*The Ringmaster gets to his feet and makes a discrete getaway through the opposite entrance way, rubbing his behind. The band stops playing and resumes the quiet march. The five clowns enter, leaping.*

THE FIVE CLOWNS: Long live Mister Clown! Hurrah!

MISTER CLOWN: Conscious clowns of all sorts, wily and dumb... come and see! I've killed the Ringmaster!

BABYLAS: Where is he?

MISTER CLOWN: In the middle of the ring!

*All run to the middle of the ring and search.*

PICCOLO: He's not there!

MISTER CLOWN: Scour the area!

AUGUST: All that's left is the outline of his backside in the sand! He's gone!

MISTER CLOWN: That doesn't matter in the least, since he's dead! Clowns! Come! To work!

PICCOLO: No!

MISTER CLOWN: Yes!

BABYLAS: No, no!

MISTER CLOWN: Yes, yes!

AUGUST: No, no, no!

MISTER CLOWN: Yes, yes, yes!

DUDULE: No, no, no, no!

MISTER CLOWN: Yes, yes, yes, yes!

CASIMIR: No, no, no, no, no!

MISTER CLOWN: Why?

AUGUST: The Ringmaster is dead! The clowns are free!

MISTER CLOWN: I beg your pardon! I'm not talking about working for the audience. I'm talking about starting a revolution!

DUDULE: And after the revolution, will we be ringmasters?

MISTER CLOWN: Are you ever dumb, Dudule! We're going to start by doing our act!

CASIMIR: Oh no we won't! Doing our act is work!

MISTER CLOWN: Not in the least! Since the title of the act is "Mister Clown Doesn't Want to Work!"

PICCOLO: Well, we don't either! [*to the clowns*] Mister Clown may not have to work in this act, but I, Piccolo, I sure will!

CASIMIR: And I, Casimir!

DUDULE: And I, Dudule!

BABYLAS: And I, Babylas!

AUGUST: And I, August!

MISTER CLOWN: You won't have to work, word of honor!

AUGUST: Then what will we have to do?

MISTER CLOWN: Nothing!

PICCOLO: How do you do that?

MISTER CLOWN: What?

PICCOLO: Nothing!

MISTER CLOWN: You sit comfortably! And you tell everyone else who's there doing nothing with you: Chin up!

CASIMIR: And why do you have to say that?

MISTER CLOWN: Because you either have worked or are going to work! To have worked is in the past. To work is in the future! To sit and do nothing is the present!

DUDULE: And how did it come to pass that it's never the past or future, but always the present?

MISTER CLOWN: Well, you sit down and you stay sitting!

DUDULE: Ah!

MISTER CLOWN: When you're sitting, you're not past, and you're not future. You're present!

PICCOLO: But what if I go somewhere else?

MISTER CLOWN: Then you are absent! Everyone go sit down!

*The five clowns take their places on the edge of the rink. Silence. The band stops playing. Mister Clown takes out his watch.*

BABYLAS: Is this doing nothing going to go on much longer?

MISTER CLOWN: Five of! In five minutes the revolution breaks out! [*He sits in the middle of the rink.*]

DUDULE: [*calling out*] Chin up!

MISTER CLOWN: Are you telling me to keep my chin up?

DUDULE: Absolutely! All the rest of us are supposed to be doing nothing!

MISTER CLOWN: Right you are! I'm going to kick things off with a manifesto! [*He gets up.*]

CASIMIR: Why?

MISTER CLOWN: Because you can't have a revolution without a manifesto!

BABYLAS: Chin up!

MISTER CLOWN: Who are you saying that to?

BABYLAS: To whoever's going to have to listen to you!

CASIMIR: Well, I know how to have a revolution without a manifesto!

MISTER CLOWN: How?

CASIMIR: Give me the floor and I'll tell you!

MISTER CLOWN: No, no! Only me, I'm going to speak!

PICCOLO: You're going to speak! You just want to be a star! That's why you're making us do nothing!

AUGUST: I'm registering a complaint against the

entire way the act "Mister Clown Doesn't Want to Work Anymore" is being conducted! Why doesn't he take a break?

MISTER CLOWN: After I've finish my manifesto and declare the revolution! [*He looks at his watch.*]

BABYLAS: Where's the manifesto?

MISTER CLOWN: [*searching his pockets*] I can't find the thread of it anymore! [*He searches again and takes out a thread at the end of which is a little paper.*] Here it is!

THE FIVE CLOWNS: Hush! Shush! Hush!

MISTER CLOWN: I cough! [*He coughs.*] And I begin! [*in one breath*] "My dear Clown, I will meet you at ten o'clock in the exact center of the ring. Adoringly, your unblemished horsewoman." [*He coughs.*]

AUGUST: That — that's a declaration of love!

MISTER CLOWN: Revolutionary manifestoes are declarations of love! Let me read you the rest! [*He turns the paper over.*] The circle of the ring is the world. And Mister Clown is at its center!

BABYLAS: Silence, Center! Would Mister Clown care to explain this manifesto?

MISTER CLOWN: It is symbolic! The dear clown is the revolutionary! The meeting at ten o'clock is the time of the revolution! And the unblemished horsewoman who adores her dear clown is the revolution!

DUDULE: [*aside*] The revolution is of the feminine gender!

MISTER CLOWN: One of! Attention! Since there are four exit doors to the circus, four of you... go shut the doors... and the fifth, empty the cash box!

CASIMIR: And the manifesto?

MISTER CLOWN: When the revolution's over! I name you all clown ministers!

AUGUST: Of what?

MISTER CLOWN: Of finance, if you bring back the cash box!

CASIMIR: And I?

MISTER CLOWN: You're a musical clown? I name you Minister of the Arts!

DUDULE: And I?

MISTER CLOWN: You're an acrobat on the high wire? I name you Minister of International Affairs!

PICCOLO: And I?

MISTER CLOWN: You, you're a sword swallower. I name you Minister of War!

BABYLAS: And I?

MISTER CLOWN: What do you do in the circus?

BABYLAS: I help roll up the carpets and walk on them at the same time. Then I run around the ring, I shout, and when everyone else has finished rolling up the carpets, I dust off my costume!

MISTER CLOWN: You are Minister of Labor! Clown Ministers... Go! [*The five clowns disperse and exit. Mister Clown looks at his watch.*] Zero of!

> *The band plays a muted, languorous waltz. Mister Clown gets down on one knee. Luna, the unblemished bareback rider, enters. She dances on the tips of her toes and whirls around Mister Clown, who is bewitched.*

LUNA: Hello Mister Clown!

MISTER CLOWN: Miss Luna, moon of beauty in the sky of my passion, I kneel before your lunar charms!

LUNA: He's so nice! You know what, my little Clown? I heard you were doing a sensational act tonight!

MISTER CLOWN: *Oui*, my angel! The revolution!

LUNA: Oh! How nasty! [*She looks around her.*] And where is this revolution?

MISTER CLOWN: In my heart!

LUNA: Oh! Silly! So you're a revolutionary?

MISTER CLOWN: Revolutionized, miss!

LUNA: Oh! Flatterer! Well tell me all about your ideas.

MISTER CLOWN: I love you!

LUNA: You aim high!

MISTER CLOWN: I aim for the heart! I'm starting the revolution all for your sake!

LUNA: And how will things be when it's over?

MISTER CLOWN: You will love me!

LUNA: Why?

MISTER CLOWN: Because I'm going to overthrow the government! I will be emperor of all the clowns. And you will be empress! All circuses everywhere will belong to me!

LUNA: That sounds perfect! Of course I'll love you! Good luck!

MISTER CLOWN: Luna of my dreams! Moon at the zenith of my future felicity! Oh my wife-to-be!

> *Luna dances out. Mister Clown blows kisses to her. The waltz stops.*

MISTER CLOWN: [*standing*] Hey there, orchestra! A military march! [*to the audience*] Ladies and gentlemen! The revolution has begun! [*beating of a bass drum*] I'm stripping myself of all my old-hat ideas and all my old hat routines. I am a new clown!

*Drum roll. Mister Clown does a series of somersaults. Then:*

MISTER CLOWN: Silence, orchestra! Now, I am going to get the radio so I can announce the Revolution of the Universal Circus! [*He runs out. Babylas, delirious with joy, comes in from the same entrance that Luna had gone out by.*]

BABYLAS: I just ran into the revolution! Whee! What a lovely girl! It's too bad that she has so many scruples! But even so she told me, "My little Babylas, I know you're going to become a revolutionary! Proclaim yourself emperor and I'll be your wife!!!" Wow! [*He does pirouettes.*]

PICCOLO: [*appearing from the same entrance*] Ah! How nice she smelled! She lured me into a corner and called me, "My little Piccolo. "Wow! My heart!

BABYLAS: [*Who has overheard him, gives him a kick in the behind.*] Sorry!

PICCOLO: Aiee! There it goes again! [*He kicks Babylas back.*]

BABYLAS: My heart!

PICCOLO: What's up Babylas? You know we're supposed to be getting this revolution on the road!

BABYLAS: But Mister Clown isn't here!

PICCOLO: We're clowns too! We can start the revolution without him!

BABYLAS: Absolutely! Don't tire yourself out, Piccolo, I'll do it myself!

PICCOLO: No, no, me, I'll do it!

*Enter Dudule, glowing.*

DUDULE: She took one look at me and I got an electric shock, a lightning bolt right on the lightning rod of my feelings! She told me, "Oh my little Dudule, you're the funniest clown of all!"

PICCOLO: [*furious with Dudule*] I bet your heart leapt, didn't it?

DUDULE: I've been betrayed! No, no... no leaping!

*Babylas kicks Dudule who returns it to Babylas, and Piccolo gets up and kicks the behinds of the other two. Panic.*

BABYLAS: Enough leaping! It's more than our clown hearts can take!

*Enter Casimir, glowing.*

CASIMIR: She told me... my little Casimir... You're a real sketch. You're bound to become monarch over all!

*Babylas, Dudule, and Piccolo set off in pursuit of him.*

THE THREE: Hey! Casimir! Listen!

CASIMIR: [*fleeing, holding his behind*] I'm sick at heart!

*Enter August, indifferent, who walks on the rim of the ring.*

AUGUST: It's strange. Anyone who's in love would rather make someone else's heart leap than have their own leap. But to me she said, "My little August, you're no idiot! I'm not asking you to become emperor, just to betray the others. I'm not saying I'll be your wife, but you shall have my favors!"

THE FOUR: [*hurtling toward August*] August! Your heart!

AUGUST: [*calm*] I'm no poet!

*The other four are bewildered.*

PICCOLO: Didn't you run into anyone?

AUGUST: Yes, the cashier! I robbed her! We're starting the revolution right now!

BABYLAS: Let's start! Who's the boss?

PICCOLO: Me!

CASIMIR: Not you, me!

BABYLAS: Neither of you! Me!

DUDULE: I nominate... me!

AUGUST: We have to enter a contest. The winner of the ring race... I'll be umpire!

BABYLAS: What's this contest all about?

AUGUST: Starting a revolution means standing the world on its head. Since one of you will have to control the world, he'll have to know how to live upside down. The first one who manages to stand on his hands is the winner!

THE FOUR: Fine!

*They stick their legs in the air, one next to the other.*

AUGUST: Careful!

CASIMIR: Are we supposed to start with the left leg?

AUGUST: I'll count to three.

*Resounding din in the wings. The clowns collapse and tremble with fear.*

THE FOUR: Help! The revolution! Help!

*Mister Clown enters, dragging a strange apparatus mounted on wheels boxes, ropes, canned food, lamps. This is the wireless telegraph. The clowns remain frozen. Mister*

*Clown installs his apparatus in the center of the ring and sets it up. Then:*

MISTER CLOWN: Orchestra, silence! [*to the clowns*] Comrade Clowns. . . the revolution is declared! Proletarians of the circus, slaves to public opinion, dawn is breaking! You shall all, swear loyalty to me. Whoever doesn't go along, I'll shoot dead. Now cry out: Long live liberty and liberated clowns! [*He takes out a billy club and shakes it.*]

THE CLOWNS: Long live liberty and Mister Clown with his billy club!

MISTER CLOWN: That's right! I'm going to announce the clown liberation to the world! This is my telegraph machine, which keeps all other telegraphs from working! [*He fiddles around with the apparatus.*] I'm going to start it up.

AUGUST: I forgot to tell you that I've got the money! Should we split it up? This is such a touching moment!

MISTER CLOWN: Go take that money to the bank! [*Mister Clown listens to the boxes of canned food, and takes on the air of technician.*]

*August runs out, but soon returns, provided with various accessories: phonograph speaker, horn, a roll of string, whistles. He hides behind the edge of the ring and tosses the string onto the radio apparatus.*

MISTER CLOWN: I'm beginning! Roger! The Great Circus of Europe here. The clowns have taken over!

Clowns of all nations, unite! Assassinate the ringmaster! The whole universe belongs to clowns! Be a clown or die! [*to the clowns*] Clap!

THE CLOWNS: [*in unison*] Long live the revolution!

MISTER CLOWN: Roger! Did you get my message?

THE TELEGRAPH MACHINE: [*via the interception of August*] Quack! Quack! Brrr! Sshhoof! Boom!

*A siren and whistle finish off the response.*

MISTER CLOWN: Do you read me? Revolution here...

BABYLAS: Ask them for a translation!

MISTER CLOWN: Roger! Clowns! What was your answer again?

THE TELEGRAPH MACHINE: [*via interception of August, through the phonograph speaker*] That all the ringmasters have been killed! The imbeciles have been locked up in the circuses and are waiting for us to decide their fate!

MISTER CLOWN: [*to the clowns*] What shall we do to the imbeciles?

CASIMIR: In the first place, we've got to know if there are a lot them!

MISTER CLOWN: [*transmitting*] Roger! What is the total population of the world not including clowns?

TELEGRAPH MACHINE: Roger! 3,741,975,427,092,510,295,321, and 25!

MISTER CLOWN: And two fifths! Thank you! Clown Comrades, what to do about the imbeciles?

THE CLOWNS: [*in unison*] Kill them!

MISTER CLOWN: [*transmitting*] Roger. They must be executed, but not all of them! Keep hold of a few specimens, 'cause you can't do entirely without imbeciles! Save the least idiotic ones!

THE TELEGRAPH MACHINE: Roger! Should we start in the ones, tens, hundreds. . .

MISTER CLOWN: Start by relieving them of their wallets! Good night! [*to the clowns*] So you really want to proclaim me boss supreme?

*He raises his billy club.*

THE CLOWNS: [*in unison*] Long live the supreme boss with his billy club!

THE TELEGRAPH MACHINE: I object!

MISTER CLOWN: What impudence! [*Slams the machine with the billy club.*]

TELEGRAPH MACHINE: Ouch, ouch, ouch! All right, I'll stop!

MISTER CLOWN: And since I'm the boss, I'm going to get married! In a few seconds, you'll proclaim me the big cheese of the free federated clowns! [*transmitting*] Roger! My love! Luna!

THE TELEGRAPH MACHINE: Rahrahrahrahrahrah! Quack! Quack! Boom!

MISTER CLOWN: She's so happy she's delirious!

BABYLAS: No, that's the screams of the imbeciles on their way to being executed!

MISTER CLOWN: Hello, Luna. You promised to love me! I'm the boss!

THE TELEGRAPH MACHINE: Miss Luna is busy!

MISTER CLOWN: With what, if I may ask?

THE TELEGRAPH MACHINE: I'll put you through to her compartment!

*The four clowns squirm. Billy club.*

MISTER CLOWN: Silence! I hear her voice!

*He goes down on one knee.*

THE TELEGRAPH MACHINE: [*woman's voice via the intercession of August*] I love you. I adore you. I'm crazy about you!

MISTER CLOWN: Music divine!

THE TELEGRAPH MACHINE: My dear little ringmaster! We're going to massacre all those nasty buffoons who imagine I love them! And then we'll get married! I love kissing your waxed moustache! I hate clean-shaven men!

MISTER CLOWN: Goodness gracious! I've been betrayed!

THE FOUR CLOWNS: [*in unison*] We've been betrayed!

BABYLAS: Not to mention cuckolded!

MISTER CLOWN: You haven't, I have! The unblemished bareback-rider's cheating on me with the ringmaster!

CASIMIR: So the ringmaster wasn't dead after all?

MISTER CLOWN: He was only pretending!

PICCOLO: Well maybe he's only pretending to cheat on you!

MISTER CLOWN: No! It's possible to fake death, but love, never! [*He cries.*] I've been screwed! And the revolution, she's been screwed too!

*He demolishes the telegraph machine by kicking it.*

THE FOUR CLOWNS: [*in unison*] The revolution is dead. Long live the revolution!

MISTER CLOWN: You've all betrayed me! We shall all go to our doom together, silly clowns, painted clowns! You don't deserve freedom! [*He exits, shaking his fist.*]

BABYLAS: One less boss! Now we'll start a revolution all on our own! First, the telegraph machine must be repaired!

DUDULE: Let's fix it! This is the transmitting station for fake news!

*They go to work on the machine.*

PICCOLO: What's this string here? A wired wireless!

BABYLAS: Give a tug. I bet there's a clown at the other end!

*The four pull. August rolls around the ring, clutching his tools.*

CASIMIR: It's August! Wasn't he supposed to be at the bank?

AUGUST: I was listening to the stock market report!

PICCOLO: So you must have been the voice of universal clowns and the unblemished cuckolder!

AUGUST: I'm the one! But I didn't tell the truth! I was off by seven in the total number of imbeciles! And as for the unblemished bareback rider, she was just letting herself be led around by the nose! She's still waiting for one of us to be leader! I've succeeded in overthrowing Mister Clown, who was full of it. And now we'll see who'll be the boss from here on in! [He runs to the entrance and comes back with four pairs of boxing gloves which he passes out to the four clowns.] You're all dying to be boss, and each of you's just waiting for the opportunity to betray all the others! There is, however, one amongst us to whom Miss Luna has promised her love! Luna hopes that he will be the winner! She gave me a little flower to pass on to him!

*He takes the flower out and shows it off.*

THE FOUR CLOWNS: It's mine! No, mine! Luna meant it for me! The flower's for me!

*August eats it. A free-for-all. The four clowns box, howl, roll in the sand, pirouette. A bass drum sounds. One after the other Casimir, Piccolo, and Dudule drop, knocked out, and cry hot tears. Babylas continues to box by himself with empty space. August gives him a kick in the behind. Babylas is knocked out in his turn. A concert of tears.*

BABYLAS: This has ceased to be a legitimate craft! I resign from the revolution!

AUGUST: Be quiet! You're all knocked out! [*The clowns stiffen. August puts on white gloves and a collapsible top hat that he had in his pocket and leaves triumphantly.*] They're dead. I, I am the victor! Luna, I come to claim my reward! [*Exits.*]

BABYLAS: [*getting up*] Once again we've been betrayed! Brothers, clowns. . . death must come! Which is no problem! They'll see that clowns know how to die! Piccolo, you commit suicide on Casimir!

Dudule, you commit suicide on Piccolo! And I'll commit suicide on Dudule!

PICCOLO: And who's going to commit suicide on you?

BABYLAS: I'm going to avenge all of you! I'll get even with August, the traitor, when he finds me in the arms of the unblemished bareback-rider. He'll kill me to wash his honor with my blood!

CASIMIR: That's fine! Farewell Piccolo!

PICCOLO: Farewell Casimir, chin up!

DUDULE: Farewell Babylas. See you!

BABYLAS: Farewell, Dudule. I'm so sad! We shall meet again in the great circus in the sky! Clowns in the stars!

*They kiss. August comes back in bawling.*

AUGUST: Hoohah! I've been betrayed! Luna didn't open the door, the ringmaster did! Poor clowns that we are! These ringmasters have us hornswoggled!

CASIMIR: Well, do we die, yes or no? What method should we use to commit suicide?

AUGUST: How about tickling the bottoms of our feet?

BABYLAS: Comes highly recommended! Let's start with August, since he betrayed us!

AUGUST: I couldn't stand it! [*They run after him.*]

THE FOUR CLOWN: Death to the traitor! Revenge!

*August is captured. They lay him on the ground and take off one shoe. The four clowns gently collapse one after the other.*

AUGUST: What's wrong with them? [*He puts his shoe back on.*] I'm going to get the doctor! [*He starts to leave, but returns horrified.*] This time we're going to die for real!

BABYLAS: [*coming over to him*] Ah! What a cut-rate suicide!

AUGUST: Watch out! Get the murderer!

*The five clowns flee bewildered. Mister Clown makes his appearance. He's dragging an enormous bomb on which is written "Dynamite, Very Dangerous."*

MISTER CLOWN: The jig's up for us! There'll be nothing left of us clowns but some little scraps!

*He sits down on the bomb.*

BABYLAS: Where are you coming from? We thought you were dead!

MISTER CLOWN: I've been busy making the bomb! We're all going to die! This will be a smashing finale!

PICCOLO: And the revolution!?

MISTER CLOWN: It's going fine! All the imbeciles are going up in smoke with us!

AUGUST: Couldn't you replace this act with a manifesto?

MISTER CLOWN: It's too late! Clowns forever! Get ready! [*He turns the starting crank.*]

THE FIVE CLOWNS: Watch out! Down with the anarchist! [*They hide behind each other and moan.*]

MISTER CLOWN: What? It isn't going off! [He gives the bomb a few big kicks.] I hear a little sound inside!

AUGUST: Wait! [*He runs out and comes back with a blacksmith's mallet.*] In this life you've got to do your part!

MISTER CLOWN: Thanks a lot! All set for the disaster! [*He recites.*] Ah love, how many misunderstandings there are in your name! Clowns, let us die like clowns! Without any tragedy! Tragedy is for the imbeciles! For the millionaire ringmasters and their romantic exploits! Jokes and shenanigans for us! Long live the assassinated clowns!

> *He hits the starting crank on the bomb. Small pop. The bomb splits open. Out comes the Ringmaster with a whip. The clowns fall in a faint.*

THE RINGMASTER: [*running into the ring*] Orchestra, go! A triumphal march!

THE CLOWNS: [*crestfallen*] The counter-attack!

*And they all die. The Bareback Rider enters, standing on a horse. She circles the ring juggling flaming torches. The Ringmaster hands over his whip to her. Policemen wearing little cardboard horses charge the clowns. The Ringmaster climbs onto the Bareback Rider's horse.*

THE RINGMASTER: Massacre the clowns! An end to all funnymen!

LUNA: Long live blood! Down with the corny clowns!

*Rifle fire. The Bareback Rider flings her torches aside. The Ringmaster gets down from the horse and carries Luna in his arms. Complete darkness. The vaulted ceiling of the circus lights up. The band stops playing. The six clowns are flying on the bars and trapezes, soaring like spirits in a bluish glow. The band is playing the quiet march as it did at the beginning.*

LUNA: [*in the Ringmaster's arms*] Ah, the pretty clowns in the clouds! But I prefer the worldly ring and your waxed moustache, oh my handsome ringmaster!

### THE END

# SELECTED BIBLIOGRAPHY

## OTHER PLAYS IN ENGLISH

*Seven Plays*. Trans., George Hauger. New York: Hill and Wang, 1960. Contains: *The Women at the Tomb, Barabbas, Three Actors and Their Drama, Pantagleize, The Blind Men, Chronicles of Hell, Lord Halewyn.*

*Seven Plays, 2*. Trans., George Hauger. New York: Hill and Wang, 1964. Contains: *Red Magic, Hop Signor!, The Death of Doctor Faust, Christopher Columbus, A Night of Pity, Piet Bouteille, Miss Jairus.*

*Escurial.* Trans., Lionel Abel. *The Modern Theatre, V*, Ed., Eric Bentley. Garden City, N.Y.: Doubleday, 1957.

*School for Buffoons*. Trans., Kenneth S. White. San Francisco: Chandler Publishing Co., 1968.

*Avant-Garde Drama: A Casebook*, Ed., Bernard Dukore and Daniel C. Gerould. Trans., George Hauger. New York: Thomas Crowell Co., 1976. Contains *Chronicles of Hell.*

*An Anthology of Modern Belgian Theatre*, Ed., Bettina Knapp. Trans., Nadine Dormoy-Savage. Troy, N.Y.: The Whitson Publishing Co., 1982. Contains *The Magpie on the Gallows* and *Escurial.*

*Theatrical Gestures from Belgian Avant-Garde*, Ed., David Willinger. Trans., David Willinger and Luc Deneulin. New York: New York Literary Forum, 1987. Contains *Death Looks in the Window*, *Blockheads*, *Venus*, and *Dreams Drowning*.

## FULL-LENGTH BOOKS ON GHELDERODE

Beyen, Roland. *Bibliographie de Michel de Ghelderode*. Brussels: Palais des Académies, 1987.

, *Michel de Ghelderode et le théâtre contemporain: Actes du Congrès internationale de Gênes*. Brussels: Société Internationale des Etudes sur Michel de Ghelderode, 1980.

, *Michel de Ghelderode ou la Comédie des apparences*. Brussels: Ministère de la Communauté française de la Belgique, 1980.

, *Ghelderode*. Paris: Seghers, 1974.

, *Michel de Ghelderode ou la hantise du masque. Essai de Biographie critique*. Brussels: Palais des Académies, 1971.

Blancart-Cassou, Jacqueline. *Le rire de Michel de Ghelderode*. Paris: Klincksieck, 1987.

Castro, Nadine. *Un moyen-âge contemporain: le théâtre de Michel de Ghelderode*. Lausanne: L'Age d'Home, 1979.

Deberdt-Malaquais, Elisabeth. *La quête d'identité dans le théâtre de Michel de Ghelderode*. Paris: Editions Universitaires, 1967.

Decock, Jean. *Le Théâtre de Michel de Ghelderode: Une dramaturgie de l'anti-théâtre et de la cruauté.* Paris: Nizet, 1969.

Francis, Jean. *L' étèrnel aujourd' hui de Michel de Ghelderode.* Brussels: Louis Musin, 1968.
———, *Michel de Ghelderode: Dramaturge des pays de par-deça.* Brussels: Labor, 1949.

Grossvogel, David. *The Self-Conscious Stage in Modern French Drama.* New York: Coumbia University Press, 1958.

Guicharnaud, Jaques. *Modern French Theatre from Giraudoux to Beckett.* New Haven: Yale University Press, 1961.

Jans, Adrien. *La vie de Ghelderode.* Brussels: Louis Musin, 1976.

*La Nervie,* special Ghelderode issue. Brussels-Paris, nos. VII-VII, 1932.

*Marginales.* Special Ghelderode issue, May, 1967.

Pronko, Leonard. *Avant-Garde: The Experimental Theatre in France.* Berkeley: University of California Press, 1962.

Santt, Alice. *Michel de Ghelderode.* Vieux-Virton: La Dryade, 1970.

Trousson, Raymond, ed. *Michel de Ghelderode dramaturge et conteur: Actes du Colloque de Bruxelles.* Brussels: Editions de l'Université de Bruxelles, 1983.

Vandromme, Pol. *Michel de Ghelderode.* Paris: Editions Universitaires, 1963.

Weiss, Auréliu. *Le Monde théâtre de Michel de Ghelderode.* Paris: Librairie 73, 1966.

Wellwarth, George. *The Theatre of Protest and Paradox: Developments in the Avant-Garde Drama.* New York: New York University Press, 1964.

## ARTICLES ON GHELDERODE

Allard, Robert. "Signé Michel de Ghelderode: *Le Siège d'Ostende.*" *Vers l'Avenir,* Jan 25, 1981.

Andriat, Frank. Untitled article. *Marginales,* May, 1981.

Bailly, Michel. "*Le Siège d'Ostende*: une pièce très verte de Michel de Ghelderode." *Le Soir,* Jan. 9, 1981.

Beyen, Roland. "Pour une nouvelle édition du *Siège d'Ostende* de Michel de Ghelderode." *Itinéraires et plaisirs textuels: Mélanges offerts au Professeur Raymond Pouilliart,* Brussels: Nauwelaerts, 1987.

Bovy, D. "Gigantesque mascarade et farce, le *Siège d'Ostende*, nous fait découvrir un côté inattendu de Michel de Ghelderode: son goût de l'anarchisme et du comique anticonformiste." *La Wallonie*, Jan. 2, 1981.

Castro, Nadine. "The Foibles of Society in Michel de Ghelderode's Theatre." *Chimères*, Spring, 1978.

Decock, Jean. "D'un inédit de Ghelderode." *The French Review*, May, 1984.

De Valck, Marie-Claire. "Ostende et Michel de Ghelderode vus par Guy Verdot." *Courrier du Littoral*, Feb. 2, 1968.

Doevenspeck, Wim. "Mijn vriend Renaat Verheyen." *Vlaanderen*, March-April, 1981.

Ensor, James. "Pour Michel de Ghelderode: Hommage du peintre des masques et de la mer." (1933) *Mes Ecrits*. Liège: Editions Nationales, 1974.
, "Discours adressé aux confrères masques." (1934) *Mes Ecrits*. Liège: Editions Nationales, 1974, p. 181.

Favart, Pierre. "Ostende sur Infini." *Reflets du Tourisme*, July-August, 1957.

Francis, Jean. *"Sortie de l'acteur." Pourquoi Pas?*, nos. 113-114, 1962.
, "Tribulations d'un texte de Michel de Ghelderode." *Le Soir*, Dec. 21, 1980.

———, "Michel de Ghelderode pour rire et pour pleurer." *Le Journal des livres*, March-April, 1981.

Ketelbuters, Marie-Paule. Untitled article on *Le Siège d'Ostende*. *La Cité*, Nov. 21, 1980.

Loyens, Jos. "Renaat Verheyen en Michel de Ghelderode." *Vlaanderen*, March-April, 1981.

Matthys, Francis. Untitled article on *Le Siège d'Ostende*. *La Libre Belgique*, Nov. 17, 1980.

Migeot, Luc. "Un nouveau Ghelderode." *La Nouvelle Gazette*, Dec. 11, 1980.

Pouilliart, Raymond. "Michel de Ghelderode." *Les Lettres Romanes*, August, 1983.

———, "Ensorien." *Porquoi Pas?* Dec. 18, 1980.

Quaghebeur, Marc. "Balises pour l'histoire de nos lettres." *Alphabet des lettres belges de langue française*, Brussels: Association pour la promotion des Lettres belges de langue française, 1982.

Stevo, Jean. "Une belle exposition en hommage à Michel de Ghelderode." *Courrier du Littoral*, Dec. 4, 1963.

Vanina, Suzanne. "La 'version Lheureux' du *Siège d'Ostende*." *Tribune des Amis de Ghelderode*, no. 16, 1987.

Verheyen, Renaat. "Renaat Verheyen" (An interview with the actor). *Nieuwe Rotterdamsche Courant*, Jan. 15, 1930.

Willinger, David. "Michel de Ghelderode," *European Writers*. New York, Scribners, 1990.

## RELEVANT DOCTORAL AND MASTERS THESES ON GHELDERODE

Clément, Lucile. *Archaisme, néologisme et régionalisme dans le théâtre de Michel de Ghelderode.* Free University Brussels, 1976.

Farcy, Gérard. *Approche de la notion de spectacle dans l'oeuvre théâtre de Michel de Ghelderode.* University of Paris, 1982.

Gerard, Danielle. *Michel de Ghelderode: "Sortie de l'Acteur."* (Edition critique) Catholic University of Louvain, 1972.

Miclotte, Christine. *Michel de Ghelderode "Le Siège d'Ostende." I. Edition critique. II. Etude des archaismes, régionalismes, et néologismes.* Catholic University of Louvain, 1987.

Op de Beeck, Ludo. *Nonstandard French Elements in the Language of Michel de Ghelderode.* University of Pittsburgh, 1973.

Van den Driessche, Jan. *Le personnage de l'artiste dans le théâtre de Michel de Ghelderode*. Catholic University of Louvain, 1985.

Verelst, Marie-Claire. *Archaisme dans le théâtre de Michel de Ghelderode d' après seize oeuvres publiées entre 1928 et 1938*. Catholic University of Louvain, 1977.


## BOOKS ON THE HISTORICAL SIEGE OF OSTEND

Gérard, Jo. *Quand la Belgique était espagnole*. Brussels: Paul Legrain, 1975.

———, *La Belgique à l'heure espagnole*. Brussels: J. M. Collet, 1985.

Lanoye, Robert. *Oostende's Epos*. Ostend: Erel, 1981.

Lefèvre, Joseph. *Spinola et la Belgique*. Brussels: La Renaissance du Livre, 1947.

Monteyne, André. *Les Bruxellois: Un Passé peu ordinaire*. Brussels: Vander, 1982.

Pirenne, Henri. *Histoire de Belgique des origines à nos jours*. Brussels: La Renaissance du Livre, 1923.

Schama, Simon. *The Embarrassment of Riches*. Berkeley: University of California Press, 1988.

Willaert, L. *Histoire de Belgique*. Tournai: Casterman, 1946.

## BOOKS ABOUT JAMES ENSOR

Avermaete, Roger. *James Ensor*. Antwerp: De Sikkel, 1947.

Croquez, Robert. *Ensor en son temps*. Ostend: Erel, 1970.

Cuypers, Firmin. *Aspects et propos de James Ensor*. Bruges: A. G. Stainforth, 1946.

Damase, J. *L'Oeuvre graphique de James Ensor*. Geneva: Motte, 1966.

Demolder, Eugene. *James Ensor*. Brussels: P. Lacomblez, 1892. Reprint Paris, 1899.

De Ridder, Andre. *James Ensor*. Paris: Rieder, 1930.

*Ensor*. Catalogue for an exhibition at the Art Institute of Chicago and the Guggenheim Museum in New York. New York: Braziller, 1976.

Ensor, James. *Mes Ecrits*. Liège: Editions Nationales, 1971.

Fierens, Paul. *James Ensor*. Paris: Hyperion, 1943.

———, *Les Dessins d'Ensor*. Brussels: Editions Apollo, 1944.

———, Edebau, F. and Stevo, Jean. *James Ensor, le maître et sa maison*. Brussels: Editions de la Connaissance, 1956.

Haesaerts, Paul. *James Ensor*. New York: Museum of Modern Art, 1952.

*Ik, James Ensor*. Catalogue of an Exhibition of Prints. Ghent and Amsterdam, 1987.

Tannenbaum, L. *James Ensor*. New York: Museum of Modern Art, 1952.

Van Gindertael, Roger. *James Ensor*. New York, 1975.